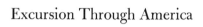

Excursion Through America

The Lakeside Classics

EXCURSION
THROUGH AMERICA

By Nicolaus Mohr

EDITED BY RAY ALLEN BILLINGTON
Henry E. Huntington Library and Art Gallery

Translated by LA VERN J. RIPPLEY
with the collaboration of
KLAUS LANZINGER

The Lakeside Press

R. R. DONNELLEY & SONS COMPANY

CHICAGO

Christmas, 1973

Ein Streifzug

durch den

Nordwesten Amerikas.

———

Festfahrt

zur

Northern Pacific-Bahn

im Herbste 1883.

———

Von

N. Mohr,

Redakteur der „Weser-Zeitung".

———

Berlin,

Verlag von Robert Oppenheim.

1884.

Original German Title Page

PUBLISHERS' PREFACE

"EXCURSION THROUGH AMERICA" is the story of a gala coast-to-coast journey to celebrate the completion of the rail link between the east coast and Oregon in 1883.

Although the excursion described in this year's edition of *The Lakeside Classics* is possibly the most extended and most well-publicized celebration of the completion of a transcontinental rail link, it was not the first. It was preceded by a celebration of the joining of the Union Pacific and the Central Pacific Railroads which met at Promontory Point, Utah in 1869, and that of the Southern Pacific and the Santa Fe which occurred in 1881 at Deming, New Mexico.

Nevertheless, when the Northern Pacific extended west from Lake Superior to meet the rails of the Oregon Railway and Navigation Company in 1883, it was a great occasion. At last the Northwest had its own rail connection with the East. Henry Villard, president of the Northern Pacific, saw it also as a great public relations opportunity to attract investors. For these reasons he invited an impressive group of British, German, and American capitalists to join the other dignitaries on the tour. As the special excursion trains rolled westward along the new route, city after city staged great celebrations, each trying to outdo the others.

Among the invited guests was the distinguished German journalist, Nicolaus Mohr. Herr Mohr described the tour and the celebrations in enthusiastic but sometimes tongue-in-cheek detail in dispatches to his Bremen newspaper. When he returned home, he rearranged and edited these dispatches to form the present book which was first printed in Berlin in 1884. Incidentally, Herr Mohr was well known among Americans of German descent because of the overseas editions of his paper which appeared in this country.

Before work on our edition of this book was actually started, we were saddened by the death of the editor we had selected, John A. Hawgood of the University of Birmingham (England). Professor Hawgood, in addition to being an expert on the American West, was fluent in the German language in which the book originally was written.

Fortunately, however, Ray Allen Billington stepped into the breach. Professor Billington is an outstanding authority on frontier America. After serving Northwestern University as their William Smith Mason Professor of History and Chicago's Newberry Library as a Trustee, he left the Middle West for California where he became Senior Research Associate of the Huntington Library in San Marino.

Excursion Through America contains a far greater number of illustrations than have previously ap-

peared in *The Lakeside Classics* series. We thus
would be remiss if we did not call attention to the
many institutions and individuals who helped us to
obtain them. Each illustration, therefore, is accompanied by its own acknowledgement.

The map depicting the Villard journey is the
third in this series to be produced by the eminent
Chicago artist and calligrapher, Robert Williams.

For the first time in this series, type for the 1973
edition of *The Lakeside Classics* was set by a new
process using high-speed computer-controlled electronic character generators. This new technique
creates type characters made up into full pages as
you see them in this book, on the face of a television-like cathode ray tube. The light pattern on the
tube exposes the pages that are formed on a computer to photographic film from which sharp, well-defined printing plates can be made.

This character generation and page composition
is done in the ultra-modern Donnelley Electronic
Graphics Division where sophisticated Donnelley-developed computer techniques are combined with
the craftsmanship of traditional typographic skills
to produce type pages at the almost unbelievable
rate of 1000 characters per second. Even the hyphenation, page numbers, and headings are dictated
by computer instructions, and are produced at the
same time the rest of the page is created.

The Electronic Graphics Division brings together

techniques developed by our pioneering research in several different fields: computer-controlled hot-metal typesetting for which we developed our own computer in the late 1950s; the utilization of electronically-controlled character generation on film, which also started at Donnelley in the 1950s with the purchase and researching of the very first photo-composing machine to be put in use; and finally, our work with the manipulation of data which we started when computers first came on the market.

With the application several years later of the cathode ray tube for type generation and composition, the technology in our Company had achieved such high efficiency that the Electronic Graphics Division was created, in 1967, to make broad commercial application of these techniques. As a result of our continuing research and development, this Division today stands in a position of unquestioned leadership in the field of computerized electronic composition.

The Division produces accurate, high-quality typesetting for a variety of our customers. Not only does it do successful typography for books such as this, but also for nationally-known magazines, catalogs, and directories.

Another first for this edition of *The Lakeside Classics* is that it was printed in our Crawfordsville, Indiana plant. These books have been bound in Crawfordsville since 1941 when our book bindery was moved there from Chicago, but this is the first time the printing was done there. Like the last two books in the series, this one is again printed by offset lithography, which continues to increase its importance in the book production field.

This preface to the 71st edition of *The Lakeside Classics*, a series which was started in 1903, again gives us an opportunity to comment on our business during the past year.

The year 1973 was characterized by challenge, achievement, setbacks, and readjustment. Overall, the Company continued to grow. Major expansions continued throughout the Company.

As the year began, however, we were faced with the loss of an old friend when LIFE magazine ceased publication. We were the major printers of this remarkable publication from its founding in 1936. Hand in hand, Donnelley developed new printing technology as LIFE pioneered new concepts in news reporting. Its acceptance by the public was so great, and its rise so meteoric, that the standing production order in the early years was to produce every possible copy before the next week's edition had to be put to press. Over the years, the magnificent accomplishments and exciting challenges of this wonderful publication did much to stimulate and develop our own production capabilities. In fact, the printing of LIFE grew to become our largest single job and was a major factor in our Company's growth and success. We look back with pride on our association with LIFE, and with sadness at its passing.

In our Chicago and Old Saybrook plants we were faced with the most serious work-force reductions in our history. Our people have faced these reductions with unusual patience and understanding, but the impact has been difficult on the many who have been affected. Every effort has been made and substantial expense was incurred to minimize the effect by transfers, retraining, demotions, augmented early retirement, and special separation payments. Assistance in finding other employment was offered to all those whom we regretfully could not continue in the work force. During the year we have dedicated major efforts to the task of revitalizing these two Divisions. A substantial number of people have been recalled and many others have been restored to former jobs. These efforts shall continue.

Even though the year began on a sad note, there were many favorable developments as it progressed. The successful start-up of the new telephone directory plant in Lancaster is meeting our highest hopes and expectations. New press equipment has been installed in Chicago and Old Saybrook to offset, in part, the loss of work which resulted from the discontinuance of LIFE magazine. Major plant additions and new press equipment are now on stream or under construction in Mattoon, Willard, Warsaw, Glasgow, and Lancaster-East.

A new financial printing office was set up in the heart of Wall Street to offer Donnelley printing services to the New York financial community. This new office is electronically connected with new financial printing facilities in the Lancaster-East plant and we are able to provide the same services as if our printing plant were located on Wall Street. This financial printing facility offers New York the same excellent printing service we have provided for forty years to Chicago's financial community.

In September, we announced the decision to establish a new gravure printing plant in Gallatin, Tennessee.

Price controls also affect our business, requiring managerial attention and administrative effort which could be more profitably directed to other endeavors. The intense competition in the printing industry controls prices far more effectively than any artificial controls imposed by the government. By dealing with symptoms rather than causes, such controls become counter-productive and severely distort the free flow of goods and services in our society. Hopefully, they will soon be terminated.

Another major concern during this past year has been the securing of an adequate supply of certain grades of printing paper. Few new printing paper facilities have been brought into production in recent years, and very few are planned for the future. This most serious problem will continue until the demand is decreased or the supply is increased, or both. However, we are making a concerted effort, which so far has been largely successful, to assure an adequate supply of paper for the immediate and long-term requirements of our customers.

In spite of the problems we face, we continue to be confident and optimistic about the future of our Company as evidenced by the substantial expenditures for expansion of our manufacturing facilities. We are taking these steps in recognition of the ability of our managers, salesmen, staff, and production employees to meet the needs of our ever-growing list of customers and the many challenges of the future.

We hope all our friends share our confidence and enthusiasm, and wish them a very Merry Christmas and a most Happy New Year.

THE PUBLISHERS

Christmas, 1973

CONTENTS

ILLUSTRATIONS

THE TEXT AND ITS EDITING

Dᴜʀɪɴɢ his travels in America in 1883 as guest of the Northern Pacific Railroad, the German publisher who wrote this book sent irregular dispatches to the *Weser Zeitung*, the Bremen newspaper that he edited. These were written, often hastily, during the infrequent intervals of leisure in his hectic schedule; occasionally on rare intervals when more time was available he re-described events that he had earlier noted briefly. When he returned to Europe in November, 1883, he arranged these extracts in book form, adding still more impressions from the storehouse of his memory. The result was published as *Ein Streifzug durch den Nordwesten Amerikas—Festfahrt zur Northern Pacific-Bahn im Herbste 1883*, and was printed in Berlin by Verlag von Oppenheim in 1884.

Many years later a copy of this book came to the attention of the Dillon Press of Minneapolis, which planned to publish an English language translation. Both Professor La Vern J. Rippley of St. Olaf College who was engaged as translator, and the editors of the Dillon Press, recognized at the outset that the book could be made readable to an American audience only if recast in diary form, and only if extraneous items were omitted. Hence Professor Rippley laid greater stress on the chronological pattern than did the original text. At the same time he eliminated lengthy descriptions of the state of the weather and of commonplace occurrences less interesting to twentieth century Americans than to nineteenth century Germans.

When the Dillon Press decided to abandon the publication and focus on other aspects of publishing, its translation and publication rights were acquired by R. R. Donnelley & Sons Company with an eye toward an addition to its distinguished Lakeside Classics series. Professor John A. Hawgood of the University of Birmingham, who combined an intimate knowledge of the American West with a thorough familiarity with the German language, agreed to prepare the volume for publication. His death in September, 1971, forced Donnelley to seek another editor. I agreed to assume the task, even though I am shamefully lacking in knowledge of German, with the understanding that an expert in that language would be engaged to help remedy my deficiencies. Professor Klaus Lanzinger of the University of Notre Dame, who assumed this role, has not only reviewed the earlier translation, making a number of significant changes, but has prepared the brief essay on Nicolaus Mohr's contribution to American travel literature that appears as an "Epilogue" to this volume.

Professor Lanzinger is not alone in having aided immeasurably in the editing of Herr Mohr's account. Dr. Lucile M. Kane, Curator of Manuscripts of the Minnesota Historical Society, has been generous beyond the call of duty in supplying me with newspaper and manuscript materials from the collections that she administers as well as saving me from numerous errors by her extended knowledge. I am similarly indebted to Mr. John L. Vantine, Research Associate, the State Historical Society of South Dakota, for aid in obtaining copies of newspapers published in that state. Mr. Louis W. Menk, Chairman of the Board of the Burlington Northern, successor to the Northern Pacific Railroad, has aided me in the search for elusive materials, as well as granting me permission to use the railroad's archives, now housed in the Minnesota Historical Society. Both the Burlington Northern officials and Mr. Henry H. Villard of New York have generously allowed the use of photographs and illustrations from their collections, many of them extremely rare. My gratitude to the Henry E. Huntington Library and Art Gallery is particularly great, for most of the materials needed in editing this book were among their collections.

In editing this work for publication I have taken certain liberties with the text. The introduction is somewhat longer than I had planned, largely because the "Villard Party," as the expedition joined by Herr Mohr was known, was singled out for a great deal of publicity by the nation's press and the temptation to tell its story in full was too great to be resisted. Too, I have made a number of deletions in Herr Mohr's account, omitting especially sections describing his visits to eastern cities during the later stages of his journey. By this time he was obviously tired, and more inclined to parrot the guidebooks he was reading than to pen original observations. All his own comments on life in the United States have been retained.

Nicolaus Mohr's narrative lacks the deep insights into the American character of a Tocqueville or a Bryce, but it does offer modern readers a fascinating description of frontier psychology in one of its most unusual aspects. The intense rivalry between western cities as they vied in honoring a man who had opened the world's gates to their commerce reveals the urge for material self-advancement that sustained the nation's expansion, just as it illustrates the unquenchable optimism with which every frontier hamlet saw itself as the future metropolis of all the West. These were heady times for those willing to brave the hardships of pioneering for the chance to grow up with the new country, and Herr Mohr observed and recorded that spirit faithfully. For today's reader, the visions of perpetual progress that buoyed the business leaders of St. Paul and Bismarck and Portland as they celebrated the completion of the railroad should be a reminder that faith, not distrust in tomorrow, carried the United States along the road to greatness.

RAY ALLEN BILLINGTON

San Marino, California, 1973

HISTORICAL INTRODUCTION

WHEN Henry Villard issued the invitation that lured Nicolaus Mohr from Germany to the United States—and thus inspired this book—he had reached the pinnacle of a career that must be judged spectacular even in the economic wonderworld of the late nineteenth century. His genius had rescued the Northern Pacific Railroad from financial chaos and extended its tracks westward to link the Pacific seaboard with the Mississippi Valley. His vision had opened the Pacific Northwest to the world's commerce and assured it of perpetual growth and prosperity. His energy had laid the basis for the extension of the farming frontier across an unpeopled domain that dwarfed many of Europe's nations. From Minneapolis to Portland he was hailed as a savior who had opened the gates into a golden future that would everlastingly benefit the people of the Northwest and of the whole country. These were truly accomplishments worthy of international attention, and Henry Villard was not one to deny himself the fame that was his due.

He had only to think back over the forty-eight years of his life to realize how very rapidly he had climbed the ladder of success. He was born Ferdinand Heinrich Gustav Hilgard in Speyer, a city in Baden, on April 10, 1835, and educated for the law at München [Munich] and Würzburg. He seemed destined for the legal career that had already won his father the presidency of the district court at Zweibrücken when his whole course was upset by the outbreak of the 1848 uprisings that rocked German authoritarianism. Young Heinrich, swayed by two liberal-minded uncles who played leading roles in the Bavarian revolutionary movement, embraced the republican cause with such conviction that he broke with his father, became an active revolutionary, and finally fled to America in October, 1853, when the uprisings failed. There, fearful of retaliation, he changed his name to Henry Villard. For a time he sought oblivion in the German communities of Cincinnati and Chicago, thus perfecting his knowledge of English before moving to Belleville, Illinois, to join a great-uncle who had migrated in the 1830s. There he read law and peddled books for a time, but when he joined the tiny editorial staff of a small-town newspaper he knew that he had found his true profession. Journalism would be his career.

A successful career it was. During the next decade Villard pursued his new craft from triumph to triumph, first as a correspondent for the *New York Staats Zeitung*, then as Rocky Mountain representative of the *Cincinnati Commercial* where he produced his well-read book on *The Past and Present of the Pike's Peak Gold Region*, published in 1860. He reported the Republican convention that nominated Lincoln for the *Commercial*, the presidential campaign for the *New York Herald*; the first years of the Civil War for the *Herald* and *New York Tribune*; the last years for a syndicate that assigned him to the Army of the Potomac; and the dawn of peace for the *Chicago Tribune*. Along the way he found time to marry a young lady who was destined to play a prominent part in his career: Miss Fanny Garrison, daughter of William Lloyd Garrison of abolitionist fame. By 1868 Henry Villard seemed to be settled into a journalistic career that he would follow through his lifetime.

So he might have, but for an invitation that year to join the staff of the *Boston Advertiser* as an editorial writer. Humanitarian reform was a way of life in that city. Given Villard's belief in republicanism his involvement was inevitable, principally as secretary of the American Social Science Association which was laboring in behalf of federal civil service. These new duties required a respectable knowledge of finance, corporate organization, and business administration. Typically, Villard labored so mightily to perfect himself in those subjects that his health was threatened. In 1871, and again in 1873, he found it necessary to spend long months in Germany to seek recovery in rest.

That second visit changed his whole future, for there he met an anxious group of German financiers with a mission for him to perform. They were, they explained, representing a larger group of their countrymen who had purchased the bonds of the Oregon and California Railroad Company which planned to connect Portland and San Francisco by rail. That railroad, like most others building at the time, had fallen victim to the Panic of 1873 and was threatened with bankruptcy. The bondholders were concerned, and wanted more information. Would Henry Villard use his newly acquired expertise in finance to investigate the whole situation and tell them how to protect their investments? Villard would, and in 1874 reached Oregon to probe the problem at its source. The solution, he reported, was obvious. The Oregon and California Railroad could never succeed so long as it competed for trade with the Oregon Steamship Company which operated vessels between the two ports. That firm was also in trouble. Therefore, why not merge the two and thus protect the German investors who were major shareholders in both concerns. His recommendations were greeted with such acclaim that Villard was not only authorized to handle the merger but was elected president of the joint company in 1876.

Henry Villard was launched on a career in railroad finance now, and would never return to the less challenging world of journalism. For a time he was drafted into the receivership of the troubled Kansas Pacific Railway where he matched wits and bravado so successfully with Jay Gould of the Union Pacific that he laid the basis of his own fortune. But his heart was in the Pacific Northwest and there his interests soon turned. That potentially rich region needed only proper commercial outlets to blossom, and Villard's mission was to provide them. He had revitalized the Oregon Steamship Company, and had replaced its wooden hulks with steel vessels; but the railroad was the way of the future and only rail connections with the East would provide the catalyst for future growth. Moreover, such a line would logically follow the low-level route along the Columbia River that led to Portland. Here was the gateway to eastern trade, and here the city that was destined to emerge as the metropolis of the Northwest.

This was the line of reasoning that led Villard in 1879 to acquire the Oregon Steam Navigation Company, a concern operating steamboats on the Columbia. His next step was to broaden the company into the Oregon Railway and Navigation Company and begin track-laying eastward from Portland along the south bank of the Columbia. Villard had no illusions of building eastward to the Mississippi Valley, for the remaining link in the trans-continental road that he envisioned was already under construction. The Northern Pacific Railroad, chartered by Congress in 1864 with a generous land grant, had laid its rails from Lake Superior to Bismarck, in the Dakotas, when the Panic of 1873 forced it to suspend operations. Now the road was showing new life, with building west of Bismarck resumed in 1879, and plans to continue along the north bank of the Columbia to Puget Sound. Here was a threat to Villard's whole grandiose scheme. If the Northern Pacific reached the Pacific it would monopolize the dreamed-of trade with the Orient, for the navigational hazards of the lower Columbia River meant that shippers would bypass Portland for the safer harbor at Puget Sound. Oregon's future, not to mention his own sizeable investments, could be saved only if the Northern Pacific could be persuaded to use the tracks of the Oregon Railway and Navigation Company on the south bank of the Columbia, with Portland as its western terminus.

Villard did try persuasion first, but when he was rebuffed, he took the only step possible: he won a controlling interest in that road. For two months, between December, 1879, and January, 1880, he quietly bought Northern Pacific stock.[1] Then, with his own resources exhausted, he sent a confidential memorandum to fifty friends asking them to subscribe to an $8,000,000 fund—with no questions asked. Such was his reputation in financial circles that not $8,000,000 but $20,000,000 poured into Villard's "Blind Pool." The rest was easy. By September 15, 1881, he had won control of the railroad and its presidency as well. His next step was to form the Oregon and Transcontinental as a holding company for both his railroad and steamship lines. By

[1] Neither a biography of Henry Villard nor an adequate history of the Northern Pacific Railroad has been written. An excellent brief account is in James B. Hedges, *Henry Villard and the Railways of the Northwest* (New York, 1930), which has provided the bulk of the information compressed into these pages.

the close of the year Henry Villard controlled the future of the Pacific Northwest, and was ready to crown his achievements by linking East and West with the steel rails that would shower it with prosperity.

This meant a flurry of construction on the two roads that would meet to form that bond. The tracks of the Oregon Railway and Navigation Company were laid first and by November, 1882, trains were operating regularly between Portland and Wallula Junction. At the same time other crews were working feverishly on the Northern Pacific, some moving eastward from Wallula Junction, some westward from Bismarck. By the summer of 1883 Villard realized the two would meet near Helena, Montana, sometime during September, 1883. Here was an event worthy of a proper celebration.

Such a celebration was needed, he knew, for a less happy reason. During the early summer Villard traveled across the entire route of the Northern Pacific, cheered by what he saw but depressed by what he heard. Superintendent after superintendent with whom he talked told the same tale: estimates far below costs, mounting expenses, the need for more money. At St. Paul, Minnesota, the road's eastern headquarters, his chief engineer was ordered to prepare an immediate estimate of money requirements. This came as a shock: the Northern Pacific was to cost $14,000,000 more than planned. Once this news leaked out he would lose the faith of the large investors on whom he leaned so heavily. Even now rumors that the company was in trouble had started its securities on the downward path after years of steady advance. This must be checked.

What better way to restore confidence than to complete the road with a flourish that would be noticed throughout the world? Once investors realized that commerce would begin flowing along that road in September they would rush to buy Northern Pacific stock, driving its price upward, and providing the extra funds needed to meet the unexpected construction costs. But how best to spread those tidings? Villard's answer was sensible. He would stage a grand opening ceremony "so pretentious, so glittering in spangled brilliance" (to quote but one observer) that the whole world would have to pay attention. This celebration would be attended by the cream of governmental and financial titans of America and Europe, beginning with the President of the United States and then descending through representatives of the British and German rulers to cabinet ministers, diplomats, congressmen, and governors—with a liberal sprinkling of bankers and businessmen thrown in. The latter were especially important, for Henry Villard wanted something more than world attention.

By mixing bankers and commercial magnates and newspaper correspondents with glamorous royalty and governmental leaders he would accomplish two needed miracles. One was to win friends in the right circles against the not-too-distant day when the Northern Pacific would need financial aid. The other was to interest the prospective investors in three principal sources of more capital for the American West—the East, Britain, and Germany—in helping develop the sparsely settled northern tier of states through which his road operated.[2] Henry Villard might rival P. T. Barnum in his flamboyant plans, but he never forgot to court the almighty dollars that would be needed in the future.

Now he must plan a ceremony—and compile a guest list—that would assure the world-wide publicity he needed. The list was to be a "Who's Who" of the world of government and finance. To the Queen of England and the Imperial German Government went handsomely engraved invitations: "In view of the international character of its enterprise, the company begs leave to extend a most respectful and cordial invitation . . . ." Would Her Highness, would the Chancellor of Imperial Germany, deign to send representatives? All expenses would be paid for the six-week journey, and the most lavish entertainment that money and influence could buy would be provided. Six "cards of invitation" were enclosed. "This railway," the invitees were assured, ". . . will not only open new and vast fields of commerce and industry in the states and

---

[2] Henry Villard, *Memoirs* (2 v., Boston, 1904), II, 304-308, contain his own reasons for inviting the German and English guests.

territories named, but also an expeditious and attractive route for travel and trade across the American continent, and to Asia and Australia."[3] This was the message—with that politely worded boost for the railroad—that went to the glittering guest list that Henry Villard and his staff compiled. If all accepted, the assemblage would outshine any in the nation's history.

Unfortunately they did not. President Chester Arthur would be otherwise occupied; also would be most of the members of his cabinet and an alarming number of senators, diplomats, and industrial titans, not to mention the elite of England and Germany—so many, in fact, that a printed circular was distributed among the laggards who had not replied by the end of July, warning that transportation arrangements could not be made until all responded.[4] Yet even though refusals far outnumbered acceptances, enough were attracted by the promise of six weeks as guests of the Northern Pacific to make a

[3] Northern Pacific Company Records, Department of the Secretary, Villard Excursion File, 1883, Folder 2, contains page after page listing guests, reproducing letters of invitation, and the like. The "Villard Excursion File" is among the papers of the Northern Pacific Railroad deposited by its successor, the Burlington Northern Railroad, in the archives of the Minnesota Historical Society. I am grateful to the Burlington Northern Railroad Inc., for permission to use this file, and to Dr. Lucile M. Kane, Curator of Manuscripts at the Society, for making the necessary arrangements.

[4] *Ibid.*, Folder 7. Dozens of letters of refusal are in Folders 4 to 7.

respectable party: from England came the Earl and Countess of Onslow, Lord Carrington, former Chief Justice Charles Russell, Lord Justice Charles Bowen, James Bryce, Sir William H. Gurdon of Her Majesty's Treasury, H. H. Gibbs of the Bank of England, a half-dozen members of Parliament, and a handful of lesser lights; from Germany came the eminent jurist Dr. Rudolf Gneist, Dr. Eduard Lasker who led the National-Liberal Party, Dr. A. W. Hofmann the chemist and Professor K. A. Zittel whose reputation as a biologist was world-wide, the writer Paul Lindau, representatives of most of the leading cities, and such financial giants as Dr. Georg Siemens of the Deutsche Bank and Otto Braunfels of the Jakob S. H. Stern Company.[5] These eye-catchers were much to Henry Villard's liking, but even more to his taste was the fact that the German guests alone, according to his own estimate, represented about $100,000,000 in capital.[6] Such good friends might be needed in the days ahead.

He was more than satisfied as he directed his underlings to inform the guests of the delights that lay ahead: steamship travel to New York, private cars

[5] Lists of the guests, all varying in degree, are in Villard, *Memoirs*, II, 308–310, the *New York Times*, August 15, 1883, p. 2, August 28, p. 3; *Chicago Tribune*, August 31, p. 2; [St. Paul] *Daily Pioneer Press*, September 3, p. 2; and particularly in *The Northwest*, I (September, 1883), 9–12. The latter also included numerous letters praising Villard for his project.

[6] Villard made this statement in an interview in Minneapolis. *Daily Minneapolis Tribune*, September 1, 1883.

on the railroads to Chicago and St. Paul, special trains for the journey to Montana, sight-seeing in the Puget Sound country, a chance to visit either San Francisco or Yellowstone National Park, hotel accommodations along the way at the finest hostelries—all at the expense of the Northern Pacific Railroad. These were tempting prospects indeed.

AMONG THOSE who prepared for the journey that summer, none was more delighted at the prospect— and none more apprehensive—than Herr Nicolaus Mohr, publisher of Bremen's *Weser Zeitung*, one of Germany's most influential newspapers. Born in Bremen July 12, 1826, Mohr had studied philology at the University of Bonn, traveled for several years in France and Spain, taught briefly at an English boarding school and for some years at the School of Economics in his native city before beginning his journalistic career in 1853. Like many of his countrymen he supported a united Germany in the hope that political, religious, and economic freedoms would be strengthened; unlike most, he was so faithful to the principle of non-violence that he opposed the events of 1866 and 1870 from which an Imperial Germany emerged.

His liberal views won him the respect of much of northern and central Germany and elevated his *Weser Zeitung* to a position of unrivaled influence among the diplomatic leaders and commercial elite there. Mohr was also known to a sizeable number of

German-Americans, for since 1866 he had printed a weekly edition of the *Weser Zeitung* for overseas distribution. His fame decreed that he would be welcomed wherever he went in the United States; his political leanings meant that he would view the nation through sympathetic eyes yet not be blind to its social and political defects.[7]

To Herr Mohr the journey that lay ahead was not an unmixed blessing; he was fifty-seven years old, not too well, and unabashedly apprehensive at risking his life in the Indian-infested wilds of the American West. He recognized, too, that the hardships and dangers of such a trip into an area just being opened to civilization were uncomfortably real. Yet the opportunity to visit a land that he admired but had never seen, and to rub elbows with his country's political bigwigs, was not to be avoided. On the night of August 14, 1883, Herr Mohr, his trunk packed, felt only elation as he joined his fellow-travelers from Germany at the Bremen *Ratskeller* for a farewell party staged by the Senators of that city.

What a gala party that was. Albert Gröning, Senator from Bremen, raised his glass first to toast the Northern Pacific Railroad and its president, Henry Villard, proud in the knowledge "that a fellow Ger-

[7] For this information on Johann Nicolaus Richard Mohr's background and career I am grateful to Dr. Lührs, Archivist of the State Archives of Bremen. It is contained in a letter to Professor Klaus Lanzinger of the University of Notre Dame dated March 23, 1972, and is based on extensive research by Dr. Lührs.

man is the leader of this tremendous achievement."
Toasts and speeches flew thick and fast, with Rudolf Schleiden of Freiburg honoring the Hanseatic
cities in general and Bremen in particular. Lord
Mayor Bugg answered, and Richard Gördeler, general agent of the Northern Pacific in Berlin, voiced
the thanks of Henry Villard for all the praise he had
received. The hour was late when the "Villard Party" (as it came to be known), all filled to repletion
with food, wine, and oratory, adjourned for a few
hours' sleep before the next day's sailing.

They were away at seven that morning, somewhat the worse for wear, by train to the port at
Bremerhafen where they struggled to load their luggage into the small boats that were to take them to
the North German Lloyd steamship *Elbe* which lay
at anchor in the harbor. By eleven they were on
their way. The crossing was hardly an undiluted
delight; the weather was unusually cold for August,
the seas rough, the winds constant, and clouds or
rain daily companions. But even the seasickness
that plagued most of the party (although not Herr
Mohr) was forgotten as the vessel passed Nantucket
Lighthouse Saturday morning, August 25, and
steamed into New York harbor after ten days at sea.

Waiting on the dock was a distinguished reception committee, headed by Henry Villard and the
famed German-American, Carl Schurz. Greetings
first, then a steam yacht to the foot of West 24th
Street where carriages waited to drive the visitors

about the city (with special attention paid the
Northern Pacific headquarters in the Mills Building
on Broad Street), deposit them at the Hoffmann
House for a "smile" (as a local reporter phrased it),
and leave them at the luxurious Brunswick Hotel at
the corner of Fifth Avenue and 26th Street.[8] Each
guest presented the special card that was furnished
him, authorizing the hotel to supply his every need
and charge it to the Northern Pacific, then turned
into his room for a needed rest.[9]

The next days were crammed full of busyness: a
visit to Coney Island, dinner at the Union League
Club with speech following speech, luncheon at
Villard's country estate near Dobb's Ferry, a steamboat journey up the Hudson River to Newburgh, a
Geselliger Abend at the Liederkranz Society where
1,500 guests consumed 15,000 steins of beer amidst
songs and still more speeches.[10] By the evening of
August 28 they were ready to board the special
train that awaited them at Grand Central Station to
begin the trip westward.

The journey was interrupted with the inevitable
day at Niagara Falls where the Germans marveled at

[8] *New York Times*, August 26, 1883, p. 2; *New York World*,
August 26, 1883, p. 7.
[9] Copies of this card are in the Villard Excursion File,
Folder 4. They are signed by George V. Sims, Mr. Villard's
assistant.
[10] The entertainment lavished on the visitors in New York
was described in the *New York Times*, August 27, 1883, p.
8, August 28, p. 2; *New York World*, August 28, p. 5.

the giant cataract, viewed the whirlpool, and descended into the Cave of the Winds. Late on Thursday, August 30, their special train deposited them
in Chicago where a committee of distinguished German-Americans waited to lead them on the usual
round of sightseeing: by open carriage to view the
stately homes on the south side and suffer near heat
prostration as they did so, to the Board of Trade
where they were awed by the babble of shouting
speculators and forced to endure another round of
speeches. By this time some, at least, among them
felt enough at home to indulge in a touch of irony;
Baron Georg von Bunsen, shouting to make himself
heard above the hubbub, assured his hosts that the
guests were delighted with the "calm, subdued, self-
conscious manner" of the Chicagoans, "the gentleness of every class of the community, which is the
most astonishing characteristic of the American
people." Few heard him. No sooner was he finished
than the hammer fell and trading resumed at such a
furious pace that the visitors left the hall unnoticed.
Over the next hours their schedule was so crowded
that they missed some of the sights they particularly
wanted to see, the famed Stock Yards especially. By
the time they returned to their special train on the
evening of August 31 they were, as one reporter
noted, "heartily glad that their treat was over."[11]

Well they might be, for Chicago had given them

[11]*Chicago Tribune*, August 29, 1883, p. 6, August 30, p. 2,
August 31, p. 2, September 1, p. 3.

a taste of the lionization that was to be their lot wherever they went in America. Here was a unique event, and the local press was determined to make an impression that would alter the course of history. "So many prominent foreigners," declared one editorial writer, "have never before been grouped together in one visiting party to this country."[12] They were stared at like so many animals in a zoo. Wherever they drove, their carriages were surrounded by gaping crowds or their steps dogged by the unabashedly curious. They were besieged by reporters who sought their opinion on everything from the state of crops in Germany to the future of European civilization, until one visitor cried out: "You are all first-rate fellows, granted, sure to become rulers of the Universe, but for the sake of humanity, let us be; we want rest."[13] Worst of all, they were constantly lectured on all the virtues of the American democracy. "WHAT WILL THEY SEE?" asked one newspaper, then went on to tell them: not vast estates of magnates, not a standing army, not a selfish nobility—only a new country where freedom and self-government had made the people more prosperous and happier in twenty years than the Old World had made them in the three centuries since the discovery of the New. They will see, the visitors were told, that monarchical governments must be overthrown and the pattern of the United States be

[12] *Chicago Tribune*, August 31, 1883, p. 4.
[13] *Ibid.*

imitated everywhere.[14] The rare moments of peace in hotel rooms must have seemed blessed to the Germans after listening to such advice day after day.

They were to listen to even more of American greatness and European decadence as they reached the heart of the Villard country. St. Paul and Minneapolis were next on their itinerary, and here the visitors were to begin to understand the significance of a new railroad to the undeveloped portions of the West. The Twin Cities, planted at the eastern terminus of the line, were to multiply their commerce, their population, and their wealth as goods flowed eastward through their portals. Here was something worth celebrating, and with a celebration that would outdo any in history. Moreover, each city was determined to out-celebrate the other. They planned a joint ceremony first, but Minneapolis failed to name the needed committee on time (due to a long-term feud between the municipal government and the Board of Trade), and the St. Paul committee, tired of waiting, decided to go ahead alone. Minneapolis, too late, sought a reconciliation; its special committee made the ten-mile trip into the enemy country only to have its plea for cooperation rejected.[15] "We crawled on our bellies to you St. Paul fellows," one member complained,

[14] *New York World*, September 1, 1883, p. 4.

[15] [St. Paul] *Daily Pioneer Press*, August 22, 1883, p. 9, August 23, p. 8, August 25, p. 3; *Daily Minneapolis Tribune*, August 18, 23, 24, 1883. Because the *Tribune* normally contained only four pages, I have omitted page numbers.

"and got kicked for our pains." Now each city would hold its own celebration, with a more lavish dinner, a longer parade, better decorations, and more speeches, than its rival.

Which would be visited first by the Villard Party? Someone on the Minneapolis committee decided to steal a march on St. Paul by persuading Henry Villard to honor their request. This was delivered by a special group that secretly visited Villard when the party was in Chicago. Here was a diplomatic *impasse* to test the skills of a master negotiator. Villard proved equal to the challenge: the dignitaries would visit St. Paul in the morning and Minneapolis in the afternoon; thus (hopefully) confining the parade planned by each city to a half-day's duration; Minneapolis could hold its banquet one night at the Lyndale Hotel, St. Paul the next at the Lafayette Hotel, both summer resort hostelries on neutral ground.[16]

The gauntlet was down now, and each city determined to outdo the other in decorations, pomp, and ceremony. Volunteers were pressed into service, mechanics and carpenters hired, business houses browbeaten into transforming their drab establishments into gaily ornamented palaces. Arches were erected at strategic intervals along the parade route in both cities, all resplendent with flags and banners and bunting; bridges spanned the streets at conspicuous points, often with models of Northern Pacific

[16] *Daily Minneapolis Tribune*, September 1, 1883.

trains; in Minneapolis a replica of Minnehaha Falls "with real water" was constructed to overawe the visitors. Minneapolis built a grandstand seating a thousand persons across from the Nicollet House; St. Paul boasted that its was even larger. And everywhere were pictures of Henry Villard, festooned with flowers by the grateful populace. "More magnificent decorations," wrote one correspondent solemnly, "never graced a city's thoroughfares."[17] Nor was this lavish display questioned, for the completion of the Northern Pacific was worth any celebration. "The event," declared one editorial writer, "will be unique in the history of the planet, and it cannot have a successor of its kind."[18] Added another: "No celebration can be too magnificent, no paeans loud enough, no rejoicings deep enough to cover the full significance of this occasion."[19]

All of this was music to Henry Villard's ears. And to the ears of his visitors. They were welcomed to St. Paul first by the usual committee with the mayor at its head, driven about the city to admire its beauty and enterprise, and at noon escorted to Magree's Restaurant where a dinner was served which, the local scribe judged, "from soup to nuts

[17] *Chicago Tribune*, September 4, 1883, p. 1; [St. Paul] *Daily Pioneer Press*, September 4, 1883, p. 2; *Daily Minneapolis Tribune*, October 30, 31, 1883.

[18] *Daily Minneapolis Tribune*, August 24, 1883.

[19] [St. Paul] *Daily Pioneer Press*, September 2, 1883, p. 4. Much of this issue was devoted to articles about Villard and the railroad.

and including the choicest vintages of wines, has never been excelled in St. Paul."[20] Such a repast almost justified the parade of speakers which followed; they were cheered with a chorus of "Hoch, Hoch, Hoch" so long that the visitors were late for their next engagement. This was in Minneapolis, where carriages awaited their special train to whisk them away to the suburban home of the town's leading citizen, William D. Washburn, founder of the giant Pillsbury-Washburn flour milling firm. The sandwiches and light supper served there satisfied most of the guests (save Herr Mohr whose appetite must have been phenomenal). Only after the usual tributes were exchanged were the tired guests returned to the railroad station, piled aboard their cars, and carried fifteen miles to the Hotel Lafayette on Lake Minnetonka, a rambling summer-resort hotel accommodating 1,200 patrons.

They were ready to rest then, and the next day they were allowed their freedom save for a steamer tour of the lake. But on Monday, September 3, their duties began again. "The most eventful day in the history of Minneapolis," one reporter dubbed it, which none would dispute. The air was crisp under a clear sky when the visiting dignitaries reached St. Paul's Union Depot at 9:45 that morning, there to join the other notables that Henry Villard had gathered. Former President Ulysses S. Grant was much in evidence, together with cabinet ministers, ambas-

[20] *Chicago Tribune*, September 2, 1883, p. 6.

sadors, congressmen and governors, as well as the thirty members of the English party who had arrived a day after the Germans.

All climbed aboard the carriages donated for the occasion (their owners, from their driver's seats, privileged to rub elbows with the great). Villard, his wife, and General Grant joined the mayor in the first carriage, the others following. Led by a platoon of police and the Great Union Band, the little procession wended slowly through streets jammed with 100,000 people to Rice Park, then up Third Street to Market. As they passed beneath the triumphal arch at Third and Cedar, Villard raised his hat to the crowd as a shower of rose petals fell over him and his carriage.[21]

Scarcely were the guests seated in the reviewing stand than the parade began. "The measureless vocabulary of a circus advertiser," wrote one reporter, would be inadequate to describe "its bewildering magnificence."[22] An escort of police first, followed by a troupe of boys in blue shirts and red trousers riding spirited ponies, soldiers from nearby Fort Snelling led by a Negro band, Indians in war paint

[21] The fullest description of the parade, decorations, and entertainment are in John H. Hanson, comp., *Grand Opening of the Northern Pacific Railway Celebration at St. Paul, Minnesota, the Eastern Terminus, September 3, 1883. Issued by Order of the City of St. Paul* (St. Paul, [1883]), 1–60. Local newspapers also printed full accounts: [St. Paul] *Daily Pioneer Press*, September 3, 1883, p. 6, September 4, p. 2; *Daily Minneapolis Tribune*, September 4, 1883.

[22] *Daily Minneapolis Tribune*, September 4, 1883.

and feathers, more military companies, a regimental band, the Ames Zouaves who paused now and then to execute complex drills to the delight of the crowd. The Grand Army of the Republic next in endless numbers, then the fire department with a wagon crowded with poles and wires that displayed the fire-alarm system, marching societies of Germans and Irish and Poles and French immigrant societies, a little wagon drawn by a Shetland pony showing the St. Paul post office in 1846 (Total Receipts $3.43) and a giant vehicle with a replica of the current operation (Total Receipts $183,446).

This was only the beginning, though the visiting dignitaries were growing restless and wandering off to sample the sandwiches, fruits and wine that had been spread beneath a flower-decked canopy. The main feature—the industrial exhibits—was still to come. It came—and came—and came. "A dazzling and bewildering display," the press branded it, with good reason. Marching lumbermen, wood workers, wholesale manufacturers and wholesale distributors, brewers, dry-goods merchants and grocery clerks—seemingly without an end. One wholesale grocer paraded fifteen wagons loaded with saleable goods; a dealer in yard goods offered no less than twenty wagons heaped with blankets, carpets, mats, knit goods, flannels, velvets, cotton bales, dress goods, tents, awnings, calicos, flannels, woolens—everything that had any remote connection with cloth. In all, that procession was ten miles long, with 724 wagons and 4,300 marchers, and required three hours to pass a given point.

Fortunately the visitors were spared the entire ordeal, for at 11:30, with the end of the parade still far distant, they thankfully departed to retrace the journey to the Union Station and the trains that would carry them the ten miles to Minneapolis where they were due at 1:00 in the afternoon. They soon discovered that they had leaped from the frying pan into the fire. Minneapolis, angered by St. Paul's refusal to stage a joint celebration, felt compelled to outdo its rival with more elaborate exhibits, more lavish decorations, and a parade that was guaranteed to numb any watcher. Too, President Chester A. Arthur had arrived unexpectedly from a western trip, just in time to join the official party.[23] Little wonder that Minneapolis was bursting with pride and excitement when the carriages bearing the President, Henry Villard, and the long procession of visiting dignitaries reached the grandstand in front of the Nicollet House shortly after 1:30 that afternoon.

The marchers, who had been waiting in line for nearly an hour, started as soon as the lengthy cheers for the President, General Grant, and Henry Villard showed first signs of subsiding. Once more watchers were carried back into history by the first

[23] The *New York Times*, September 1, 1883, p. 4, reported that Villard had done everything possible to lure President Arthur to his ceremony, but had failed.

wagons: two loaded with Sioux Indians, and one with a statue of Father Hennepin proclaiming that while he discovered Minneapolis in 1680, Henry Villard discovered it in 1880; Red River carts and stagecoaches and cattle and pioneers. Then came the more recent arrivals, represented by the *Turnverein* and the Harmonia Society and the Scandinavian Society with their hundreds of marchers.

Again, the industrial exhibits monopolized most of the procession. Some of them were crowd-catchers—a working model of the Pillsbury flour mill, a model of a bull tossing grain in the air—but for the most part viewers suffered the sight of armies of workers and traders and clerks as they passed in procession, or of wagons loaded with saleable goods offered by every wholesale establishment and retail emporium in the city. "The Philadelphia One-Price Clothing Store and the Big Boston Haberdashery," reported a local chronicler, "made displays as elaborate as they were charming, and as perfect as the slumber of innocence."[24] Minneapolis had clearly won the battle of the parades.[25] Its spectacle was twenty miles long, took seven hours to pass a given spot, and contained fourteen bands, fifteen military companies, 134 men on horseback, 829 wagons, 2,213 horses, and several thousand marchers. The

[24] *Daily Minneapolis Tribune*, September 4, 1883.

[25] *Ibid.*, September 6, 1883. Full accounts of the Minneapolis parade are in a special eighteen-page issue of the *Daily Minneapolis Tribune*, September 4, 1883, and the [St. Paul] *Daily Pioneer Press*, September 4, 1883, pp. 5-6.

visitors, commented a reporter, looked on until they could look no longer.

Again Herr Mohr and his fellow-dignitaries were spared the entire ordeal. By 4:00 that afternoon, with the procession scarcely under way, they were on their way to the Lyndale Hotel on nearby Lake Calhoun, a summer hostelry somewhat less elaborate than the Hotel Lafayette, where they were to be served a late-afternoon "breakfast" as guests of the city of Minneapolis. An unusual breakfast that was, with an elaborate menu printed on white silk, music by Day's Band, and a buffet that ranged from *pâté de foie gras* and boned canvas-back duck to roasted buffalo tongue and broiled prairie chicken. Washburn presided, as befitting the city's leading citizen, and introduced the speakers: Henry Villard whose remarks were greeted with "tempestuous applause," General Grant, a senator from Oregon, representatives of the German party, and such others as could make themselves heard. This was not easy, for the listeners were so surfeited with oratory after the first speakers that they preferred to chatter among themselves.[26] By this time they had heard the same boasts too often to be interested.

Yet more was to come, for now St. Paul had its turn. Scarcely was the last speaker silenced than all were trundled away to the Lafayette Hotel for the final banquet. This was "the crown of the great day;" the decorations were more ornate (but with

[26] *Daily Minneapolis Tribune*, September 4, 1883, p. 7.

nothing "tawdry or bizarre in the effect"), the menu (printed in French) designed to outshine that of the best Paris restaurant, the feast "the most elaborate one that money could provide, in the matter of both victuals and drink." That, at least, was the judgment of the St. Paul press; reporters from other cities were less prejudiced when they found that the guests were served "a meagre assortment of badly cooked viands, with high-sounding French names, served shabbily, and in such small quantities that even those most easily satisfied rose from the table with their appetites unappeased."[27] The wine, they added, could be bought for seven dollars a case, but this did the guests no harm for most was consumed by the waiters who were so tipsy by the end of the meal that they served the last three courses badly and forgot the coffee altogether. "For general badness and overtaxed ambition," haughtily judged the correspondent of the *New York Times*, that meal "excelled any 'swell dinner' of which I have had the honor to partake."[28]

But the worst was yet to come, for the visitors must sing for their poor supper by enduring the overdoses of oratory that had been planned. The mayor of St. Paul, capitalizing on his brief moment in the sun, not only talked endlessly himself but followed with over-long introductions: one for President Arthur who dwelt expansively on Villard's

[27] *Ibid.*, September 6, 1883.
[28] *New York Times*, September 9, 1883, p. 9.

accomplishments and praised the builders of the Northern Pacific ("All honor to them and to their zeal and energy which have given to that enterprise such tremendous success"); others for H. M. Teller, Secretary of the Interior; the governor of Minnesota; the mayor of Minneapolis; the commandant at Fort Snelling; a representative of the foreign guests; the builder of the Great Northern Railroad; and a few more. By the time Carl Schurz was introduced to respond to a toast on "The Press," that worthy and most of the official guests had been hurried away to catch their special trains for the journey westward. The most exciting two days in the history of the Twin Cities had ended. "St. Paul and Minneapolis," wrote a St. Paul reporter, "vied with each other in celebrating an event which for importance has no parallel in their history."[29] Some of the honored guests must have wished that their rivalry had led to less competitive exhibitionism. They were bone tired as they settled into their berths for the midnight departure.

For Henry Villard there was little rest, for he was sadly aware that this last stage of the journey was studded with danger. He must transport 332 of the most influential men in the United States, England,

[29][St. Paul] *Daily Pioneer Press*, September 4, 1883, p. 4. The banquet was described in the *Daily Minneapolis Tribune*, September 4, 1883, p. 5, the *Chicago Tribune*, September 4, 1883, p. 1, and the *New York Times*, September 5, 1883, p. 4.

and Germany, riding in forty-three private cars in four trains operating a half-hour apart, across two thousand miles of virgin territory where stations were spaced at hundred-mile intervals and equipment for safety control nonexistent. True, he had made every possible preparation. A refrigerator car attached to the first train carried enough meat and fresh vegetables to last to Helena, where they would be met by a special supply train from the coast. Telegraph offices along the route were ordered to stay open day and night to be available to the special operator who rode each section, carrying a relay battery and pole-climbing equipment that would allow aid to be summoned in case of emergency. Riding on each train was a skilled mechanic trained to repair broken equipment. All other trains, both freight and passenger, were to be sidetracked while the special trains were in the same division, while the division superintendents were to ride with one of the sections within their own territories.[30] Every possible danger had been anticipated, but Villard was a good enough railroad man to know that accidents and breakdowns could never be avoided. He would not be completely at ease until the last of his distinguished guests was safely home again.[31]

For the moment, however, his apprehensions could be shelved, for the journey westward was one

---

[30] *Daily Minneapolis Tribune*, August 26, September 5, 1883.
[31] Villard, *Memoirs*, II, 311–312.

continuous celebration. Villard had seen to that; leaving nothing to chance (not even the booster spirit of a budding new town) the Northern Pacific had distributed flags and evergreens along the way with suggestions that local products be added to create special displays. The company had, one of its officials reported, "gotten up quite an interest among the citizens along the line and urged them to display samples of wheat, cereals, etc. in an ornamental way, and I have no fears but that this part of the programme will meet with satisfaction."[32] Such goading was hardly necessary, for there was not an infant community along the route but was eager to blow its own horn, tout its own products, and tell the world that it was destined to become *the* metropolis of all the West. "Every city and village along the line from Brainerd to Portland," reported the *Minneapolis Tribune*, "is purchasing bunting and gunpowder by wholesale, and the one will wave and the other explode with unique and peculiar western vigor in honor of the passing excursionists and the day they celebrate."[33]

The travelers had their first taste of western enthusiasm at Fargo where a "grand triumphal arch" spanned the track, topped by a huge cornucopia on wheels representing the railroad, pouring forth

[32] General Manager of the Northern Pacific Company at St. Paul to George V. Sims, August 14, 1883, in Villard Excursion File, Folder 4–7.

[33] *Daily Minneapolis Tribune*, August 16, 1883.

products of the fertile soil. The most imposing decorations the party had seen since they had entered Minnesota, Villard called them, doubtless hoping that Minneapolis papers would not copy. There a thousand or more people from all the countryside had gathered to greet the visitors and cheer the parade of speakers who volunteered for the occasion during the brief stop.

At every hamlet along the tracks the story was the same, for each was cocksure that the railroad would transmute it into a teeming city, bustling with commerce and prosperity. Only the publicity stemming from the visit of the official party was needed to put it on the map. Wrote one exuberant editor: "The pulsing arteries of commerce and trade of the Northwest will center here as naturally as the needle of the compass seeks the pole. Power and glory await us. Prosperity is knocking at the door and the goddess of fortune is bestowing upon us her most radiant smiles."[34] Nor was this wishful thinking alone. Already speculators were bidding the price of town lots and rural acreage sky high, confident that the land would return their investment a hundred fold within a year.[35] For all of this Henry Villard was responsible, and they must shower him with their gratitude. VILLARD THE VICTORIOUS, proclaimed one newspaper that

[34] *Bismarck* [Dakota Territory] *Tribune*, September 7, 1883.
[35] *New York Times*, September 9, 1883, p. 9; *Chicago Tribune*, September 5, 1883, p. 3.

had chronicled the westward progress of the party.[36]

One celebration overshadowed all others. Bismarck had reason to rejoice, for it had just won a tug-of-war with Yankton as the site of the territorial capital, and was surely destined for a place in the commercial sun. Why not combine the Villard visit with the laying of the capitol's cornerstone, thus assuring a burst of publicity for the event? The governor's suggestion (and his assurance that the new edifice "will be as large as the Minnesota capitol and much more imposing") was enough.[37] Villard and his guests would be happy to be there for the great occasion. Their trains would arrive sometime during the night of September 4 so that all would be available for the ceremony the next morning.

The great day in Bismarck's brief history dawned fair; the sun shown through a soft September haze; "the gentle breezes which swept over the emerald-clothed prairies fanned each cheek with a soothing tenderness which was at once both delightful and gratifying"—or so a local scribe reported, doubtless hoping that metropolitan papers would copy. The guests were less appreciative when tumbled from their cars at 7:30, but they cheerfully crowded into the waiting carriages and set off for the capitol site, escorted by a military band from Fort Yates.

The little procession hardly rivaled the parades

[36][St. Paul] *Daily Pioneer Press*, September 5, 1883, p. 3.
[37] Nehemiah G. Ordway to Henry Villard, July 18, 1883, in Villard Excursion File, Folder 4–7.

staged by the Twin Cities—the band first, a carriage bearing the governor, General Grant and Henry Villard, others holding the visiting dignitaries, more with the town's leading citizens, two fire companies, and Chief Sitting Bull with a handful of followers—nor could the decorations equal those the guests had seen. "Our fair burg," explained the local editor, "is yet but an infant in her swaddling clothes," but given time it would outshine all rivals.

It could, however, provide lush oratory to challenge any competitor, and as soon as the echoes of the seventeen-gun salute that accompanied the cornerstone laying died down, the speeches began: Henry Villard at some length, the governor at greater length ending with the presentation of a scroll to Baron von Eisendecher, the German minister, honoring Chancellor Bismarck. The German minister hoped that the city "will make its name sound in your land as highly as the name of its godfather sounds in our land" (cheers). William M. Evarts, Carl Schurz, H. M. Teller, Mayor Carter Harrison of Chicago, and General Grant (by popular demand). Even Sitting Bull[38] was persuaded to mutter a few words (that no one understood) before passing among the visitors to sell his autograph at

[38] *Bismarck Tribune*, September 6, 1883. This paper published a special eight-page edition to honor the occasion, with full descriptions of all that took place. The presence of Chief Sitting Bull was noticed especially by the correspondent of *Frank Leslie's Illustrated Newspaper*, LVII (September 22, 1883), 77.

$1.50 a copy. "The most important episode in the history of our bustling young city," the *Bismarck Tribune* branded it, and no one disagreed.[39]

By mid-morning the special trains were rolling westward once more, through mile after mile of yellow Dakota wheat fields where grain stood in shocks and threshing crews were busy, past little villages where evergreens decorated the station and the whole populace was out to cheer, on westward into the higher country of western Dakota and the Badlands. There a stop was made to let the guests walk about and marvel at nature's distortion of the earth. Even in the smallest hamlets miniature parades and receptions and music and such decorations as local ingenuity could muster greeted the visitors. This was a triumphant procession if ever one was.

At Greycliff, in the very heart of the Crow Indian Reservation, the trains paused for a ceremony that delighted the foreign guests. They must, Villard realized as he planned the expedition, be treated to the sight of Indians, and what better spot than this for a small ceremony. The reservation agent proved cooperative; he would see to it that as many as desired were waiting and that they staged one of their dances for the sightseers. All of this would be free, of course; cheap presents might be given to Indians who were farming, or those who had sent their children to the agency school, or "a few others who are considered to be chiefs or head men," but the rest

[39] *Bismarck Tribune*, September 6, 1883.

deserved nothing. On second thought, why award even these? "I think if we make them a pretty good feast and give them plenty of cigarettes to smoke it will satisfy them."[40] So much for the rights of Uncle Sam's wards. The railroad was pleased with such economical entertainment, and so were the overseas visitors who gaped in delight as several hundred Crow warriors executed a noisy war dance. "So weird a spectacle," Henry Villard wrote with satisfaction, "the like of which will never be seen again in the United States, naturally appealed strongly to all the European guests."[41]

All was not pomp and ceremony as the special trains inched westward, for as the tracks climbed steeply into the Rocky Mountain country problems multiplied. Once a locomotive failed in an isolated spot; the telegraph operator who was on the train climbed a pole, signaled for help, and watched as another engine soon arrived from the nearest station, pulling a flat car loaded with rails torn from an unused siding. When these were laid as a bypass around the stalled locomotive the journey was resumed. Unfinished portions of the road through the high mountain country triggered two near-serious accidents. Tunnels under the highest passes on the line—the Bozeman Pass in the Belt Mountains and

[40] H. J. Armstrong, Crow Indian Agency, to Thomas F. Oakes, Vice-President, July 23, July 24, 1883. Villard Excursion File, Folder 4–7.

[41] Villard, *Memoirs*, II, 311; *Chicago Tribune*, September 8, 1883, p. 7; *New York Times*, September 8, 1883, p. 2.

the Mullan Pass in the principal range—were still under construction, forcing traffic to span impossibly steep grades over the passes themselves. While descending from the Mullan Pass, a coupling gave way, sending half of one of the trains hurtling down the switchback grade. The end of the car carrying the British minister was smashed and six others damaged, but miraculously no one was hurt. Later the same car broke loose while on a ferry in Oregon, but again was restrained without serious injury. Little wonder that Henry Villard suffered the agonies of the damned until his visitors were safely at their first major destination: the site where the "last spike" would be driven.

This had been selected carefully with an eye to its scenic beauty and availability. Any would do, for the Northern Pacific had actually been completed two weeks earlier when the crews from east and west met at three in the afternoon on August 23, 1883, at Independence Gulch in Deer Valley, to stage their own unheralded "last spike" ceremony with the two construction gang foremen, M. Fitzpatrick and Michael Gilford, alternating in using the sledge.[42] Now another site five miles away, at a point where Independence Creek flowed into the Deer Lodge River about fifty miles west of Helena, was chosen; there a grassy meadow, fringed by willows

[42][St. Paul] *Pioneer Press*, August 23, 1883, p. 8, August 24, p. 7; *New York Herald*, August 24, 1883, p. 6; *New York Times*, September 1, 1883, p. 2.

and cottonwood trees against the backdrop of the towering Rocky Mountains, provided both ample room and an imposing view. Thither was sent in late August a workcrew with twenty carloads of needed lumber and materials, and instructions to build an extensive plank promenade at trackside, a pavilion seating one thousand persons, and a bandstand.[43] All were decorated with flags of the United States, Britain, and Germany, and all were gay with bunting as the great day dawned. The final step was to tear up six hundred feet of track to be relaid during the ceremony, even though this meant delaying the regular trains that were already running over the line.

The ceremonies were scheduled for early in the day, but not until mid-afternoon did the notable-bearing special trains arrive—four from the east and one from the west, laden with eminent Californians, Oregonians, and Washingtonians—and not until 3:30 did Henry Villard attempt to quiet the throng of some two thousand miners, farmers, ranchers, and railroad workers who had somehow found their way to that isolated spot. By this time a dense autumn haze hid the mountains, but the sun shone warmly—too warmly for the overseas visitors who were seated on the unshaded promenade beside the tracks. The great moment had arrived.

Band music first, provided by the Fifth Infantry military band from Fort Keogh, which accommo-

[43][St. Paul] *Pioneer Press*, August 29, 1883, p. 3.

dated with not only the usual marches but also "A Grand Triumphal March: 'The Iron Horse,'" composed especially for the occasion. Then Henry Villard, seated with his wife, his fifteen-year-old daughter, and his three-month-old son, stood up to speak, reciting the history of the enterprise that was to reach its climax that afternoon. "No light duty it was," he reminded those who could hear him, "but wearisome and brain and nerve exhausting. Still, its very grandeur inspired the will and the power to perform it, and there was comfort and elevation in the thought that we have built what cannot perish, but will last to the end of all earthly things."[44]

Villard's eloquence opened the floodgates of oratory for the endless procession of speakers who followed. William M. Evarts, orator of the day,[45] had been firmly instructed to restrict himself to half an hour, but who could restrain himself on such an occasion? Not Evarts, as he heaped commendation

[44] Full accounts of the ceremony, differing in detail, are in *New York Times*, September 9, 1883, p. 2, September 10, p. 1, September 23, p. 6; *New York Herald*, September 10, 1883, p. 4; *Chicago Tribune*, September 9, 1883, p. 6; *Daily Minneapolis Tribune*, September 9, 1883; *Frank Leslie's Illustrated Newspaper*, LVII (September 22, 1883), 70. *The Northwest*, I (September, 1883), reproduces most of the speeches in full.

[45] An undated memorandum from Mr. Villard's secretary, George V. Sims, reads: "Foreign ministers and two gentlemen from England and two from Germany to make brief speeches at the opening. Mr. Evart's speech to be restricted to half an hour. Band to play while track being laid." Villard Excursion File, Folder 4.

on Villard and the Northern Pacific. "It brings new fields to tillage adequate to feed millions, under whose healthful and happy toil their seed time and harvest shall never fail, and tens of millions more, less fortunate, who crowd the workshops and the factories, the cities and the mines of Europe and America in this age of industry. It will help assuage inequalities of Nature and disparities of fortune among our own people, and to spread peace, plenty and prosperity to other nations."

A musical interlude was welcome after those effusions, then the parade of speakers continued: Secretary of the Interior H. M. Teller who was mercifully brief, former president of the railroad Frederick Billings who was tiresome, Sir James Hannen who showed little inclination for British understatement as he lauded the road and its builder, Baron von Eisendecher and Dr. Rudolf Gneist and Dr. A. W. Hofmann who voiced the sentiments of the German delegation, six of the seven governors who administered the states and territories through which the road operated. Despite this Niagara of rhetoric, and despite a speakers' stand so ingeniously placed that the orators had their backs to their principal audience, the crowd demanded one more. General Grant received the only genuinely enthusiastic response of the lot as his listeners "whooped and yelled and hallooed like mad."

All was in readiness now for the ceremony that the crowd anticipated. Two rival gangs were ready, three hundred brawny workers in all, to lay six hundred feet of track, with a prize to the crew that reached the junction point first. At a signal they fell to the task, racing the loaded flat cars into place, slamming down the rails, hammering and pounding. Within minutes all was over, with the gang from the east judged the winner. How the crowd cheered; then, as cannon boomed, "Old Nig," a horse that had pulled the steel cart all the way from the Missouri River, was roundly applauded. As silence fell, Villard stepped forward, holding not a golden spike but one of iron that had been the first driven when construction began. The silver-plated sledge was handed to H. C. Davis, who had driven the first spike when work started in 1870. After he had struck a lusty blow it was passed to Villard who let his three-month-old son hold the handle before he took his turn. Frederick Billings "took a whack" next (in the language of the *New York Times* correspondent), and General Grant one more as the spike sank level with the tie. The tracks were joined and the ceremony was over for all save a senator from Oregon who tried to deliver a speech he had prepared but had not been called upon to deliver.

No one listened, for by this time pandemonium reigned. Cannon thundered, the crowds cheered, the band blared forth "Yankee Doodle," "Hail Columbia," "God Save the Queen," and *"Die Wacht am Rhein."* Amidst this bedlam two locomotives steamed forward, each gay with bunting and streamers, to meet and pass as the watchers cheered again. The world learned that a new link had been forged between East and West only a few hours later, for the Associated Press writer had an engine waiting, steam up, for a wild ride to Helena, fifty miles away, in three hours.[46] This was Henry Villard's moment of triumph. He left that ceremony, as he later recorded, "indescribably elated at this consummation of the peaceful conquest of the West."[47]

For Herr Mohr and the rest of the visiting Germans anything that followed would be anticlimactic. And much did follow. They again boarded their trains that evening to steam on westward, stopping along the way to marvel at the wonders of the Rockies, the beauties of Lake Pend d'Oreille where a projected steamboat ride was drenched by heavy rains, and the splendors of the Columbia Valley.

At Portland, which was reached September 11, the tired pilgrims endured more decorations, more speeches, and a parade as long as that in St. Paul, but mercifully lacking the industrial exhibits that made those in the Twin Cities so monotonous. Instead they applauded a wagon bearing the stump of a tree with woodmen chopping; a sawed beam a foot thick, seventy-feet long, and twenty-seven feet wide; salmon frozen in blocks of ice; a colorfully dressed band of young students from an Indian Training School; and a detachment of pioneers in

[46] *Daily Minnesota Tribune*, September 9, 1883.
[47] Villard, *Memoirs*, II, 311.

the prairie schooners that had carried them over the Oregon Trail.[48] These were worth viewing, even though they had to pay the piper that night by attending an official banquet at the Mechanics' Pavilion where a dozen orators repeated the clichés they had heard so often before.

Nor was the end yet, for Villard wanted his visitors to see the giant harbor that would funnel the trade of the Orient to the East over the Northern Pacific tracks. Leaving Portland, the German party journeyed by train and boat to the western terminus of the road at Tacoma where they boarded steamers for a never-to-be-forgotten cruise on Puget Sound, with brief visits to Victoria and Seattle—and one last parade. Back in Portland again the party divided, some to visit San Francisco, others to retrace their path to Minneapolis and the East.

HENRY VILLARD could accompany neither group, for he had heard disconcerting news that sent him scurrying back to New York City. His railroad, he learned, faced a serious financial crisis and needed his guiding hand. Two developments were responsible. One was the grossly underestimated construction cost; his engineers had assured him that the $40,000,000 raised by the sale of first-mortgage bonds would surely build the line and leave some $13,000,000 as a treasury reserve; instead the entire

[48] *New York Times*, September 23, 1883, p. 6; *The Northwest*, I (September, 1883), 17.

sum was needed to complete the road, leaving no cushion against emergencies. The other was his own overoptimism. Villard had persuaded capitalists to invest in his empire by promising large dividends. These he insisted on paying whatever the state of the finances, confident that commerce over the completed line would justify his extravagance. Instead expenditures outpaced receipts; by October, 1883, the deficit had risen to $9,459,921 and the Northern Pacific was in serious trouble.[49]

None of this was known to the investing public, but rumors were beginning to spread: that Villard's Oregon Transportation Company was planning to issue $15,000,000 in debenture bonds to meet its debts, and that the Northern Pacific's balance was $17,000,000 in the red. This Villard vigorously denied. Doubting Thomases were still skeptical; "a flourish of trumpets upon the part of Mr. Villard," one insisted, ". . . has become imperatively necessary to give tone to the junketing excursion which is now in progress."[50] Others, wanting to believe, were so encouraged that the company's stock, which had been sliding downward in a depressed market, showed signs of revival. All the road's problems, one St. Paul editorial writer was sure, stemmed from rival capitalists who wanted to cast a pall over his "last spike" celebration. As for the Northern

[49] Hedges, *Henry Villard*, 109–110.

[50] *New York Herald*, August 29, 1883, p. 9, September 2, p. 12.

Pacific, "it is as safe as the mountains it climbs."[51]

Wall Street was less sure, and by September 9 the road's stock began edging downward again. "In spite of its being 'spike' day," wrote one financial editor, "there was probably more effectual hammering of the stock in the Board Room and with greater results than was obtained by the physical driving in of the last nail upon the road itself."[52] For the next weeks the decline continued as Northern Pacific's common stock slid from $44.25 a share September 14 to $31.75 October 1, its preferred from $75 to $61.[53] To make matters worse the road's troubles depressed the entire market, to the consternation of investors and the annoyance of brokers. The sad state of Wall Street could be blamed, one thought, on the "general stamping upon the Northern Pacific properties, upon which, for an hour or two, the scalpers of the Board Room executed a regular war dance."[54] These were the plaints that greeted Henry Villard when he returned to New York, the plaudits of the Northwest still ringing in his ears.

Nor did his troubles end there, for the lavish festivities that he had arranged for his spike-driving ceremony made fair game for his critics. The *New York World*, the most vocal of the anti-Villard

[51] [St. Paul] *Daily Pioneer Press*, September 2, 1883, p. 4.

[52] *New York Herald*, September 9, 1883, p. 10.

[53] *New York World*, September 15, 1883, p. 3; *New York Times*, September 17, 1883, p. 3, September 24, p. 2, September 27, p. 3; *Chicago Tribune*, September 15, 1883, p. 14.

[54] *New York Herald*, September 15, 1883, p. 11.

press, compared the lot of his junketing guests with those who gorged themselves at Roman banquets in classical days while the common people starved. That extravagance, the paper estimated, had cost at least $250,000. Why waste such a sum on the decadent of Europe? Why shower them with such luxuries that "their aristocratic hands need never to descend into their pockets even to fee a waiter or pay a bootblack?" This was hardly fair to American taxpayers who had given the road a land grant worth at least $100,000,000.[55]

More sympathetic editorial writers found the road's plight deserving of tears rather than mockery. "It is really too bad," declared one in the *New York Herald*, "that the inopportune drop in Northern Pacific and Oregon Transcontinental should threaten to convert what Mr. Villard . . . meant to be a triumphal march into a sort of funeral baked meats procession."[56] Villard could take but faint comfort in such sympathy.

He could stave off bankruptcy, however, by using a second mortgage on his Northern Pacific properties to support the $20,000,000 bond issue needed to meet expenses. The money was easily raised; his German guests had been so well impressed with the economic potentials of the Pacific Northwest that they sold the bonds abroad in record time. Villard

[55] *New York World*, August 30, 1883, p. 4, September 11, p. 4, September 12, p. 4.
[56] *New York Herald*, August 30, 1883, p. 9.

could use the returns to care for construction defi-
cits and meet the interest payments on some of his
debts, but even he knew that the end was in sight.
The railroad's bonded indebtedness was now
$61,635,400, and even the most optimistic support-
er realized that years must pass before traffic on the
Northern Pacific would grow to the point where it
could pay the interest and principal on such a sum.
By the end of November he was nervously exhausted and ready to admit defeat. When a few close
friends advised him that recovery would be impossible under his discredited leadership he resigned
from the presidency of two of his other companies
in December, 1883, and from the Northern Pacific
in January, 1884.[57] Villard returned to the manage-
ment of some of his properties after two years of
recovery in Germany, but never again would he
achieve the financial power that was his when he
brought Nicolaus Mohr and his fellow-Germans to
America in 1883.

WHEN Henry Villard left his charges in Portland
they were given their choice of returning to the East
via San Francisco and the Union Pacific Railroad,
or retracing the journey over the Northern Pacific.
Herr Mohr elected the latter route, and never regretted his choice. The party, dwindled in size now
to little more than a dozen, enjoyed the luxury of a
boat trip up the Columbia River, made a brief jour-

[57] Villard, *Memoirs*, II, 313–315.

ney to Walla Walla, and finally boarded the cars
that would carry them to St. Paul. Two stops along
the way had been planned by their host. The first
proved disappointing; while their special cars waited at the hamlet of Ravali, they set out to climb Mt.
MacDonald which supposedly offered a superb view
of the Mission Range. Only a few of the more hardy
succeeded, for the distances were so great and the
trail so steep that most returned to the train more
exhausted than satisfied.

The second stop was more pleasant. Yellowstone
National Park was then only ten years old, and virtually *terra incognita* save to the most foolhardy ad-
venturers. It was, however, on the Northern Pacific
route, and an attraction that the railroad intended
to use as a bait for passengers. Herr Mohr and his
fellow-Germans reached there on the spur track
that ran from Livingston on the main line to Cinnabar, then in carriages that carried them the last six
miles to the park entrance at Gardiner. They were
comfortably housed in a spanking new hotel then
under construction at Mammoth Hot Springs, just
within the gates, where they made the last preparations for the daring adventure that lay ahead. A few
elected to make the tour on horseback but Herr
Mohr, older and more cautious, chose to travel in a
wagon. Often during the next days he regretted his
decision as they bumped over almost impossible
roads or balanced precariously on the brim of cliffs
with dizzying depths below. In the end the wonders

that he saw compensated for all his fears; the party visited both the Upper and Lower Geyser basins where they marveled at nature's display as would millions of visitors in later years. Some even dipped their handkerchiefs into Old Faithful to be washed during its regular eruptions.

This was the last of the spectaculars arranged by Villard for his guests. Herr Mohr and his friends returned to St. Paul where they scattered, he to visit in the German community there for several days before beginning a lonely tour of the principal cities of the Mississippi Valley and eastern seaboard. St. Louis captivated him for some time, for he was fortunate enough to arrive during "Fair Week" and had an opportunity to see yet another parade. Then eastward by rail, with brief stop-overs at Louisville and Cincinnati. Boston he deemed worthy of several days of sight-seeing; Philadelphia he found worth a stay of only a few hours, and Washington and Baltimore no more enticing. He was obviously tired of travel by now; his impressions as he recorded them for his readers at home were less and less his own and more and more parroted briefly from the guidebooks that he read.

Back in New York in mid-October, the little party of Germans who had left Bremen two months before gathered for one last reunion and one final chance to thank Henry Villard for the memorable tour that was ending. Only the famed Delmonico's restaurant was worthy of such an occasion, and there they assembled on the night of October 15, 1883, to eat their way through a repast that began with *Consommé Marie Stuart* and *Timbales à la Rothschild* and ended with *Gaufrés à la Crème* and *Soufflé Vanilla*, all washed down with six excellent wines.[58] All of this Herr Mohr described in his journal far more fully than did the press which had by this time lost its interest in the visiting dignitaries. Herr Mohr sailed from New York for Bremen on October 31, 1883, there to gather the dispatches describing his adventures that he had been sending to his newspaper, add a few more impressions, and in 1884 publish his *Ein Streifzug durch den Nordwesten Amerikas* which now appears in translation on the following pages.

RAY ALLEN BILLINGTON

[58] A copy of the printed menu is in Villard Excursion File, Folder 4-7.

AUTHOR'S PREFACE

THE following report is from a trip I made in the fall of last year as one of the German guests of Henry Villard. The occasion was the completion of the Northern Pacific Railroad. Most of the reports were written during the trip itself and have already appeared in the *Weser Zeitung*. The rest were written from many sketches and notes, or from memory, after my return. As far as possible I have retained the letter style and have tried in effect to let my diary do the talking. My goal has been to add to the story wherever, in the excitement of the moment, material was passed over too lightly. Thus I hope my descriptions have not lost their freshness but that they rather have gained by this. To be sure, this narrative even now cannot claim to be more than a rather superficial account of impressions gleaned from a fabulous trip.

We saw a great deal; we had the opportunity to learn much—and for this we should be thankful to our German-American traveling companions. Nevertheless, our contacts were rather fleeting and many aspects of this country and its inhabitants we could not get to know. Yet the impressions I gleaned from the trip are so manifold that I am convinced they will offer something of worth to many others.

I am especially happy for the opportunity to present this publication as a testimonial to the

Northern Pacific Railroad. Likewise I wish to express my appreciation to Mr. Henry Villard for his efficiency, his loyalty, and his overall kindness that inspired each and every one of the participants.

N. MOHR

Bremen, March, 1884

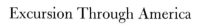

Excursion Through America

HENRY VILLARD
1835–1900

Taken from *West Shore* magazine, September, 1883
Courtesy of Oregon Historical Society

1

The Invitation

AFTER a confidential inquiry which prepared us
for the surprise, we—the participants of the
journey—received the following invitation:

The Northern Pacific Railroad Company requests the
pleasure of your presence at the opening of its Main Line
from Lake Superior to Portland, Oregon, and Puget
Sound.

The Company expects to be honored by your taking
part in the act of joining the two ends of tracks at a point
in Montana near the western approach to the tunnel
piercing the main range of the Rocky Mountains.

The arrangements for entertainment of the Company's
guests are fully set forth in the enclosures.

Henry Villard
President

An invitation of this nature had never before
been extended anywhere in Europe. It was an invitation to an opening ceremony somewhere in the
Rocky Mountains at a point that couldn't even be
pinpointed by name and it presupposed a great
journey across the ocean and over hundreds of
miles of land. Thus the invitation created a major
sensation not only among those invited but also in
wider circles.

The details were given in a letter sent by Richard

Gördeler, the General Agent of the Northern Pacific Railroad Company in Berlin, to all those invited:

Reservations have been made for thirty of the most elegant accommodations on the North German Lloyd steamer, the *Elbe*, which is scheduled to depart from Bremerhafen on the fifteenth of August of this year. All cabins are adjacent to the main lounges and saloons. For these cabins the North German Lloyd will accept only tickets that are personally signed and bear the seal of the ticket holder. Since departure will take place on Wednesday, August 15, by special train from Bremen to Bremerhafen, it is absolutely necessary that all gentlemen arrive in Bremen not later than the fourteenth. When assigning cabins—there are six for two persons and six for three persons—we will do our best to take into consideration personal preferences.

Arrival in New York is scheduled for Sunday, August 26. Rooms have been reserved in four of the best hotels in the city, the Brunswick, the Hoffmann, the Windsor and the Buckingham.

After the guests have had a chance to see the sights in New York City and its vicinity, they will depart for the West on Thursday, August 30. Following a brief visit to Boston and a stopover at Niagara Falls, they will travel by way of Buffalo, Cleveland, and Chicago to St. Paul, Minnesota. From there they will travel on the Northern Pacific Railroad to Portland, Oregon, and to Puget Sound where they will board a steamer for an excursion trip to British Columbia and back to Portland.

Then the gentlemen will be offered an option as to how they wish to return to New York. Those who wish to see the rich natural wonders of Yellowstone Park will make the return trip on the Northern Pacific. And it is suggested that from Chicago they travel to Philadelphia on the Pennsylvania Railroad and from there make a side trip to Washington and Baltimore. On the other hand, those who wish to go to San Francisco can do so on a steamer belonging to the Oregon Railway and Navigation Company. From San Francisco they can return to New York on one of the other Pacific railways. All necessary tickets will be provided. The gentlemen may arrange the return trips to Germany at their pleasure. Arrangements have been made with the North German Lloyd to allow use of the return ticket on any of its rapid passenger liners that depart from New York between October 1 and November 1.

That was the initial invitation. Included with this were vouchers for our round trip tickets and hotels as well as information about the Northern Pacific Railroad and the geography of the country.[1]

We learned who our traveling companions would be from a letter sent out by the *Allgemeine Zeitung*. Major General von Xylander and his wife, the sister of Mr. Villard, as well as Colonel von Xylander, and Dr. Schütte had departed for New York already at the beginning of the month. Dr. Delbrück had been in America already for some time.[2] The rest of

[1] For the benefit of his guests, Henry Villard commissioned three publications that were distributed to members of the party: Eugene V. Smalley, *History of the Northern Pacific Railroad* (New York, 1883), Henry J. Winser, *The Great Northwest. A Guide-Book and Itinerary for the Use of Tourists and Travellers over the Lines of the Northern Pacific Railroad* (New York, 1883), and a pamphlet filled with instructions and advice. He described these preparations in *Memoirs of Henry Villard, Journalist and Financier, 1835–1900* (2 v., Boston, 1904), II, 308–309.

[2] Bavarian Major General Robert von Xylander, husband of Henry Villard's only surviving sister, was Minister of Mil-

us were to sail together on the North German Lloyd steamship *Elbe* (departing from Bremerhafen August 15, 1883) . . . .

---

itary Affairs in the National Bundesrat; Colonel Emil Ritter von Xylander, also of Bavaria, was commander of the First Cavalry Brigade. Apparently Dr. Schütte and Dr. Delbrück failed to join the party in New York; their names were not listed in the newspapers that chronicled the course of the party.

2

The Journey Begins

Bremen
Tuesday, August 14, 1883

THE Bremen Senate would have it no other way;
they insisted on giving a party for the entire
group of guests. We are scheduled to sail tomorrow
on the *Elbe* and tonight we had the party—in the
Bremen Ratskeller.

The room normally reserved for the Senators and
the one adjoining it, both colorfully decorated with
paintings and woodcarvings, provided the perfect
atmosphere. In such a setting all formalities disappeared. And in no time at all strangers had become
friends.

At 8:00 p.m. we were welcomed by a number of
the Senators as well as some of the local citizens.
After the introductions came the speeches. Senator
Gröning[1] spoke on behalf of the City of Bremen and
raised his glass to the Northern Pacific Railroad, to
its president and to its representative at the party,
Mr. Gördeler. Dr. Schleiden followed with a toast

[1] Senator Albert Gröning joined the party as official representative of the City of Bremen; Rudolf Schleiden, who
had formerly represented the Hanseatic Cities in Washington, was another of the invited guests. Richard Gördeler was
General Agent of the Northern Pacific Railroad in Berlin.

to the future of Bremen and to its governing body,
the Senate. Then Mr. Gördeler said a few words on
behalf of the railroad and drank to the well-being of
the free Hanseatic Cities of Bremen and Hamburg.
Finally, Lord Mayor Bugg, speaking for his City of
Bremen, wished us all a successful journey.

In the amusement and casual gathering of the
evening, some of our party stayed very late. However, most of us retired to our rooms shortly after
11:00 p.m. to be ready for the early morning trip by
train to the port of Bremerhafen.

Could it be that this is our last night before leaving our Fatherland? Was the banquet in fact our
last meal before we are surrendered to the mighty
ocean waves?

If so, I only want to say that our last impression
of Germany was a most refreshing one. The stately
old arches of the Ratskeller, the centuries old barrels, the huge wine cellar filled with the rarest wines
from the Rhine and Moselle valleys, all this combined to dispel our thoughts about the New World
toward which we were heading. It allowed us to
meditate for the last moment on the Fatherland and
the past.

At the Chalk Cliffs of Dover
Thursday, August 16, 1883

THERE is always a hustle at the railroad station in
Bremen when it is sailing day for the North German
Lloyd steamers. Wednesdays there are usually two

ships leaving for America. Such a day was yesterday when the members of our "Villard party," along with many other passengers, arrived bag and baggage. (Those who were planning to emigrate to America had already boarded the night before.) As you can imagine, the experience was rather unsettling. Even if one is leaving just for a two- or three-month pleasure tour, he becomes nervous and somewhat bewildered. It was therefore a relief once the train was in motion and one could settle down inside his coach. As always the coaches were filled to the very last seat.

The trip to Bremerhafen was not exactly suited to making a passenger forget himself and whatever was occupying his mind. It was, however, long enough so that one could get acquainted with a fellow traveler, an acquaintance which might last through the whole sea voyage. Eventually we pulled into Geestemünde, circled through Bremerhafen and arrived at the Lloyd terminal. Since the *Elbe* was riding at anchor in the harbor, we had to carry all of our own belongings up the plank of a smaller steamer, the *Lloyd*. This was neither easy nor pleasant, but with some patience we made it. The *Lloyd* then took us out to the *Elbe* and here the misery was repeated all over again. We had to climb the plank from the small ship to the large one. Aboard it was no better. Each of us plowed through the crowd toward our cabins, hoping at last to be rid of the heavy luggage. Gradually everyone found his way and all seemed eager to help one another. By 11:00 a.m. everything was under control and we were on the way.

The ship was richly decorated with flags. There was music to welcome us on board and music to still the pangs of those on shore who waved good-bye. As we headed out to sea, the steamer *Lloyd* was still at our side. Then there was a blast of the horn and the little steamer knew he was to turn back to land.

Faster and faster the ship moved—past the Weser lighthouse and past the familiar Caisson; but beyond these landmarks there was not much to catch the eye. The only thing that bothered us a little was a brisk wind that caused the ship to groan and sigh. Then about noon the Weser River signal ship disappeared from view. The *Elbe* moved on confidently, untroubled by the swirling, crashing waves. She churned up a mighty wake as she headed into the strong west wind that beat the foam and spray up over the keel and far back on the deck.

When the gong sounded for lunch, the first class passengers could still rouse themselves. All thirty sat together at the two center tables. A striking feature of our party is the small number of representatives from the fairer sex. But we were joined by a large number of German-Americans and their entire families, including children of all sizes, returning from a visit to Germany. As for the lunch, it tasted all the better since it became apparent that

The Elbe

not everyone would make it back to their tables for dinner at 5:00 p.m.

After lunch we renewed the friendships made in the Bremen Ratskeller. Most of the places in the sitting rooms were soon occupied. However, in the upper lounges, in the saloon, in the smoking room, and on the promenade deck, there was a feeling of emptiness. No doubt the people in steerage will be jealous of the space that has been allotted to us.

The time until dinner passed quickly with all kinds of diversions at our disposal. From the many Americans on board we were pleased to learn that our arrival in the United States is awaited with great expectation. The hope is that the visitors whom Henry Villard has invited will help to destroy the prejudices about America that are now prevalent in Germany. Hopefully they will see the better side of America and take their new convictions back to Germany, spreading the word. These Americans maintained that in the past decade the United States has not only made material progress unequaled anywhere in the world, but also has come to deserve respect and honor for her sciences and arts. With the immense material wealth in the hands of the right people, an earnest and generally successful effort is being made to bring to culture the same prosperity that is enjoyed in other spheres. It is to be hoped that the one-sided opinions of some tourists will be superseded by the better informed insights of other observers. Thus we can look forward to a very friendly reception. The only danger is that so many opportunities for learning will be offered that we will not be able to cope with them in so short a time. So said our American shipmates.

Then came an announcement: "We will pass the Borkum lighthouse ship at 4:35 p.m." This called forth memories of the sinking of the *Cimbria*.[2] Then another tidbit: "At 5:00 p.m. we will be meeting the steamer *Donau* [Danube]."

Up to now our fortunes had been very good. Although the ship was increasingly buffeted by the waves, the swells were not so heavy that we could not stand it. Practically every person could still do justice to the excellent dinner served. Following the meal, however, the weather became rougher and rougher. At 8:45 p.m. the "Terschelling Fire" came into view and in a southwesterly direction we entered the Channel.

A quiet and vicious struggle had already begun

[2] On the early morning of January 19, 1883, the 3,000 ton Hamburg-American steamer *Cimbria*, carrying a crew of 120 and 402 passengers bound from Hamburg for New York, collided with the English steamer *Sultan* in a dense fog off the island of Borkum near the East Friesland coast. In all some 420 persons, most of them German and Russian immigrants bound for the United States, were drowned. The loss of life, and mysterious circumstances surrounding the sinking which apparently involved a third vessel, created a major sensation. *London Times*, January 22, 1883, p. 6, January 23, p. 6, January 25, p. 5, January 26, p. 6, February 12, p. 6, February 14, p. 5.

with the wicked enemy, seasickness. For a long time you fight back, refusing to admit your weakness. But what's the use? Neither age, rank nor science can save you from this malady. Sooner or later you become a victim . . . .

When we appeared on deck bright and early the next morning, a monotonous drizzle was falling. On the other hand, the sea itself was throbbing with action on all sides. Steamers and sailing vessels were either passing us or we were passing them. Along came a capsized hull, either a steamer or a yacht, and the waves played a game with their booty. As we passed the signal ship of East Goodwin, the number of vessels around us increased and we could see the coast of England on the horizon. A shaft of sunlight suddenly pierced through onto the Chalk Cliffs of Dover. Not long afterward the signals on the masts of the *Elbe* were raised as an indication to the Dover station to report back to Bremen.

Now Dover lies before us, beautifully bathed in light. Beyond, on one hill, Dover's ancient castle rises menacingly against the sky. Military installations and enormous fortifications dominate the other high hills. Along the shoreline there is a row of impressive looking hotels. The pier extends far out into the water. Over to one side lies a double ship with its four smokestacks. A closer look reveals that it is two ships joined together by a single deck. This type of construction is supposed to prevent seasickness and it probably does help, but it is doubtful whether it could withstand the pounding of the waves of a stormy sea.

Just now we recognize that the port has understood our signal. At this moment the people in Bremen probably already know that the *Elbe* has passed Dover. From this point, the coastline rises gradually away from the sea with treeless hills that are scarcely even green in the background. Now and then nature has dashed off sharp slabs of chalk cliffs forming mighty precipices.

We expect to be in Southampton tomorrow at the first light of dawn.

3

The Atlantic Crossing

Off Newfoundland
Wednesday, August 22, 1883

I T WAS a gorgeous day at sea as we sailed into the
sound between the Isle of Wight and the English
mainland. In the distance we could see the island
cloaked in a light haze and before us lay the sound
as smooth as glass.

Over on the mainland appeared Portsmouth with
its fortifications, its docks, and its forest of ship
masts. A mighty five-masted sailing ship lay at the
wharf and nearby was a torpedo ship with seven
small torpedo steamers on board, all equipped with
mighty cranes. Opposite Portsmouth was Ryde,
where yachts and steamers were moving hither and
thither. Somewhere on the right lay Southampton,
where we were to pick up mail and on the left Os-
borne came into view. How charming were the
fields encircled by clusters of trees and the old castle with its ivy-covered walls. Then came Cowes,
built on a row of terraces stretching along on both
sides of the Medina River. At the wharves were a
number of warships as well as the royal yachts, distinguished by their yellow smokestacks. These are
the sail and steam yachts that have long been the

pride and privilege of England. On both land and
sea the prosperity of this country shines forth. The
English have spared no effort in making this a show-
place. They have a certain quality about them.
When they like something, they do it up exquisite-
ly, and this principle applies particularly to their
love of ships. What the Englishman achieves in his
ships is unequaled by any other nation.

We sailed up the Southampton River as far as
Netley Hospital and there met the small steamer
Lloyd. As our band struck up a greeting, the passengers and mail came on board. Included among the
newcomers was Mr. von Bunsen, who joined our
party.[1] Letters and newspapers were distributed.
Here we were barely twenty-four hours at sea and
already people were envious of those lucky enough
to receive mail from the hand of the steward. A
newspaper boy offered the *Times* and other newspapers for sale, but his supply in no way satisfied the
demand.

Making a wide turn, we sailed out the same way
we came in. Then we learned that our sister ship
the *Fulda* had passed the Isles of Scilly that morning and that we would probably meet her at the
famous Needles about 6:00 p.m. Sure enough, just
as we approached those strange rocky spires—the

[1] Georg von Bunsen, who joined the party at Southampton, had been in the public eye since 1862 when he became
a member of the Prussian legislature. He had served with
distinction as a member of the German Reichstag since the
unification of Germany in 1871.

remains of cliffs that have been devoured by the waves—the *Fulda* came steaming toward us. Everybody hurried up on deck and formed a solid line at the rail. Over on the *Fulda* the scene was no different. With hats waving and music blaring, we shouted hurrahs to each other. The ships slowed for the meeting. Then we took aboard the pilot of the *Fulda* along with letters and newspapers and likewise handed our pilot over to our sister ship.[2] Then we continued westward while the *Fulda* steamed up to Southampton to deliver the American mail, then east to the Weser River, where she would arrive either late on Friday evening or early Saturday morning.

Unfortunately the weather did not hold as we believed it would following that splendid afternoon. By evening it was overcast and soon the coastline was hidden from view. During the night the captain had to be on duty and even had to perform some delicate maneuvers to avoid a collision. By the next morning a thick gray fog had closed in and it began to rain. The sun broke through the clouds several times, raising our hopes for a nice day, but the fog triumphed and our hopes were dashed. For the first time now we heard the siren, a foghorn sounded by a special steam mechanism—a dull reverberating tone beginning as a low roar and

[2] The North German Lloyd *Fulda* sailed from New York August 8, 1883, bound for Bremen. *New York Times*, August 8, 1883, p. 3.

then ascending to a treble key. All of the Lloyd
ships on the New York route are equipped with this
noisy gear that generates a blast heard for five nauti-
cal miles. As soon as the siren sounded once, the
cabin stewards closed the heavy iron doors to the
interior sections. A moment later we heard through
the dense fog the whistle of another ship, but we
never did get to see it.

Thus the coastline of Europe drifted away without our being able to bid it good-bye. The fog even
took the Isles of Scilly from our view. There must
have been quite a storm on the ocean for the swells
were very high and we were fighting a strong wind.
Consequently the ship rolled and pitched severely
and has continued to do so day after day.

The discomfort has taken its toll and as of today
many have already paid their tribute to the sea.
Others experience chronic seasickness. Under these
circumstances moods grow sour and passengers begin to criticize. Some grumble that the Lloyd gives
them too much to eat, some say their cabins are not
comfortable, others complain about the heat and
the smells or the noise when they are trying to get
some badly-needed sleep.

Just as drunkenness affects men differently, so too
does seasickness. One man simply makes mournful
sounds while another laments that his wife was correct in opposing this trip of his altogether. Yet another is quite irritated. He takes his bout with this
misery as a personal offense and attempts to argue

with the gods of fate. Most, however, try to hide their suffering in the quiet loneliness of their cabins, especially when their roommates are likewise suffering. But the ill-tempered shipmate can indeed upset everyone's balance.

To be sure a certain number of the travelers are always alive and ready. Most of these are people who have crossed the ocean ten or twelve times. One veteran talks of having gone across forty-two times; he is now on his forty-third trip. These are the businessmen who are returning from business affairs in Europe. For them, a journey like this is little more than part of a job and they do everything they can to lighten the burden. They travel on the fastest ships during certain seasons and spend most of their time playing cards. Of course they know America well and can make suitable comparisons with similar conditions in Germany. We enjoy talking with them and learn something about the situation there.

We are altogether thirty people in the Villard party on the ship. Some of the members in the group were personal friends of Villard from Southern Germany. Others, belonging to the world of finance, were invited because they maintained business connections with the Northern Pacific. There were also many prominent men representing the sciences and learning in our group, most of them well known in Germany and the United States. The professors Hofmann, Gneist, von Holst, and Zittel accepted the invitation because of their special interest in the great republic. The geologist Zittel pursued special scientific projects, while von Holst, the author of several significant works on the American legal system, wanted to study the American government.[3]

For an August crossing the weather is unexpectedly raw, windy and foggy. It is the combination of the steady head wind and heavy swell that causes the ship to pitch and toss so badly. Periodically the crew tries to erect sails in the hope of lending the steamer a little more stability. But usually the effort is in vain and within a few hours they lower them again. Shipping and flapping in the wind, the sails seem only to slow our speed.

On all Lloyd ships the waiters in second class get together and form a band. In the middle of the morning they usually assemble to play a half dozen melodies, dances and other tunes. On this trip the

[3] Germany's financial elite were represented by Dr. Georg Siemens, director of the Deutsche Bank, Otto Braunfels of the Jakob S. H. Stern house from Frankfurt am Main, Senator von Schauss of the Süddeutsche Land Bank, and Hermann Narcuse. Dr. A. W. Hofmann was a privy councilor as well as professor of chemistry at the University of Berlin, Rudolf Gneist a prominent jurist, professor of constitutional law at the University of Berlin, and a member of both the Supreme Court and the German Reichstag. Hermann von Holst, later to be professor at the University of Chicago, was recognized as Germany's leading historian of the United States. Dr. K. A. Zittel was a well-known geographer and explorer who held a professorship at the University of München [Munich].

performances did not start until the third day out; but as soon as they did, a few lively couples began dancing and a circle of bystanders gathered to watch. The number of actual dancers was rather slim. But among them were two young, vivacious American girls with Bremen-sounding names. With their charming and uninhibited style of dancing, they did a great deal to cheer up us men. They even taught us several nice variations of German dances. (Perhaps it is due to their initiative that the very next winter after our journey, new American dance styles appeared in the German ballrooms.)

In the mornings we get up early—in fact earlier than we would choose. On the *Elbe* we gain a half hour every day. It may sound pleasant back home to wake up at seven and know that it is only 6:30 a.m., but here at sea this adjustment to astronomy means that the morning coffee arrives a half-hour late every single day.

On days when the weather is somewhat tolerable, the majority of us are up on deck between seven and eight in the morning. If you arrive any earlier, you will encounter sweeping, polishing, scrubbing, mopping, swabbing, dusting, and buffing—all of such intensity that would put most housewives to shame. In the saloon, on deck and in the hallways, everything is spic and span. The longer we are on board the more we come to admire the organization. In all there are about 1160 passengers on board. Add to this the crew of 120 and you have the population of a village whose entire bed and board is provided on this ship. Every need must be taken care of each day without any resources beyond those that are stored somewhere on this ship. And all of this is done without the slightest hesitation or interruption. Each and every meal is served punctually to the very minute.

Here in first class we enjoy a lazy existence. We are becoming more and more unwilling to do any work. Hardly anyone does any reading anymore, and an inner voice keeps warning us that when we get back to terra firma, we will be good for little more than a labor colony. But is this surprising when they feed us to the point of demoralization? I have already mentioned that the morning coffee is awaited with increasing impatience. About 7:30 a.m., the gong sounds through the halls as the first welcome indication that the breakfast hour is approaching. Actually this bell is intended for the stewards, who within a few minutes set the tables in the dining room for 110 persons. On the long tables they lay out a choice of breads, including the popular "Bremen Zwieback." On the menu are listed several hot dishes such as beefsteak, baked fish, and buckwheat pancakes.

At 8:30 a.m. the gong sounds again and the dining room is quickly filled. Although on this particular voyage every place at the ten tables is assigned, it is not uncommon to find empty places as long as the sea remains so unfriendly. A sympathetic inquiry about the fate of an absent neighbor is a favorite starting point for conversation . . . .

Barely three hours after breakfast—at noon—we again sit down to a gourmet meal. This second breakfast is a meal for which we Germans still have not found a name. Spread out on the tables is a huge assortment of food, enough to satisfy anyone's desire: several hot dishes, cold cuts, herring, anchovies, caviar, a variety of cheeses, etc. Once again those of us in good health do justice to the delicacies. This does not mean, of course, that we won't have an appetite for dinner at 5:00 p.m. We tell each other that the sea air burns up all the calories and we go ahead and eat as if we had gone twelve hours without a morsel.

Actually the noon meal is kept fairly short because the smoking of pipes and cigars is permitted only up on deck or in the smoking room. The gentlemen excuse themselves immediately and withdraw to the promenade deck. Quite a number of the passengers have obtained deck chairs to relax outside. The moment the weather is halfway decent, rows and rows of these chairs appear on deck, occupied mostly by the ladies. The men usually stroll up and down or gather in the smoking room to play cards. Thus time passes in this sort of inactivity, interrupted only now and then by some conversation or perhaps a bit of hand work. Really, everything depends on the weather . . . .

Today was terrible. All through last night the

wind blew violently. In the morning for breakfast we found little fences on the edge of each table to prevent the dishes from sliding all over the room. This was an ominous sign that heavy rolling could be expected and our supposition proved quite correct. Up on deck already much had happened. During the night the topsail had been ripped to shreds. The sailors were sent up to tie down the square sails and were greeted by a driving rain in their faces. Right in the middle of all this commotion the band began to play a concert. Just one or two of the ladies showed up for breakfast and even the weakness of the stronger sex was in evidence with the many empty places at the tables. Under the impact of the southwest wind, the sea became ever more turbulent. On all sides the wind was skimming the foam off the waves and driving it at us like a rainstorm. Once in a while the clouds split for a moment and a shaft of sunlight pierced down on the roaring waves. The immense ship bobbed up and down in the rough sea like a cork.

Guy lines were tied on the upper deck to make a handrail for the passengers. Sailing canvasses were stretched across the open stairwells between the decks. Not surprisingly the breakfast mood was rather despondent. Though only half of the passengers were present, two-thirds of our party made it.

At noon the Captain allowed himself some conversation with the passengers. But when someone commented to him about the storm, he acknowledged only that there was "a nice fresh breeze." All afternoon the storm continued. Our speed declined from twelve knots to nine knots, but this evening we have again accelerated to fourteen knots . . . .

Friday, August 24, 1883

THIS morning things were very much in motion. The Captain prepared to take the pilot on board and sent a crew man up to the lookout to search out the pilot's schooner. Meanwhile everything is astir in preparation for disembarkation. Still the fog continues to play its little game with us. Bright sun is above us but all around are walls of mist.

At our noon meal Senator Gröning expressed our good wishes to the Captain, but the Captain himself had to stay at the bridge.[4] As we were eating, Nantucket lighthouse came into sight and we comforted ourselves that we must be on the right course.

Early Saturday morning, August 25, 1883

WHAT a beautiful morning. How magnificently the sun rises and floods the gray coast of Long Island. Last night at midnight the pilot finally arrived on board. Now before us lie the Highlands; the picture becomes ever more beautiful.

[4] Senator Albert Gröning, representative of the Free City of Bremen, was to be the most called-upon speaker during the party's stay in the United States.

4

The Arrival in New York

HOW CAN I even begin to report the immensely varied impressions that I have gained since Saturday morning? As is well known, Americans are not sparing of praise of their country, and often they arouse in us Europeans a certain sense of disbelief. Well, he who arrives in the New World for the first time through the Lower Bay of New York can take heart. When the hills of New Jersey first became visible, they were only vague outlines. Gradually we saw them in greater detail and before us lay Long Island with its countless bathing beaches, summer resorts, and massive hotels. There was no end to the questions of the sightseers on board.

Attention was constantly distracted—first to the right, then to the left. Impatiently we peered into the distance to catch a glimpse of New York City. There was a great deal of restlessness everywhere. One man was tense with the anticipation of seeing his family once again; another was visibly shaken by the uncertainties that faced him in the new country. The expressions on the faces about us showed many more emotions in those last few hours on board than they did at the time we first boarded the ship. However, there were only a small number arriving

with no contacts whatsoever. The majority had
been brought over by relatives and friends and they
at least could point to a spot on the map to which
they were headed and intended to settle down.

Our ship continued westward past the fortress of
Sandy Hook, then a sharp turn to the north toward
the Narrows, a narrow channel well-guarded by
forts. The high hills of New Jersey were studded
with houses, but in general the parched lawns and
meadows rather spoiled the view. Even the leaves
on the trees were turning brown.

At the quarantine area the ship came to a halt.
An officer boarded and those in steerage lined up
from one side of the ship to the other while doctors
examined them and looked over their vaccination
records.

Meanwhile the head agent of the North German
Lloyd and several other men climbed aboard, including Carl Schurz. For a moment we did not recognize the furrowed face and gentle countenance of
the young man we had known long ago in Bonn. In
spite of the outstanding role Schurz has played in
the political growth of the United States, he has
never cast off his German character nor has he the
slightest touch of feigned Americanism about him.[1]

[1] Carl Schurz, the most prominent German-American of
this era, had been born near Köln [Cologne] in 1829 and fled
to the United States in 1852 after the failure of the liberal
revolutions of 1848. There he rose rapidly as a journalist
and Republican politician, serving in the Union armies and,
after the war, contributing to the rise of the Liberal Repub-

Then we moved on through the Narrows. On
both right and left were rows of houses and piers;
then on the right Forts Lafayette and Hamilton and
on the left Forts Wadsworth and Tompkins. Gently
the inner bay opened up before us. Then suddenly
the great panorama of the gigantic city unfolded,
split by the Hudson on one side and the East River
on the other into three cities—Jersey City, New
York, and Brooklyn.[2] Politically they are distinct,
but for all practical purposes they form a single im-

lican faction. At the same time he served as correspondent or
editor of several newspapers. In 1868 he was elected to the
Senate from Missouri, and in 1877 was named Secretary of
the Interior, a post that allowed him to practice his liberal
beliefs concerning treatment of the Indians and the conservation of natural resources. On leaving the cabinet he became an employee of Henry Villard, who had just purchased
the *New York Evening Post* and *The Nation*. His brilliant
journalistic career had just ended in 1883 when he differed
with Edwin L. Godkin, editor of *The Nation*, over editorial
policy. Schurz was to accompany the Villard Party westward.

[2] Vessels entering New York's picturesque harbor first
passed Sandy Hook, an outer bar guarded in 1883 by a fort,
then Fire Island, before steaming into the Narrows. On the
left were the battlements of Fort Wadsworth and Fort
Tompkins, on the right those of Fort Hamilton and old Fort
Lafayette. Passing through the Narrows, the panorama of
the city unfolded, with Bedloe's Island (soon to hold the
Statue of Liberty) on the left and Ellis Island, guarded by a
fort, farther along the New Jersey shore. At the right was
Governor's Island, with Castle William and old Fort Columbia. Directly ahead lay the city with its towering six-story
buildings; Brooklyn was on the right and Jersey City on the
left. *Appleton's General Guide to the United States and Canada. Illustrated* (New York, 1884), 6.

mense city, growing steadily and destined to become within a few decades one of the largest cities in the entire world.

The activity in the water defied explanation. Mighty steamers and sailing vessels were shuffling hither and yon, ferry boats were dashing in all directions. The many water inlets in the New York area make travel by boat almost mandatory. Castle Garden, the tip of the Island of Manhattan, the world famous suspension bridge, the estuary of the Hudson known as the North River—all of this now came into view. It was one great sea of buildings bordered by ships and docks, backed up by a fantastic array of warehouses—everything shining brightly in the pure air uncontaminated by dirty black smoke. Rising above this man-made complex were the suspension bridge and several striking towers.

We steamed up the Hudson. On both sides of the river were the docking piers, the warehouses, and the dock cranes, one next to the other. Finally we arrived at the North German Lloyd dock and with seeming ease the big ship tied up.

Back in Bremen we struggled to get our baggage and ourselves on board. But that was nothing compared to the confusion here—the pushing and shoving such as we have never experienced before. To leave the ship that had been our only home for nine days and on which we had come to feel so at home aroused a twinge of sadness in the final minutes. We shook hands with our fine Captain Willigerod and promised to make the return voyage on his ship.

Finally we were on American soil. After the relative peace and quiet on board, it seemed like a wild affair. Suitcases and trunks came shooting down the ramp and clear across to the middle of the shed. For some of us passengers the stewards carried the hand luggage, but even so we had to scramble for the rest of our things. Then of course there was the customs check. Members of our party were permitted to make a declaration on board and thus we were spared the inconvenience, but it still took a long time to get everything together.

Meanwhile Henry Villard himself arrived on the scene and introduced himself to his guests.[3] He is a stately man with distinct facial features, bright eyes, and a serene but friendly manner. He makes the finest impression. He led us immediately to the ferry boat that would transport us across the Hudson to New York City. The short crossing completed, we found carriages waiting for us at the landing. On our drive through the city to the hotel we formed our first impressions—the tramways level with the ground, the elevated trains overhead, and a net of telegraph wires woven and meshed like a piece of cloth, a preview of the communication needs for

[3]The official greeting party consisted of Henry Villard, Gustav Schwab, of the New York firm of Oelrichs & Company which served as the New York agent for the North German Lloyd Steamship Company, and Paul Schultze, general land agent for the Northern Pacific Railroad. *New York Times*, August 26, 1883, p. 2.

such a gigantic city. Certain features made us feel right at home, but others reminded us that we were thousands of miles away.

We were driven along famed Fifth Avenue, down Broadway to the lower part of the city, to Wall Street, then to the Mills Building where the Northern Pacific Railroad has its offices. Here we went out on the roof of the building for a panoramic view of the city. To the south lay the great Upper Bay of New York with its narrow exit to the sea; on the left the East River and Governor's Island, to the right the Hudson. For a panorama that deserves several hours we were allowed only a few minutes.[4] Next we drove to the suspension bridge which links New York to Brooklyn.[5] We merely drove over and came back as soon as we could turn around.

Permit me to give you a description of the bridge

---

[4] A steam yacht carried the party from the pier to the foot of 24th Street where carriages waited. They were driven down Broadway to the Battery, saw Wall Street, and visited the company headquarters in the Mills Building, an immense brick structure on Broad Street opposite the Stock Exchange. *New York World*, August 26, 1883, p. 7; *Appleton's General Guide*, 8.

[5] Brooklyn Bridge, or the "East River Bridge" as it was then known, had been opened only a few months before, May 23, 1883. More than a mile long and 85 feet wide, with a promenade for foot passengers, two railway tracks, and two roadways for vehicles, it was the longest suspension bridge in the world and considered the engineering marvel of the age. Designed by John A. Roebling and completed by his son, the bridge had been under construction for thirteen years and cost $15,500,000. *Appleton's General Guide*, 11.

Courtesy of The Huntington Library

*The East River Suspension Bridge between New York
and Brooklyn (Brooklyn Bridge) c1883*

Taken from Rudolf Cronau's *Von Wunderland zu Wunderland*

as well as a few statistics. You have heard about the
essentials when it was opened, but statistics do not
do justice to this structure. It is truly one of the
wonders of the New World. Each time one turns
toward this structure, hovering gently over the East
River, the eye is struck by its gracious lightness. It is
used for pedestrians and vehicles, as well as trams
that are pulled across it by a cable. The bridge also
provides a spectacular promenade. A walk at this

ethereal height with its view out across the bay or in the other direction up the East River into the sea of houses on land is one of the memories that will never fade. The suspension bridge and the pressing traffic in the streets as well as on the river below all make a very deep impression on the foreigner.

The numbers of men on vehicles and on foot and the streetcars running back and forth in endless streams continually cause us to marvel. It is possible that the traffic in London is greater and that there is not much less in Berlin, Paris, or Constantinople, but with its river traffic New York is surely in first place. The mighty ferry boats plying back and forth without a break, the river steamers, the heavy traffic of ocean-going vessels—all taken together—provide the picture of a surging life force that encompasses the "Empire City" and makes it great.

Too often, when we try to explain, when we try to bring our readers nearer the reality of something, we make comparisons and then end up by saying there is no comparison. This is our problem. But if I were to point to one thing that seemed to detract from New York I would say it lacks distinguishing lines. At the edge of the water the distinctiveness is blurred immediately by the petty details of the houses. The docks extending out into the water one behind another stretch far into the distance. But because they are so bunched together in rows, they cannot be distinguished enough to perceive the tremendous traffic. In the city there is no point from which to view the long lines of ships. One sees no great forest of ship masts.

The same holds true for the squares and streets that we have seen. The streets are straight and endlessly long. They could be shorter than they are and still not alter the basic design. Likewise, one misses a distinctive line in the facades on the main streets. The individual buildings, even the largest, lose their identity in the great length of the streets.

The stores are splendid. They tend to show rather gaudy colors, but this gives the show windows a lively look. Down in the lower section of the city there is a great mass of pedestrians. The masses of people seem to be pushed forward and back as if in a rhythmic, rocking motion. I would have expected them to be more hurried in their movement. It seemed to me there was a characteristic, pensive gait about them. Thus the traffic regulates itself with a remarkable calm and gentleness. Nothing has impressed me so much as the disposition of moving crowds whether on foot or in carriages or on ship. With typical self-assuredness each person goes his own way. For example, when a ferry boat suddenly dumps a hundred people on the shore in the midst of this mass, the ball of yarn simply unsnarls itself with little pushing or shoving. Nowhere are the crowds noisy and nowhere are the police to be seen. The police are in evidence only at the street crossings where the carriage traffic is heavy.

There were practically no historical monuments

to be seen anywhere and what there were had little meaning. But this is understandable. Also, the architecture was not much to boast about. One has the feeling that the buildings cost a great deal of money, but taste cannot always be bought.

The drive completed, we arrived at Madison Square and entered the lobby of our hotel, the Brunswick.[6] We were greeted by a number of distinguished New York Germans as well as the former governor of Wisconsin, Edward Salomon, Consul Kühne, Gustav Ottendorfer, the publisher of the *New York Staats Zeitung*, and friends and relatives.[7]

[6] *Appleton's General Guide* rated the Brunswick Hotel at the corner of 5th Avenue and 26th Street as second only to the Brevoort House among the city's luxury establishments conducted on the European Plan. Room rates were judged high—two or three dollars a night—but the extras and sundries that made European hotel bills so annoying were unknown and guests were assured that "the practice of feeing servants, though it has some slight and irregular observance, has never attained the force of custom." The hotel was directly across the street from Delmonico's, "one of the best restaurants in the world." *Appleton's General Guide*, xii, 1.

[7] Edward Salomon had fled Germany after the collapse of the liberal revolutions, entered Republican politics, and served as Lieutenant Governor and Governor of Wisconsin. In 1869 he moved to New York where he established himself as a leader of the large German community. Oswald Ottendorfer (as he preferred to be called in America) had also found refuge in the United States after participating in the 1848 outbreaks. There he found employment on the *New York Staats Zeitung*, married the widow of its publisher, and in 1859 became its principal publisher. He was also active in Republican politics and a leader in the city's German settlement. Frederick Kühne was German Consul-General in New

To our great joy we were informed that several of the New York Germans, including Carl Schurz, would accompany us on our trip west. Each of us received a copy of the itinerary[8] and then were allowed to retire to our rooms for a short rest.

In the evening we were entertained by the Northern Pacific Railroad at dinner in the Union League Club, one of the finest in New York. This meal gave us the opportunity to pass judgment on the New York cooking. After all, New York is famous as the place where one eats the best and after that evening I should decline to quarrel with that boast. The dinner was excellent with plenty to eat and added embellishments of all kinds. The only detraction was its length. We had already had eight courses when we arrived at the dessert. This does go a little beyond the limits of pleasure. The wines were flawless. One of the outstanding features was the table decorations—beautiful flowers that filled the room with their fragrance. This was the first time in our lives that we had been served by black men. The

---

York. *National Cyclopaedia of American Biography*, III (New York, 1893), 411; and XII (New York, 1904), 75.

[8] The revised itinerary, calling for the German party to leave New York on the evening of August 29, and detailing every move to be made until they reached the site of the "last spike" ceremony the morning of September 7, was published in the *New York Times*, August 15, 1883, p. 2. Guests were advised to bring umbrellas and overcoats, but assured that there would be no occasions when evening dress would be worn. The schedule was to be more often violated than observed.

dinner was supposed to take place without toasts or speeches. But a chance occurrence opened the flood gates and by the time we were finished we even had the pleasure of hearing Carl Schurz.

The Union League Club is one of the best in New York.[9] As you might imagine, its furnishings are rather expensive and as for comfort, our every expectation is more than fulfilled. However, at the moment there is in New York a trend in design that is fairly strange to us. They display a peculiar preference for the bizarre that we can't really understand. Even in the Hotel Brunswick, which supposedly cannot be surpassed anywhere in the United States, this peculiarity in decorations has occasioned raised eyebrows. The impression was strengthened later in the Union League Club.

Sunday was set aside for a trip on the Hudson. We were picked up by a chartered steamer with the German flag flying on the stern. A special band was there to play German melodies. Our party was expanded by a few New Yorkers to whom we are grateful for the interesting information they could give us. For some time we moved along between docks on both sides, then we followed the natural shoreline of the river's right side, while on the opposite shore the city of New York still stretched along the river.

[9] The Union League Club was then housed in a "spacious and handsome building" at the corner of Park Avenue and 39th Street. *Appleton's General Guide*, 16.

From the street layout, one can see how the planners have calculated the future growth of the city. As is commonly known, the map of New York is very simple. A tongue of land extending from north to south between the East River and the Hudson is partitioned off by twelve avenues, which in turn are intersected at right angles by numbered streets. Plans provide for more than one hundred streets, and afterwards they can be extended north onto the mainland area.

The Hudson has often been called the American Rhine but this comparison is not really justified.[10] Such a statement actually does injustice to both rivers, for neither has the characteristics of the other. This portion of the Hudson is more or less an arm of the sea, banked on each side by low mountains. The tide, after all, floods more than fifty miles up river. It has a depth that permits ocean liners to travel up as far as Newburgh, farther up than West Point. Thus even far upstream the tides have a great influence on the Hudson. The Rhine on the other hand is more like a mountain stream. The Hudson is so broad in places that one is reminded of the sea. Even in the lower regions the mountainous shores are covered with forests and the formations of the cliffs at the ridge are craggier than along the Rhine.

[10] Americans were less tolerant than Herr Mohr. Said a popular guidebook: "The Hudson River has been compared to the Rhine, and what it lacks in crumbling ruin and castle-crowned steep it more than makes up for by its greater variety and superior breadth." *Appleton's General Guide*, 60.

By contrast the ridges of the Rhine are speckled with medieval ruins, fortresses with cities below, and the river flows along at a determined pace.

The trip was wonderful and blessed with good weather. It took us all the way to the thriving commercial city of Newburgh. On the return trip we had an opportunity to pay a visit to the Military Academy of West Point.[11] This Academy trains the officers for all branches of the military in the United States. About 250 young men receive their training there, all at the expense of the country. It has an excellent setting. The training ground is a plateau surrounded by full-grown trees and for the moment covered by troops out there on maneuvers. The officer candidates were dressed in white linen uniforms and they wore felt helmets with brass trimming. It was not easy to leave this charming spot for the return to New York.

On Monday we were given a reception by Mr. Villard at his villa at Dobb's Ferry, not far from the

[11] The journey carried the German party past the three-hundred-foot high Palisades, past Yonkers with its 19,000 inhabitants, through the Tappan Zee where the Hudson widened to four miles, past the "elegant villas" that ringed the shore near Tarrytown, past the grim stone buildings of Sing Sing State Prison, past Peekskill, "one of the prettiest towns on the Hudson," through the lush highlands to West Point, the site of the National Military Academy, fifty-one miles from New York. Nine miles beyond this the river widened into the broad Newburgh Bay, with the city itself and its 18,000 dwellers on the west shore. There the steamer turned about for its return trip. *Appleton's General Guide*, 62–63.

Hudson. We were picked up at the railroad station by horse-drawn carriages and driven through an area of many villas, among them that of the famous Jay Gould.[12]

The day finished with a concert in the richly ornamented building of the German "Liederkranz"—the center for German-American activities in New York.[13] I can assure you that the German taverns on

[12] The thirty-one members of the German party were picked up at their hotel at 9:00 a.m. that morning, driven to the Grand Central Station, whisked in special cars to Tarrytown, and taken in another fleet of carriages to visit the estates of Washington Irving and Jay Gould. At noon they arrived at Henry Villard's own estate, elaborately decorated for the occasion; there they were seated on the veranda to enjoy the superb view of the Hudson while a band "discoursed music on the lawn." The food was abundant and the speeches few, although Rudolf Gneist thanked Villard for his hospitality and agreed that the Rhine and Hudson could not be compared. "We have in octavo," he told his host, "what you have in folio." *New York Times*, August 28, 1883, p. 5; *New York World*, August 28, 1883, p. 5.

[13] The Liederkranz Society had planned only an intimate *Geselliger Abend* for a few friends at its new headquarters on 58th Street, but instead 1,500 members demanded the right to be present. William Steinway, the club's president, welcomed the guests; then with a flourish of music 1,500 beer steins were raised as a chorus sang "The Jolly Wanderer." Once more Dr. Gneist was called upon for an address, and once more he voiced the visitors' awe at the size of the nation, the speed of American life, and the hospitality showered upon them. Others followed for what seemed an interminable time: Dr. A. W. Hofmann who named the three necessities of life (beer, thirsty throats, and friends to welcome to the festive board), Paul Lindau the well-known novelist, Hermann von Holst who discoursed for too-great length on the significance of American civilization, Oswald

this side of the ocean have lost none of their original authenticity. Everything here was so festive, so *gemütlich*, so musical, and everyone so happy with his beer—just as in the old homeland. Without the slightest difficulty we could imagine ourselves back, each in the middle of his own home town. It is difficult to realize that the great majority of those present made their homes and their fortunes here on foreign soil, and that they live here in a culture that is in many ways outstanding but yet does not have the same homogeneous philosophy and way of life as ours. Only by realizing this can one have a full appreciation of what that evening meant to us; it helped us understand the bonds that tie the German to his Fatherland.

Ottendorfer of the *Staats Zeitung* who advised his colleagues to do justice to American affairs, and Carl Schurz, who dwelt on the glories of a Germany that was "the original hive of the Anglo-Saxon race so rapidly spreading over the world." The 15,000 steins of beer consumed on the occasion apparently made this dose of oratory palatable. *New York Times,* August 28, 1883, p. 5; *New York World,* August 28, 1883, p. 5.

5

From Niagara to Chicago

Chicago
Friday, August 31, 1883

No doubt you have already received my reports that all is going well. As a matter of fact, if there is anything at all that can be done to add comfort to a trip like this, surely Mr. Villard has already thought of it and provided for it. We are traveling in such comfort that traveling has virtually ceased to be toilsome.

The train that carried us away from New York Tuesday evening consisted of six splendid units, most of which were Pullman Cars. The majority of these were built for the Board of Directors. This means that in addition to the kitchen and ordinary conveniences each has a special salon and living rooms that convert to bedrooms at night. Two Negroes provided for our every need. Each morning we received a substantial breakfast, then went visiting from car to car.[1]

[1] The party left New York in a special train of seven private cars, most of them borrowed from their owners or from other railroads for the occasion. Letters from the Northern Pacific soliciting these cars, together with the assignments to them, are in the Villard Excursion File, Folder 2. At the rear was Villard's own private car. Carl Schurz, ex-Governor

By Wednesday morning we reached Syracuse,
New York. We passed through a series of cities,
all with classical names and a very modern look
—Troy, Rome, etc. With increasing expectation
we approached Buffalo and Niagara Falls. Finally
about noon we were close enough to see the large
clouds of spray. The sky also was cloudy and dark
so that it was difficult to distinguish the earthbound
clouds from their heavenly kin. Our anticipation
continued to grow as we observed hordes of people
streaming across the bridge that leads to the Canadian shore. Our train came to a stop. We got out,
were packed into a carriage, and then driven in the
same direction.

In the dark and gloomy weather we rode across
into the Dominion of Queen Victoria filled with
silent awe. Yet I must admit we were at first a little
disappointed. We descended to the Falls from the
Clifton House and there the view improved. Then
we returned to the hotel for lunch. After lunch, as
we stepped out on the terrace, the clouds suddenly
parted, allowing the sun to break through. A fantastic drama of nature took place before our eyes—the

Edward Salomon of Wisconsin, and Consul-General Frederick Kühne, all from New York, accompanied the party.
They were driven to the Grand Central Station in carriages,
admitted through a private door, and escorted to the train by
conductor F. B. Eldred of St. Paul, resplendent in a bright
new uniform. He had been commissioned to accompany the
party over the entire route. At 9:15 p.m. all were aboard and
the train pulled from the station, bound for Niagara Falls.
New York Times, August 29, 1883, p. 2.

whole sky turned blue and the clouds gathered into fluffy white balls rolling across the heavens so that the light and shadows alternately played on the scene below. How different everything now looked, but it would be hopeless for me to try to recapture in words a complete picture of this mighty natural wonder. Never before had we seen anything that even faintly resembled it.

Niagara Falls excites an overpowering admiration for the whole with its parts—the swift stream above, the plunging water, the whirlpool, and the miles of swirling and frothing water downstream. Nowhere does it have an equal.

From our reading we had been under the impression that the Falls would tumble down at us. To the contrary, we stood on the same level with the river as its waters thundered down into the depths, into a gorge formed by the water that flows from the Great Lakes and seeks the lower level of Lake Ontario. As we proceeded from the Clifton House on the Canadian side to the Horseshoe Falls, we could see the magic effect of the sunlight on the falls. How much deeper was the blue-green color in contrast to the white foam, how transparent were the rising clouds of steam. A sightseeing platform afforded us the opportunity for a sweeping overview of the broad and exciting terrain.

But we were not permitted to get the full enjoyment of the view. Side by side with the beauty of this natural wonder was a carnival atmosphere.

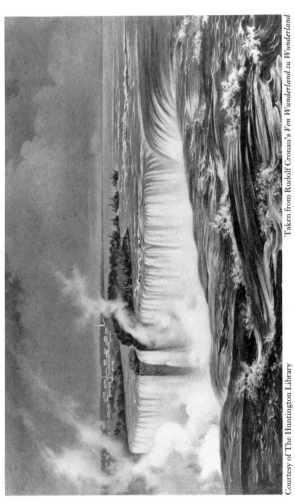

Taken from Rudolf Cronau's *Von Wunderland zu Wunderland*

The Falls of Niagara, view from the Canadian side, 1883

Hotels and stores lined the river and everywhere were obtrusive merchants, offering all kinds of articles for sale—low quality photographs, reproductions in wood and stone, glass, and china—the junk was disgusting. I envied the first Europeans who arrived here in time to see an unspoiled wilderness. They had the good fortune to see this great natural beauty cloaked in its lonely majesty.

But immediately we ourselves again fell victim to civilization. Without our carriage we would not have seen as much as we did. Some of my companions had themselves photographed, then we hurried to our comfortable coach and quickly crossed the bridge back to the shore of the United States. We have no right to criticize the progress of civilization. As we casually sat in our seats, the carriage glided down to the lowest point, where we got out and descended on a boardwalk to the lower end of the American Falls.

The water seemed to plunge right at us. Out of the mysterious depths into which it then disappeared, clouds rose up and split the sun's rays into a rainbow. The drama was so tremendous, so splendid, so beautiful that none could resist turning to it again and again. From there we returned by carriage to the bridge that connects the narrow arm of the river to Goat Island. This island includes about sixty acres and is covered with trees of particular interest to tree fanciers. But the trees are destined to disappear as the island itself is slowly disappearing.

After Goat Island we visited the small Luna Island, where we had a close look at the American
Falls as well as the Canadian Falls. From there we
descended Biddle Stairs to the foot of the rock that
forms Luna Island, the only point where one can
actually get under the falls. Many of our group
donned waterproof clothing and made the eerie expedition into this Cave of the Winds behind the
American Falls.[2]

Once again we went over to the Canadian side via
the suspension bridge. We sped along the river at a
quick trot, down to the second bridge, also a suspension bridge, that is used for railroad traffic. For a
time we followed a path close to the edge of the
river. At one point there was a land slide and we
hurried back to the carriages to move on to the final
act of this drama—the whirlpool. It was already
growing dark, so we had to view this sight from half
way up. Yet the impression equaled those we had

---

[2] Goat Island was reached by a bridge from the rear of
Cataract House; a short walk beyond was a foot-bridge to
Luna Island, a high rock mass lying between the Center
Falls and the American Falls. There the best view was obtained of the American Falls, 1,100 feet wide, where the
river plunged 164 feet into the chasm below. Just beyond
Luna Island a spiral staircase, fastened to the rock with iron
braces and named after Nicholas Biddle of United States
Bank fame who had ordered it built, led to the foot of the
cliff. There two paths diverged, one leading to the Cave of
the Winds, a spacious recess behind Center Falls. Visitors
were allowed in the cave only when clothed in special waterproof suits and accompanied by guides. *Appleton's General
Guide*, 168–173.

experienced elsewhere at the Falls. Here the turbulent river is driven into long-drawn-out whirlpools within a huge bowl formed by the cliff-like banks.[3]

At the sight of the whirlpool with its mysterious churning and surging, we recalled the unfortunate Captain Webb, who lost his life here in an insane attempt to swim through the vicious currents of the Niagara.[4] If this were an age of myths and sagas, then Niagara Falls would surely be clothed in poetic and philosophic garments. In our time reality has its own fascinating lure and the proof of this is that a swimmer would make a bet and in response to the challenge would plunge into the swirling waters to his death. Perhaps in some future time this story will become legend.

For lack of poetic sagas, our age tries to improve on nature's wonders by means of electric lights. As we returned from Canada to the United States, walking across the bridge, we could see the American Falls bathed in electric lights—first in silvery white, then in red. This too was an impressive sight,

[3] The whirlpool, three miles below the falls, was caused by a sharp bend in the river which at this point was only 220 feet wide. According to the contemporary guidebook, the water rushed against the bank "with prodigious fury, and being turned back almost at a right angle is converted into an angry and swirling eddy." *Appleton's General Guide*, 173.

[4] Captain Matthew Webb, a world-famed daredevil who had attracted wide attention when he swam the English Channel, had been killed July 24, 1883, in an attempt to swim across the whirlpool. *New York Times*, August 12, 1883, p. 10, August 13, p. 2, September 1, p. 5.

but no comparison to the glory of the sunlight.

Through the city of Niagara we walked to the Niagara City Depot. All along the main street were hotels and stores and it was evident that the city thrives on the tourists who come to see the Falls.

That evening we returned to Buffalo, where our train had to stop for a few hours. Thus we had the opportunity to take a late evening stroll up and down the main street. We were very surprised at the big city feeling of this town. On the other hand, some of the more thirsty souls in our party were just as surprised that they could not find a single tavern open in this famous beer city, not even one spot where the German stroller could enjoy a sip in friendly *gemütlichkeit*.

During the night we chugged on toward Chicago. We reached Cleveland on Lake Erie in the morning, just as we were coming out of our berths to gather in the salon. It was a disappointment that we could not leave the train station, for Cleveland is supposed to be one of the most charming cities in the United States, with a population of over 160,000 people. To our right Lake Erie stretched out in the distance, much like the sea.

We moved on through Ohio and Indiana with little change of scenery. It really was not much different from what we are accustomed to seeing back home in our hilly areas. We passed Toledo and then proceeded across to Lake Michigan. It was growing dusk and the land looked more and more barren with thinly overgrown dunes, swamps, and brush. For us this meant that we were approaching Chicago, the queen of the West and the rival of New York. Slowly we crept across a maze of tracks into the train station.

Quite a number of Germans were present at our arrival and with gallant courtesy they took care of every detail.[5] The entire group was taken to the Palmer House, a huge and elegant hotel. The traffic and milling around was a far cry from the comfortable little inns that we know so well in Germany. The loud commotion even provided a contrast to the quiet restfulness of the Brunswick Hotel in New York. Late into the night and early this morning people were congregating in the lobby, trying to get in and out of the reception room.

Even after New York, the streets of Chicago are very impressive. The city for the most part has been

[5] Conflicts and rivalries within Chicago's German community threatened to prevent any official reception. Villard at last called on Carl Schurz to settle the dispute. He did so by asking George Schneider to take charge; Schneider, another refugee from the 1848 revolutions, was editor of the *Chicago Staats Zeitung*, president of the National Bank of Illinois, and such a power in Republican circles that the opposing factions dared not dispute him. Under his direction the visitors were loaded into carriages and taken directly to the Palmer House where they were served a sumptuous luncheon, complete with sufficient liquid refreshments to dissolve all animosities, and then introduced to such leading citizens as Marshall Field and George M. Pullman who welcomed them with short speeches. *Chicago Tribune*, August 31, 1883, p. 2.

Courtesy of The Chicago Historical Society   Engraving from *Picturesque Chicago*, Chicago Engraving Co., 1875/1882/1884

State Street, Chicago, looking south from Monroe Street, with Palmer House in foreground

rebuilt since the fire and has profited greatly in the process. In my judgment there is a better building style here—larger fronts and better lines. The immense stores reflect the fact that Chicago has become the great emporium of the vast West. This morning at 10:00 a.m. our German friends are to take us for a sightseeing tour of the city.

Friday evening

THIS forenoon we took our tour of Chicago, came back for lunch, then went out for several more hours. An entire row of elegant carriages was placed at our disposal. And in each of the coaches one Chicago German came along so that we would have an explanation for everything we saw.

The Palmer House is a colossal structure. The lowest level is open to the public, half stock market and half cafe; and it has become a gathering place for the curious, for idlers, and for certain businessmen. All of the corridors are lined with white marble.[6] At the pillars and along the walls are upholstered chairs and divans, usually occupied by men reading newspapers. There are no ladies around; they seem to stay on the balcony above, looking down on all this commotion.

[6] The Palmer House was an immense fire-proof structure of sandstone occupying nearly an entire block on State Street at Monroe Street. "The building," proclaimed a contemporary guidebook, "is one of the most imposing in the city, and its interior decorations are very fine." *Appleton's General Guide*, 301.

After our morning coffee, served with a good variety of cold cuts, we drove through the big wide streets. Actually neither the avenues nor the streets give one the impression of much friendliness. Smoke has blackened the walls and the pavement is horrible, but the high and massive buildings are powerful as is the life that pulsates in the streets below. One can instinctively feel the surging of life that carries everything with it as Chicago proceeds to outstrip her rivals and achieve the title of the most feared city in the Union.[7]

We wound back and forth through an endless number of streets, but there were few details that really stood out. Chicago is still a young city, having just celebrated its fiftieth anniversary since it had been incorporated. One of the citizens who voted for its incorporation is still alive. Only twelve years have passed since the city was largely destroyed by fire and then immediately rebuilt. The growth of Chicago is often cited as an example of the fabulous progress that may be expected for all American cities.

The people here are in a constant state of excitement. They cannot contain themselves in their eagerness to tell the visitor about the size, the fantastic

[7] Chicago had yet to earn the reputation for lawlessness that made it America's most "feared" city in the 1920s. Instead Herr Mohr referred to the city's aggressive spirit, its determination to outstrip such rivals as Cleveland and St. Louis as a commercial center, and the cocksure self-assurance of its citizens.

progress, and the growth of their city. The number of inhabitants is already estimated at 700,000 although the census of 1880 gives a quarter of a million less.[8] It is estimated that the population of the city increases by at least 50,000 a year. In total population Chicago still is behind Philadelphia, but in the volume of trade, the city is second only to New York. And that position of the young giant city remains uncontested. However in just one day we were not able to form an accurate picture of the role commerce plays in this city. Particularly since several hours of our sightseeing were taken up by a tour of a park on the south side of the city, one of the many parks of which Chicago boasts. They are all linked together by boulevards.

In such a superficial visit, one cannot find an answer as to why Chicago grew up at this precise spot. Possibly the Chicago River, with its two arms—the North and South rivers—may have been the factor that brought the first settlers. Also, at the point of the estuary in Lake Michigan, the terrain affords a natural harbor. But the size and rapid growth of Chicago is due unquestionably to the hard work of its inhabitants. When the great fire of 1871 reduced a major portion of the city to ashes, like a Phoenix it arose more beautiful and more elegant than before. With capital loaned from the eastern seaboard the blow dealt by the fire was completely overcome

[8] Chicago's population in 1880 was 503,304. The 700,000 figure for 1883 was obviously unduly optimistic.

Courtesy of The Chicago Historical Society Engraving from *Picturesque Chicago*, Chicago Engraving Co., 1878/1882/1884

Pine Street, Chicago, looking north from Huron Street (Pine was later called Michigan Avenue)

in a few years and trade grew at a spiraling rate.

On Michigan Avenue we saw some of the homes of the rich. When looking at villas and castles in our country, we usually tell about the noble origins of the family that lives in them and we talk about their connections to other great families and their inherited estates. Here in Chicago our colleagues characterized them in the same way, giving their hereditary lines, how they earned their millions, who were the owners and the inhabitants of this or that villa. However, the three main "lines" here seem to have been that of "pigs," "wheat," and "lumber," in addition to real estate speculation.

The avenue is an imposing, wide drive, faced by the villas and palaces, each with its small open front yard. The street makes an excellent impression. Unfortunately, though, there is no direct view onto Lake Michigan. Michigan Avenue opens onto the boulevards that tie into the many parks, interconnecting the whole of Chicago. I believe there are no less than five large parks, the nicest of which must be Lincoln Park.[9]

[9] The visitors spent the morning viewing the stately "villas" with their elaborately ornamented grounds that made Wabash, Prairie, and Michigan Avenues the show-places of the city's south side. The hot mid-day sun, beating into the open carriages, made the trip less than enjoyable. Even the tastefully decorated parks on the south side, consisting of a lavishly planted 1,055-acre public estate that stretched for more than a mile along Lake Michigan, failed to spark enthusiasm among the visitors. Or so the local reporter noted. *Chicago Tribune*, September 1, 1883, p. 3.

*The Lakeside Building at Clark and Adams Streets,
Chicago, occupied by the Donnelley
Company from 1873 to 1882*

After the long drive in the environs we returned to the city, impressed again by the energetic hustle and bustle in the business streets. Every single building has five, six, or more stories that tell much about the excellent state of business. The city is after all the provider for the entire West of the industrial products of the East and Europe.

Unfortunately our time was far too short to visit

some of the astounding warehouses, the stock yards, and the slaughter houses.[10] They did want us to get a glimpse of the business life, however, so they took us to the grain exchange.[11] There we were given a reception that calmed the wild tumult for a few moments while we were taken to a balcony to over-look the activity. But the minutes of quiet did not last very long. They paid tribute to Villard; he responded; another gentleman spoke; and finally von Bunsen. But what each said was not heard by a single soul, if indeed by the speaker himself. There

[10] A few of the more hardy visitors, scorning rest, did make the trip to Pullman that afternoon, supposedly to be guests at the estate of George M. Pullman. They found no one to greet them when they arrived at the station, and were happily drinking at the nearest saloon when George Pull-man finally appeared to show them about his factories. *Chicago Tribune*, September 1, 1883, p. 3.

[11] When the visitors entered the great hall of the Board of Trade Building at the corner of Washington and La Salle streets, trading in grain futures was in full swing and the hall a bedlam of noise and confusion. Quiet fell at once when the president of the board rapped with his hammer and the trad-ers rushed to gather about the platform. Villard spoke brief-ly, calling Chicago one of the wonders of the age, before introducing Baron Georg von Bunsen of the German party who did his best to address his restless audience and was wildly applauded, even though no more than a dozen had been able to hear him. Scarcely had he finished than the president's hammer fell again and trading resumed. The vis-itors were unnoticed as they made their way from the hall. *Chicago Tribune*, September 1, 1883, p. 3. As Herr Mohr noted, the building was soon to be replaced by a magnificent million-dollar structure then being built across La Salle Street, fronting on Jackson Street.

The Chicago Board of Trade

was an incredible screaming, shouting, and yelling by the young traders. I suppose they thought they had already made too much of a sacrifice by letting us interrupt their business for a quarter of an hour. As we were leaving, the screaming and yelling seemed to double. To all of us who were unfamiliar with the operations, it seemed like an asylum full of mad men, though in reality it was the transactions of the grain exchange. The quotations made amidst this crazy screaming are instantaneously announced in the major centers of America and Europe. The grain exchange building is in very bad repair, but a new one is under construction.

In the Palmer House we made our first acquaintance with a real American hotel.[12] A large number of Negro waiters were serving in the dining room. We chose our food from a menu that offers a rich variety of dishes. You can order whatever you like and as much as you can eat since everything is included in the one price for "board and lodging." We have learned that Americans do not drink wine with their meals. We Germans cannot seem to get along without this nourishment, so we go ahead and

[12] Fortunately for the visitors, arrangements were so badly made that the carriages supposed to take them to Lincoln Park and the water works that afternoon did not arrive at the hotel until 4:00 p.m. This allowed most of them to snatch some much-needed rest. When they left for the railroad station that night one was honest enough to tell his hosts that they were "heartily glad that their treat was over." *Chicago Tribune,* September 1, 1883, p. 3.

order it while the native-born Americans get along on ice water, coffee, tea, milk, or buttermilk.

At seven o'clock this evening we were told to be ready for our departure, and on the way we had the opportunity to travel once more through the city. In New York we marveled at the elevated railroad. Chicago has its counterpart in a streetcar drawn by a cable. The arrangement is peculiar to Chicago and is said to have stood its test. It is quite a sight to see a whole train of railroad cars moving through the streets at considerable speed with no visible power source. The power comes from a tightly woven cable, an inch in diameter, which is driven by a stationary machine. The long so-called endless rope stretches to the machine station where it is wound on a large revolving spool. The cable covers a total distance of sixteen miles round trip; the system seems to work well but it is said to be expensive because the cables wear out rapidly under the heavy use.[13] The streets were also filled with horse drawn vehicles, cars drawn by locomotives, and a flood of wagon traffic.

At traffic centers, houses are covered from top to bottom with colorful billboards. We saw many firms with German names advertising. According to the last census about 70,000 immigrated Germans

[13] While Chicago's North Side was served by horse cars, cable cars were used exclusively on the south side. The system, which cost $2,500,000 to install, was viewed as "the most perfectly organized in the country." *Appleton's General Guide*, 302.

should live here. If you add to that the first generation children born here, then Chicago must have
100,000 German-speaking inhabitants; perhaps they
may be estimated at 150,000.

As a final treat on our way to the terminal of the
Chicago and North Western Railroad, we stopped
for a few minutes with our countrymen at a beer
garden in the vicinity of Lincoln Park. There we
met Hermann Raster, one of the most outstanding
German journalists in America and publisher of the
Illinois Staat Zeitung. Raster has just returned from
Germany and unfortunately could not join our tour
of the Northwest.[14]

Yet we had left many things unseen as we boarded our railroad cars and took leave of Chicago. We
would like to express our genuine gratitude to the
Chicago Germans, who so graciously made our
stopover there so pleasant and informative.

[14] Before being driven to the North Western Railroad depot on Wells Street, the group gathered for a final drink at
De Berge's Beer Garden, a well-known hostelry on Clark
Street near North Avenue. There they met a prominent German-American who had been a victim of the feud that divided the community, Hermann Raster, an 1848 refugee who
had since 1867 edited the influential Republican paper, the
Illinois Staat Zeitung. Despite his prominence, Raster had
not been invited to serve on the committee to welcome the
Villard Party. Incensed by this, he refused to have anything
to do with the visitors until they were ready to leave.
Chicago Tribune, September 1, 1883, p. 3; John Moses and
Joseph Kirkland, eds., *The History of Chicago* (Chicago,
1895), II, 52.

6

A Minnesota Interlude

Hotel Lafayette
Saturday night, September 1, 1883

AFTER leaving Chicago last night there is little to report of our trip through the dark night. We do know that we passed through Madison, the capital of Wisconsin, because this morning there were several beautiful bouquets of flowers on board, a gift to us from the Germans in Madison. A large group of our countrymen had gathered at the train station to greet us as we passed through, but due to the late hour their good intentions were in vain.[1] We sent our thanks by telegram.

My recollections of today begin with Eau Claire, three-fourths of the way from Chicago to St. Paul. The city lies at the confluence of two rivers, the Eau Claire and the Chippewa, and it has a varied collection of churches. Huge piles of wood and wood products indicate that Eau Claire is situated near

[1] The large party of Madison German-Americans had been waiting for several hours when the special train paused briefly at the station shortly after midnight to take on fuel and water. Despite the late hour, they serenaded the dark cars with vocal and instrumental music, and left a basket of buttonhole bouquets to be given the guests the next morning, *Chicago Tribune*, September 2, 1883.

large tracts of forested land and that the city owes its life to the wood industry. The landscape around there is very pleasant. But before we had the chance to observe very much, we were rushing westward again with about one hundred miles still before us to St. Paul.

Soon, however, we passed Hudson and after moving across Lake St. Croix arrived in Minnesota and finally in its capital, St. Paul. As we disembarked from the train, I was overcome for a moment by a kind of homesickness. Suddenly it came to me just how far I was from home. For in my imagination, St. Paul was always the *ultima thule*, the last extremity of the northwestern United States, the very last refuge for beings who could find no other spot to take refuge. Now I stood at the train depot of St. Paul, surrounded by a crowd of people who stared at us with genuine interest. Into this crowd I peered, trying to recognize at least one face. As far as I can tell, I knew no one out there; yet I could not help feeling that German countrymen living in St. Paul must have known about me and I kept hoping someone would come up to me and tell me so. But none did and I had no more time to feel sorry for myself.

Following a brief introductory greeting we were taken to the horsedrawn carriages for a tour of the city, a St. Paul citizen accompanying us in each vehicle. Shortly thereafter, my premonitions about St. Paul were corrected. The city is very new and is thriving but it has an unfinished look about it. Between the tall and substantial buildings they are still leveling off the hills to improve the terrain for more buildings. Our first stop was at the administration building of the Northern Pacific Railroad. It has just been completed and decorated with motifs showing the fruits of the local countryside as well as a selection of the wild life from the local forests and fields.[2]

Then we were driven up and down and back and forth through the downtown and far beyond. St. Paul is all decked out in festival decorations and there is great excitement. Everywhere there are flags and banners, wreaths and triumphal arches, and everywhere you see that business plays a major role here. The suburbs are attractive, houses with fresh green lawns and beautiful oak trees in the yards. We were served lunch in a restaurant back downtown and of course there were several speeches. Dr. Albert Wolff of the German *Volkszeitung* greeted us and Henry Villard talked about the significance of

[2] When the Villard Party arrived at ten on the morning of September 1 it was greeted by a sizable portion of the city's German-born population, headed by Mayor C. D. O'Brien. After the usual "strains of martial music" and the inevitable formalities, the guests were driven about the city, stopping first at the headquarters of the Northern Pacific Railroad on Fourth Street, a building "strikingly notable in point of architectural beauty," that had been elaborately decorated for the occasion. *Daily Minneapolis Tribune*, August 31, 1883. [Because this newspaper normally printed only four pages, page numbers have not been added.]

the new Northern Pacific Railroad, emphasizing the pleasure for him to be a German called to complete this tremendous task. Dr. Schleiden then offered a toast to the hospitable city of St. Paul. He remarked that he had become acquainted with the city nearly a quarter of a century earlier and that even then he had recognized its great future.[3]

In the afternoon we went north to Minneapolis where we also received a friendly welcome. These two cities have much in common and their outer limits are only a few miles from each other. No doubt for this very reason, there is a jealous rivalry between them. Minneapolis has grown up even faster than St. Paul. It has a natural source of wealth

[3] The visitors were taken to the city's leading restaurant, Magee's, where an elaborate repast was served, followed by the usual speeches. The first was given by Albert Wolff, a German-born political exile who had reached Minnesota in 1853 and by 1877 was editing the *St. Paul Volkszeitung*. This time Dr. Rudolf Schleiden, former representative of the Hanseatic Cities to the United States, responded for the guests. He was followed by O. H. Lienau, one of the visitors, who raised his glass to "The health of Mr. Villard, the Pathfinder." Villard responded with a brief speech in German recalling his first visit to the city twenty-five years before and noting its growth which he predicted would be accelerated by completion of the railroad. A typically German "kommers" at Grote's Beer Garden had been planned, but by the time the last orator had finished, no time remained. *Chicago Tribune*, September 2, 1883, p. 6; [St. Paul] *Daily Pioneer Press* August 29, 1883, p. 3. The speeches are given in full in John H. Hanson, comp., *Grand Opening of the Northern Pacific Railway Celebration at St. Paul, Minnesota, The Eastern Terminus. September 3, 1883. Issued by Order of the City of St. Paul* (St. Paul, [1883]), 6–10.

that its sister city does not have, namely: the water power furnished by the Falls of St. Anthony of the Mississippi River. The river falls sixty feet there and this gift of nature is exploited to its maximum. Minneapolis has just as large a population as St. Paul, its streets are straight and wide, though not all complete, and life is bubbling over everywhere one looks. Three bridges span the Mississippi here and a huge viaduct over the river is under construction. Quays and loading facilities have been built to expedite commerce and trade.

The milling industry in the city of Minneapolis is very great. The Falls of St. Anthony provide the water power for dozens of mills, among them some whose sizes outstrip anything of their kind in the world. The waterfalls appear to be protected like a precious property. Large rocks in the river indicate that the power of the water is taking its toll on the river's bed. The edge of the falls is gradually breaking off and threatening to move up stream. In order to prevent this, the rim of the falls as well as the incline and the striking area at the bottom have been overlaid with heavy planks so that the water glides smoothly across the edge and on down the trough.[4]

[4] The Twin Cities were not as closely joined in 1883 as today. St. Paul, the state capital, with a population of 41,473 in 1880, was built on terraces on both sides of the Mississippi. Ten miles to the north lay Minneapolis, with 46,887 population in 1880, covering a broad plain high above the Mississippi's bluffs. Its prosperity rested on the

One of the huge mills, the Pillsbury, was shown to us in every detail. We started at the lowest level where a large shaft of water is brought in through a special channel. This then turns a monstrous water wheel which generates 2,500 horsepower and which in turn drives all the mechanical parts of the mill. The grindstones of the mill are recessed in the machine. A steel cylinder, or rather hundreds of such cylinders having various types of rough surfaces, roll together and thereby grind the wheat. Almost every activity here is done by machine. Human hands only regulate the machines or assist in various small tasks. The wheat is driven through hundreds of little cavities, if I may put it that way, and in these apertures it gets finer and finer. When it is fine enough, the flour flows together into a large hopper and from there it is put into sacks or barrels. Workmen either sew shut the sacks or nail shut the barrels. They work with feverish energy as if they were trying to keep in step with the mighty forces

Falls of St. Anthony, where the river fell eighteen feet perpendicularly, then dropped another 82 feet in two miles. As Herr Mohr noted, the beauty of the falls had been marred by a broad wooden apron constructed entirely across the river, sloping from the edge of the falls to a point near their base. Over this the water slipped smoothly, preventing the rock edges from wearing away. The best view of the falls was from an iron suspension bridge, one of the three spanning the river. Henry J. Winser, *The Great Northwest. A Guide-Book and Itinerary for the Use of Tourists and Travellers over the Lines of the Northern Pacific Railroad* (New York, 1883), 26–27. This was the official guidebook prepared for the railroad and distributed to the Villard Party.

of the natural water power. I don't think I have ever seen any place back home where people work so ferociously.

We climbed from floor to floor until at last we stood high on the roof and enjoyed the panoramic view of the city and its countryside, including the towers of St. Paul off in the distance. The Pillsbury mill turns out five thousand barrels of flour every day but it has rivals for this record on the other side of the river.[5]

Minneapolis is also astir with preparations for the festival. One is impressed by the number of vehicles on the streets.[6] In this land of such great distances,

[5] Minneapolis flour mills pioneered the "New Process" technique by which wheat berries were gradually reduced to flour in a series of successive grindings through metal rollers, with sifting after each reduction. The result was a highly glutenous flour widely in demand. The Pillsbury "A Mill," the largest then operating, was seven stories high. Its basement contained two fifty-five foot water wheels, each weighing thirteen tons, that produced 2,400 horsepower. This was transmitted through giant drive shafts on the first floor, where pulleys twelve feet in diameter turned forty-eight-inch belts at the rate of 4,260 feet a minute. The belts, in turn, conveyed power to the rollers in the attic. The grain was ground eight times as it descended by gravity from floor to floor; the flour was discharged at the bottom so rapidly that a freight car could be filled every twenty-five minutes. Normal production was 5,200 barrels a day. In all twenty-one mills were clustered in Minneapolis. Earnest Ingersoll, "The Home of Hiawatha," *Harper's Magazine*, LXVII (June, 1883), 75-77.

[6] That Sunday, the press reported, was the noisiest and busiest in the city's history as displays were hurried to completion after the late start. "Innumerable novel or happy

driving is an absolute necessity. As in St. Paul we took a drive through the city. In the suburbs we were pleased by the lovely villas and the well-manicured lawns which testify to the affluence of the inhabitants here. Nowhere does one see evidence of poverty.

At the conclusion of our tour we were invited to a dinner by the Honorable W. D. Washburn, which had the character of a luncheon. The Washburns are closely connected with the fate of Minneapolis and their villa is not very large but very pleasantly furnished. A new palace-like residence of Mr. Washburn's is just being completed.[7]

Evening had already closed in by the time we arrived at Hotel Lafayette on Lake Minnetonka.[8]

---

devices were springing into existence on all the byways, while scores of mechanics worked like beavers upon the less substantial decorations, arches, miniature representations of railway bridges, ships, waterfalls and other ingeniously constructed odds and ends." [St. Paul] *Daily Pioneer Press*, September 3, 1883, p. 6.

[7] William D. Washburn was indeed closely connected with the fate of Minneapolis. Born in 1831, he was a founder of the Washburn & Crosby Milling Company which eventually merged to form the Pillsbury-Washburn Company and dominate flour milling. He was also the organizer of two railroads, and was at this time a member of Congress.

[8] Lake Minnetonka, fifteen miles by rail from Minneapolis, was considered by Minnesotans the most beautiful in the world. Said a guidebook author: "Its depths have that deep blue azure that belongs to the purest water under summer skies, and its charming irregular shores, forested clear down to the shining beach, break into new combinations of woodland beauty at each advance of your boat." The lake's shores

We wonder if anything has ever occurred either in modern or in ancient times comparable to this trip to the Far West. Now we finally have our entire party together. We are to travel to the festive completion of the Northern Pacific Railroad track at a point thousands of miles west of the Atlantic Ocean. The joining of these tracks will connect the Pacific and the Atlantic Oceans with rails stretching from Portland, Oregon, to New York through St. Paul and Chicago, and across an enormous distance of land.

I am not yet certain exactly how many are in the entire troop that is supposed to depart from here tomorrow evening, but most likely there will be in the neighborhood of three hundred.[9] And we will travel with every conceivable comfort. Discounting the fact that the rooms are smaller, our accommodations on the train offer the same peak of excellence as any New York hotel. Our party of Germans arrived here on board a train with eleven cars. I have

were dotted with the summer homes of wealthy southerners, and by a number of resort hotels. Of these the largest was The Lafayette, with accommodations for 1,200 guests. Winser, *The Great Northwest*, 29–30.

[9] The English dignitaries invited by Villard to view the "last spike" ceremony arrived in St. Paul a day after the Germans, traveling in their own special train. Another train had also arrived from Chicago, filled with American notables. A fourth was soon to be added when the whole party started westward from St. Paul. In all the Villard Party included some 180 Americans and German-Americans, and about sixty visitors from overseas. Villard, *Memoirs*, II, 308–310.

already mentioned that despite their sleeping berths the famous Palace Cars by Pullman are actually second class accommodations. We occupy the cars built for the Board of Directors, which offer an extra plush in accommodations. We enjoy a salon in which six or eight men can comfortably sit together and not be too crowded to converse comfortably, and we each have a living room that converts to a bedroom in the evening. We also have a washroom, a dressing room, a kitchen, and a pantry in the car; and what the kitchen and pantry have to offer is incredible. But then, the train cars will be our domicile for some time.

Today we have a free day to wander about. We are as happy about that as young boys on a free day from school. Just where Minnetonka lies, you may never have known. And if you have never even heard of Lake Minnetonka before, you still should not harbor a guilty conscience about your deficient knowledge of geography. Neither Appleton's guide nor the guidebook for Englishmen mentions either Lake Minnetonka or Hotel Lafayette.[10] Yet the latter claims to have but one rival among the countless American resort hotels.

But from today on, Lake Minnetonka and Hotel Lafayette will be famous. A crowd of important

[10] Mohr was right. Neither Montgomery Gibbs' *The Englishman's Guidebook to the United States and Canada* (London, 1883), nor *Appleton's General Guide to the United States and Canada, Illustrated* (New York, 1883), mentioned either the lake or the hotel.

personalities is gathering here that will attract the eyes of the entire United States. Tomorrow evening there is to be a banquet given by the mayor and the city councilmen of St. Paul, with many important speeches that will resound from every corner of this land. Former President Grant arrived this morning and with him a swarm of politicians—former senators, ambassadors, governors, and members of Congress. In short, Hotel Lafayette is momentarily the focus of American life as well as the center of an international gathering. The English[11] are here with their notables from both houses of Parliament and from the worlds of science and commerce. Our German party has grown with the addition of several important German-Americans while in Chicago,

[11] Villard had assembled an impressive gathering, although not nearly as impressive as he would have liked. In addition to former President U. S. Grant, the list included Henry M. Teller, Secretary of the Interior; Attorney General Benjamin Brewster; L. S. Sackville West, Minister Plenipotentiary from Great Britain; Count Lippe-Weissenfeld, Charge d'Affairs from Austria-Hungary; Count Steen Anderson de Bille of the Danish legation; Count de Bilat, Charge d'Affairs from Sweden and Norway; Baron von Eisendecher, the Imperial German Minister; a number of governors and congressmen, as well as cabinet members and such business leaders as Jay Cooke and George M. Pullman. The English guests numbered about thirty, including Professor James Bryce, Lord Justice Bowen, Lord Carrington, the Earl and Countess of Onslow, the Earl of Dalhousie, H. Gibbs, Governor of the Bank of England, Chief Justice Charles Russell, and a number of members of Parliament and lesser title holders. *New York Times*, August 15, 1883, p. 5.

Messrs. Lasker[12] and Adolf Meier from St. Louis, and the Consul General Feigel.

Tomorrow the entire Villard party will unite for the first time at celebrations in Minneapolis and St. Paul. Both cities are making preparations for the opening of the railroad. It will be a full holiday with all the stores closed. From this you can see how much emphasis is placed on the completion of the railroad. The mere fact that such a large number of important American politicians are coming here proves it is a major milestone. Even with the high level of comfort on the trains, taking part in a trip of this sort does demand stamina. Nevertheless they are coming to pay their tribute to the significance of this event that has far more than a local effect.

Now let me tell you exactly where Lake Minnetonka is. You will see on the map in Stieler's Atlas[13] that it is twelve miles from Minneapolis and can be reached from the city in a half-hour. The shores rise gradually and the lake is enclosed by forests and corn fields. Steamers give excursion rides on it.

[12] Eduard Lasker of Berlin, a member of the German Reichstag and an outspoken opponent of Bismarck's policies, had been touring in the United States and joined the party in Chicago. Adolf Meier, who had migrated from Germany to St. Louis in 1837, was a prominent manufacturer in that city. *Chicago Tribune*, August 29, 1883, p. 2.

[13] The excellent German atlas prepared by Adolf Stieler, *Händ Atlas Über Alle Theile der Erde und Über das Weltgebäude* (Gotha, 1881) did show the points mentioned by Herr Mohr.

Hotel Lafayette is a gigantic wood building, lofty, simple, clean but not luxurious, with huge covered terraces and spacious salons. It reminds one of a building we would erect for a marksman tournament or a song fest. I might add that the activity here today was not much different.

Except for a few minor inconveniences that come with summer heat, we arrived here in comfort last night, not really tired, rather excited by what we have seen so far. Just imagine what we have already seen! We can hardly believe that barely a week ago the *Elbe* brought us to American soil and that only two-and-a-half weeks have passed since we left home. In one sense the multitude of impressions as well as the rapid change make the length of time seem much longer than it is.

Hotel Lafayette
Monday morning, September 3, 1883

I MIGHT BEGIN by saying that I'm *still* at Hotel Lafayette. To spend a lovely long day in one spot with only a short interruption for a steamer cruise on the lake is for this trip a very unusual day. I did spend two restful nights sleeping in the hotel and it is in gratitude that I report a few details about Minnetonka and its hotel. A moment ago I picked up a brochure about Minnetonka down in the office, so I could probably tell you more about it than you care to hear. But I will spare you the poetic exuberance of its prose. If I may venture a little comparison, I may say that the Berliners in our group see a similarity between Lake Minnetonka and their Havel lakes in Berlin. Our enthusiastic guidebook maintains that in all of the great Northwest, Minnetonka has neither equal nor rival. "Although its reputation has spread far and wide, no magic in a painter's brush, no sensational words of a writer's pen have yet been able to capture its beauty and its bountiful charm."[14] I will neither confirm nor deny this boast, but I will admit that Lake Minnetonka is a very charming spot in spite of its insignificance on the map. It has so many bays and inlets, islands and peninsulas, isthmuses and narrows—there seem to be enough for an entire continent. The shorelines are beautifully forested, and in the bays are inviting hotels and villas half hidden by the trees. The lake is one of countless water basins that cover the "lake regions" of Minnesota.

Out on one of the islands, the St. Paul Germans have built up a pleasant spot where they can get away from the rush of the world and peacefully enjoy a cool drink. St. Paul and Minneapolis are not far from here and the hotels along the lake get many of their clients from the Twin Cities. Our hotel is built in true American dimensions and it is expanding from one season to the next. It is seven hundred feet long and one hundred feet wide with four floors

[14]This quotation did not appear in the two guidebooks that Herr Mohr was using: Winser, *The Great Northwest*, and *Appleton's General Guide*.

in all. All around this gigantic Queen Anne style structure is a covered veranda. On the ground floor there is a large dining room on the left, and on the right the parlor or conversation room. On the upper floors through the middle of the building runs a wide hall with rooms on both sides. The walls have been covered over with plaster but not painted; the furnishings are simple but nice; and as everywhere in this country, the beds are exquisite.

When there is bright sunshine and warm weather, Hotel Lafayette is a wonderful place to be. I do not know how many hundreds of people can be accommodated here at one time, but there is room for our entire Villard party in addition to the other guests. Yesterday a list of all banquet guests expected from Germany, England, and America was made available to us. It may not be an accurate list because at the last moment this one or that one may have had to decline, but on the whole one can get some idea of what kind of company he will be in.

The English historian Bryce[15] and Dr. Burchardt, a German from Manchester, have taken the initiative to promote some social mixing. Nevertheless, so far the nationalities have kept pretty much to themselves. Introductions do not always help very much

[15] James Bryce, at this time a professor at the University of Oxford, was a prominent historian and public figure, famed for his history of the Roman Empire. This was his third visit to America but his first to the American West. His remarkable work, *The American Commonwealth*, was to be published five years later.

Hotel Lafayette, Lake Minnetonka (burned 1897)

because it is virtually impossible to keep all the names and personalities distinct. In addition to the guests of the Northern Pacific Railroad there are many here from St. Paul, Minneapolis, and other cities.

Monday evening, September 3, 1883

WHAT A DAY ! This morning the big festival in St. Paul, this afternoon in Minneapolis, this evening the banquet in the Lafayette Hotel, and tomorrow morning at 1:00 a.m. we will pull out for the great West. Today President Arthur, former President Grant, and various secretaries and American state officials of the highest rank were a part of our Villard party.[16] Both the young cities of St. Paul and Minneapolis tried today to show the world what they can do in the fields of commerce and industry. And indeed they have succeeded in awakening great wonderment on the part of all who watched the very interesting parades. It is difficult for people in Europe to imagine what these cities have accomplished. Situated one on each side of the Mississippi only a few miles from each other, they have in a few short years demonstrated a truly fantastic rate of growth. Both are approximately the same size, each

[16] President Chester A. Arthur had been touring in the Far West for six weeks, climaxing his visit with a fishing expedition in Yellowstone National Park. His return schedule allowed him to join the ceremonies, much to Villard's delight. *New York Times*, August 30, 1883, p. 2, September 3, p. 1.

having about ninety-thousand inhabitants, and they are rivals in many aspects.

St. Paul has the advantage of having a larger volume of trade, but Minneapolis has the advantage for certain industries in its location at the Falls of St. Anthony on the Mississippi. Both cities have expanded vertically. In a very few years hotels, warehouses, and factory buildings have shot up—high structures that would give distinction to any city. All kinds of things have been started and a few are already being abandoned. The streets still leave much to be desired, but there are horse-drawn streetcars, and in Minneapolis, even some with locomotives running through the city. Everywhere in these cities there is a vitality and vigor that affects and inspires the mood of any visitor.[17]

Today we were supposed to see these cities as they see themselves. Each has tried to demonstrate that it will be capable of dominating the massive extra territory which the railroad is now opening up. Unfortunately we had to watch two similar displays in one day. The effect blunted and confused our general impressions.

[17] Five railroads, and 150 trains a day, entered St. Paul; in addition, its Mississippi River commerce was large. In 1883 the city was showing every sign of continued growth; most of its streets were still unpaved, but a sewage system was being installed and gas lights provided some illumination. Minneapolis was also booming as water power from the Falls of St. Anthony was brought into use. In 1882 the value of its flour milling products alone was $11,000,000. *Appleton's General Guide*, 355–357.

In New York we had already heard that trouble between the two cities was brewing. As the story was related to us, it was not only petty jealousy that prevented cooperation between the neighboring cities for this occasion. In Minneapolis relations between the community and the city government have not been very cordial. A large portion of the population, under the leadership of the Chamber of Commerce, had split off from the mayor and the city council making its own festival arrangements in a private undertaking. In St. Paul the whole program was accomplished officially by the city. Thus any cooperation between the cities on this venture was rendered impossible.[18] So there was a parade in St. Paul and another parade in Minneapolis. And what parades! In each case it took hours to pass.

It would of course far exceed my powers to give you a complete picture of what took place. I can

[18]So intense was the rivalry between the two cities that a cooperative reception for the Villard Party was impossible. Henry Villard first learned of this when met in Chicago by a committee of four from Minneapolis, headed by Washburn. Acting in his usual decisive way, he told the Minneapolis committee that it could have either the morning or afternoon of September 3 for its parade and reception, and could provide one of the two banquets. The committee chose the afternoon, providing the party could reach there by one o'clock. Telegrams announcing these arrangements could not be sent from Chicago until August 31, allowing only four days to plan the parade and dinner, and to provide decorations. *Daily Minneapolis Tribune*, August 23, September 1, 1883; [St. Paul] *Daily Pioneer Press*, August 22, 1883, p. 9, August 23, p. 8, August 25, p. 3.

only say one thing, and I must emphasize it, that we Europeans were astounded in the fullest sense of the word. And the entire drama was organized in only a few days. Someone remarked, "The entire business community, the composite of all our industries, was put on wheels for several hours." One could say it was a traveling exhibition.

This forenoon when we arrived in St. Paul from our country resort, carriages were again waiting for us. (By the way, General Grant chose our carriage, firmly convinced apparently that he could sit with us and smoke his cigars undisturbed.)[19] We were driven to the festival square through streets ornamented by large flags, small flags, wreaths and garlands. We passed several triumphal arches. On top of one of the arches, decorated in arabesque style, stood young ladies in colorful native costumes. From one of the platforms, young girls in national costumes showered the passers-by with flowers.[20] Villard's picture was everywhere.

[19] According to reporters who were present, General Grant rode in the first carriage of the procession with Mr. and Mrs. Villard and Mayor O'Brien. For a full account of these ceremonies see the "Historical Introduction" to this book, pp. xliv–xlviii. *Chicago Tribune*, September 4, 1883, p. 1; *Daily Minneapolis Tribune*, September 4, 1883, p. 5. The fullest description of the parade is in Hanson, comp., *Grand Opening of the Northern Pacific Railway*, 26–41.

[20] One reporter noted that General Grant sat grim and silent amidst this shower of flowers, wearing a white plug hat, and holding between his fingers the remains of an "old stogie" that he had been smoking. *Daily Minneapolis Tribune*, September 4, 1883, p. 5.

Parade in St. Paul

Taken from *Frank Leslie's Illustrated Newspaper*

We were driven to Rice Park, the large square where the procession was to pass by. Here we were introduced to the mayor, the bishop, the commanding general of Fort Snelling, former President Grant and other distinguished guests. It was an excellent spot from which to view the parade. We could move about freely and yet we were protected from the sun by the foliage on the trees. A great number of young men on horseback opened the parade.[21] Next came a unit that was of special interest to our party, several groups of Negro troops from the regular army, led by white officers. They are stationed at neighboring Fort Snelling.[22] Their uniforms were dark blue and they had light blue trimmings and the young men looked strong and robust. Then came the artillery. Next there was a troupe of authentic Indians who had been moved out of the land which they once possessed as civilization pressed in.

The militia also paraded. By the spit and shine of their equipment one could tell that even these sons

[21] After the usual police units, the parade began with a troupe of boys on ponies under the direction of Marshal Isaac Doblay, all making a "pleasing appearance" in their blue shirts and red trousers and white skull caps. [St. Paul] *Daily Pioneer Press*, September 4, 1883, p. 2.

[22] The Negro troops, a detachment of the 25th Colored Infantry some two hundred strong, were at this time stationed at nearby Fort Snelling. "The colored band and regiment from the Fort," a local scribe noted, "was a source of wonder to the foreigners." [St. Paul] *Daily Pioneer Press*, September 4, 1883, p. 2.

of the Republic find the gay uniform attractive. Very impressive were the Zouaves of Minneapolis, who performed here under the command of the mayor of their city. Also impressive were the Old Volunteers and the fire department with its luxurious-looking sprayers and equipment. Then came units from all the local clubs: the Catholic Charities Society, the Irish, the French, the Bohemians wearing emblems, sashes and other markings, the Free Masons, the German singing societies as well as the German mutual aid organizations.

Next we saw the commercial and trade union groups. First the knights of the Cloven, who represent the cattle trade, all on horseback; then the fruit dealers and growers riding on floats; also other trade groups. Then came promotion and advertising of all types; next the post office department with the mail carriers dressed in gray. A float depicting the St. Paul post office of 1846 drew many cheers; it was a little cupboard with many pigeon holes. Right behind it was a model of the post office today which handles millions of letters. Also the Express Company came by, as it was years ago, and now. Finally, there appeared a gigantic map of the Northern Pacific Railroad line carried on a float drawn by six horses; and behind this all the craft unions and professionals who were and are responsible for building the railroad. Then came displays of the products that will be transported by the railroad. Next came the elaborate press exhibits. The

Pioneer Press had set up a printing press and staff on its float and was turning out a newspaper which contained descriptions of the City of St. Paul. As it moved along in the parade, the papers were printed and scattered immediately among the crowds.[23]

There were many floats characterizing the industries of St. Paul. There was an endless row of dry goods businesses. Auerbach, Finch and Van Slyck had no less than fifteen wagons loaded with articles from their stores and factories.[24] The milling and wood products firms outdid each other with their characteristic trappings on wagons and teams. Every minute our surprise grew greater at the incomprehensible number and diversity of industries here, and the high degree of perfection they have achieved. I must add that there were some excellent bits of humor and boastful tall tales illustrating the enviable confidence of certain industries which already have plans for expansion from St. Paul all the way to Japan and China.

We enjoyed our lunch in one of the tents and watched the parade for a while afterwards until we

[23] This miniature, four-page paper, called *The Pioneer Press Extra*, and dated September 3, 1883, was devoted to an account of St. Paul's growth and prospects, and to praise of Villard. A copy is in the Minnesota State Historical Society library.

[24] Actually the wholesale dry goods firm of Auerbach, Finch & Van Slyck had no less than twenty wagons in the procession all laden with goods that it marketed. It was, judged one reporter, "certainly a creditable display." [St. Paul] *Daily Pioneer Press*, September 4, 1883, p. 2.

Parade on Third Street, St. Paul

finally had to get in our carriages again. Once more we drove through the streets of St. Paul and to the train station. By train we dashed over to Minneapolis where a similar drama was to take place. As we pulled in, President Arthur was also arriving with his entourage. He came from the West where he had been visiting a national park. The busy festival committee from St. Paul had gone through much difficulty to get the Chief of the Republic to their celebration. They claimed that President Arthur traveled at the train's highest speed to donate his presence to St. Paul's rival, Minneapolis.

Henry Villard accompanied the President to his carriage and rode with him into the city, and the rest of us followed closely behind in happy confusion. I tried in vain to get closer for a better look at the President. In circumstances like this you regret the lack of a uniform. If you are wearing your braids and your buttons, of course, people can judge what sort of a person you are in terms of your worth and position.

We were driven to the Hotel Nicollet, where they had erected a monstrous tribune.[25] We took our places on it and could look down the street almost an infinite distance. The entire stretch was jammed with heads and in the far background we could see the beginning of a parade. Opposite us were pictures of Minnehaha Falls and other interesting scenes from the Northwest. When General Grant arrived at the tribune, there was a tremendous roar from the people. It is with such terrifying shouts that the people in this country try to show

[25] Facing the thousand-seat grandstand erected in front of the Nicollet House was a model of the famed Minnehaha Falls, with real water tumbling over a mass of evergreens, and beside this, large pictures of Henry Villard and Jay Cooke, wreathed in flowers. By the time the Villard Party and President Arthur arrived at 1:30, the procession had been waiting for nearly an hour. *Daily Minneapolis Tribune*, September 4, 1883, p. 8; *Chicago Tribune*, September 4, 1883, p. 1.

their affection. Grant is really very beloved by the common people, for they see him as the man who preserved the Union and they honor him as a brave general. It would have been fine if Grant had been satisfied with that reputation. As president he earned little praise and has fallen considerably in the eyes of educated Americans. The other famous personalities were greeted in similar style. Perhaps the greatest outburst of them all was for Villard and President Arthur.

After the arrival of the celebrities the procession could begin. Minneapolis makes the typical mistake of youth. It tries to act older and thus reaches back into the past. Opening the parade following the militia was the missionary Hennepin with Bible in hand and the words in his mouth, "I discovered these Falls." Then came the Indians with their wigwam and canoe under the motto "In 1859 this place belonged to us."[26] Next came the immigrants in their famous covered wagons drawn by oxen.

[26] Father Louis Hennepin accompanied Robert Sieur de La Salle, westward from Quebec in 1679 when that French colonizer established Fort Crevecoeur in the Illinois Country, then in 1680 led a small expedition northward to explore the Upper Mississippi. Herr Mohr recorded half of the sign which read: "Hennepin Discovered the Falls in 1680 and Villard Discovered them in 1880." The Indians who claimed that "this place" belonged to them in 1859 could not have been referring to the Minneapolis area which was ceded to the United States by the Sioux in 1853 and 1857. According to the press, however, Herr Mohr misread the banner which read: "This Was Our Home in 1849." *Daily Minneapolis Tribune*, September 4, 1883, p. 8.

Thereupon followed a depiction of the rapid development of the area—the progress from the days of extreme hardship to the way of life today. Huge models of cattle herds called to mind the cattle business. Then the parade became much the same as the procession in St. Paul—militia, fire department, veterans, and the various nationality clubs. The Germans were very well represented—one singing group called "Harmonie" even had its own float. The Scandinavians, whom we have met often here, displayed the motto: "Our adopted Country, first and last."

"Wheat is king and the Northern Pacific its throne" was the motto used to introduce the industries of Minneapolis. First to be represented were the flour mills. They depicted how flour was milled in 1870, in 1875, and how it is done now in 1883. The Pillsbury Mill which I have already mentioned was represented by a huge model; in one way or another every mill was displayed—and not only the mills but also the elevators and the other associated industries. There was an endless parade of millers accompanying these floats.

After the mills came the wood products. Then came the trades, in short everything that Minneapolis either produces itself for shipment to the interior of the country, or stores in transit and ships out later. I simply cannot enumerate all we saw nor can I describe it. Everything was swimming before my eyes and my hand was lame from taking notes.

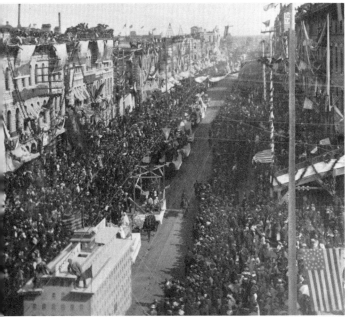

Courtesy of the Minnesota Historical Society

Parade down Washington Avenue, Minneapolis

Long before the end of the parade was in sight I was relieved from my task. We were told to get into our carriages.[27]

[27] Villard's guests were fortunate, for those with no excuse to leave were forced to watch for seven solid hours before the last float passed. "Such a vast industrial procession has probably never been seen in this country," wrote a newspaper correspondent, who might well have added that he hoped it

We were to be entertained by the city of Minneapolis at the Lyndale, a summer resort similar to the Lafayette Hotel but smaller, situated on Calhoun Lake, several miles outside of the city. There we found what we really needed—food and drink. An abundant selection of excellently prepared cold dishes was spread out on large tables and black men poured champagne. When breakfast was finished, if you can call breakfast a meal that is served at three or four in the afternoon, there followed some pleasant oratory.[28] General Washburn, who had recently been our host, was president of the festival committee. He began with a highly flattering toast to Villard, "whose tremendous talent for organization places him among the conquerors of the world, for indeed the victories of peace are no less glorious than those of war." Following such a speech Villard could only say a few modest words to decline the flattering tribute. General Washburn then brought up the thesis that Jay Cooke, the first to undertake the construction of the Northern Pacific Railroad, also deserved to be mentioned along with the man

---

never would be seen again. *Chicago Tribune*, September 4, 1883, p. 1.

[28] The "breakfast" menu included oysters, salmon, lobster, deviled crabs, chicken, buffalo tongue, prairie chicken, ham glacé, roast beef, turkey, boned canvasback duck, shrimp salad, pâté de foie gras, and an extended array of delicacies that ended with a dozen types of pastry. Most of the speeches given afterward are printed in the *Daily Minneapolis Tribune*, September 4, 1883, p. 7. For an account of the affair see "Historical Introduction," p. l.

who completed the job. He called on General Nettleton to tell why.[29]

General Grant was asked to speak as was former Secretary of State Evarts, who is an excellent dinner speaker.[30] I was not able to understand much of what he said because his witty comments were submerged in a flood of laughter. But it was a pleasure just to watch Evarts' face, a haggard, spiritual countenance. Whenever he was about to turn a phrase, a charming, ironical smile swept across his face. Grant is no public speaker. His voice is not strong enough, but apparently he has a sense of humor.

Once again, before all the speeches were finished, we were ordered back to our carriages. We still had the most important task of the day before us—the great banquet in Hotel Lafayette, to which we had been invited by the city of St. Paul. Moreover we still had to pack and get ready for the night trip. So we returned again to Lake Minnetonka. Fortunately

[29] Alfred B. Nettleton, founder and editor of the *Daily Minneapolis Tribune*, had between 1870 and 1875 been associated with Jay Cooke, the New York financier who had controlled the Northern Pacific's destiny during those years.

[30] William M. Evarts (1818–1901) was one of the nation's most popular statesmen and legal authorities, having served in the three most famous cases of the generation: the impeachment of President Andrew Johnson (for the defense), the litigation arising over the disputed election of 1876, and the Geneva Arbitration of 1871–1872 concerning claims against England for damage done by Confederate privateers. He also served as Secretary of State between 1877 and 1881. Evarts had been selected by Villard as the principal orator for the events celebrating the opening of the railroad.

we have been excused from wearing tuxedos so it will not take too long to get dressed.

Late Monday night, September 3, 1883

I FIND I have a spare quarter of an hour to add a description of the banquet which I took part in— for the first and last time—with a president of the United States. I might add that our acquaintance did not grow a bit more intimate from the experience. Most likely he did not learn about my existence and unfortunately I came away with only a very far removed observation of him. Since I had assumed that a head of state under all circumstances would take his place in the middle of the head table, most of the time I was making respectful glances at the mayor of St. Paul instead of the president of the United States. It was only when Mr. Arthur stood up to answer a toast that I became aware of my error. Up to that point I had envied the president for his youthful appearance. The real president is not so youthful, but he appears to be a very distinguished-looking character. Mr. Arthur spoke briefly and at a good pace, turning the attention to Henry Villard who sat on the other side of the mayor. Villard answered by giving to others the credit for completion of the Northern Pacific.[31] Also

[31] Herr Mohr seems to have been unaware that the speeches inflicted on the guests on this occasion were as carefully planned as those at the other banquets. The mayor of St. Paul, C. D. O'Brien, presided, calling first on President Arthur who introduced Henry Villard after a few com-

at the head table were the ambassadors, secretaries, governors of the states, Carl Schurz, and others.

The banquet took place in a dining room fantastically decorated with flags and coats of arms. In all there were about five hundred people and as is usually the case for overcrowded parties, the service was not up to standard. Although there were excellent things described in the elaborately printed menu, by no means did everybody get all he was promised.[32] Long before the speeches and the dinner were finished we had to be off. The baggage has already been delivered. We are looking forward to peace and quiet after these eventful days.

---

plimentary remarks. Villard's usual glowing recital of the economic boom sure to multiply the Midwest's prosperity with the completion of the road was followed by an endless succession of toasts: to "The Northwest" (response by former governor Alexander Ramsey of Minnesota), "Our Foreign Guests" (British Minister L. S. Sackville West), "The United States Government" (H. M. Teller), "The State of Minnesota" (Governor L. F. Hubbard), "The Army—Holding the Savages in Check while the Shores of the Continent were United" (General Albert H. Terry from Fort Snelling), "The City of Minneapolis" (Mayor A. A. Ames), "The Railroad System of Minnesota" (James J. Hill), and "The Press" (no response, for Carl Schurz, who had been scheduled to speak, had joined the other guests in a parade to their private cars, and some needed rest). The speeches are printed in Hanson, comp., *Grand Opening of the Northern Pacific Railway*, 45–58.

[32] For hostile accounts of this dinner recorded by representatives of the press see "Historical Introduction," pp. l–lii. The menu is printed in French, as the press pointed out in Hanson, comp., *Grand Opening of the Northern Pacific Railway*, 47.

7

Through Dakota and Montana

The far side of Fargo
Tuesday afternoon, September 4, 1883

PERHAPS I should have headed my letter simply "the Prairie." You see, one of the trains preceding us—I am in the third train—has had an accident. There is some damage to its tender and some gashes in the sleeper, as if someone had struck it with a piece of iron. A farmer has just come by in his wagon and we have learned from him that the damage is not too bad. So here we are sprawled out on the grassy prairie of Dakota.

Since noon we have been in the golden Northwest, the granary par excellence of the United States. The wheat fields are on all sides of us, farther than the eye can see. Actually it was not until we reached Fargo that we got on the Northern Pacific tracks. The connecting link from St. Paul to the main line at Fargo at present is provided by tracks of the St. Paul, Minneapolis, and Manitoba Railroad. The main Northern Pacific line itself runs from Duluth on Lake Superior to Wallula Junction on the Columbia River, a distance of 2100 miles. At St. Cloud we crossed the Mississippi River early in the morning. The countryside was lovely—rolling and cultivated. Later, however, it became somewhat monotonous. Then we passed out of the Mississippi watershed.

The Red River of the North, as it is called to distinguish it from the Red River in Louisiana, flows north into Lake Winnipeg. It forms the border between Minnesota and Dakota and north of Fargo it is navigable. An entire flotilla of river steamers, some as large as 250 tons, travels it. The Red River Valley is wide and rich, partly due to the river's flooding.[1] It is no wonder that at the point where the railroad crosses the river, a thriving and populous settlement has developed and is growing rapidly.

Fargo lies in Dakota; and on the opposite side of the river, in Minnesota, is the city of Moorhead. Thus a second pair of sister cities has been formed though in their rivalry they are not very sisterly— much like St. Paul and Minneapolis. Certainly Moorhead is not as large as Fargo; but it does have its own bank, several newspapers, a Grand Pacific Hotel, a park, an academy, and churches for a number of confessions and sects. As a shipping point it is just as well situated as Fargo, but Fargo is far ahead in every respect.

[1] Herr Mohr was obviously relying heavily on the guide-book furnished him by Henry Villard. This described the Valley of the Red River as a beautiful prairie, sixty to eighty miles wide, level as a garden bed, and with a rich black soil from three to seven feet deep that produced twenty to twenty-five bushels of wheat to the acre. Winser, *The Great Northwest*, 81–82.

Fargo now finds itself in a state of transition—from a settlement that provided only the bare necessities to a modern city with all the niceties.[2] The contrast between what is still unfinished and what is considered acceptable in normal civilization is more evident here than in any of the cities we have seen so far. The city is laid out in vast dimensions. Rough outlines define the main street on a scale so grand that it would be adequate for any one of our major capital cities. Along the street next to the modest little wood stores stand massive, glittering department stores, edifices that resemble palaces. Almost every third building houses a farm machinery dealer and at the railroad station there are countless numbers of these machines in their bright colors. The main street intersects with wide cross streets, still unfinished with open spaces for new buildings. But everywhere new stone buildings are springing up and right beyond these wonderful new structures lies the prairie.

Even in Fargo there was a celebration to honor

[2] Fargo was indeed in a state of transition. Founded about 1871 as an outfitting point for emigrants bound for the wheat lands of Dakota Territory, it grew so slowly that by 1880 it boasted a population of only 2,693. With the approach of the railroad it boomed so spectacularly that by 1883 some 10,000 persons lived there, and the number was doubling every year. At the time of Mohr's visit it claimed seven churches, eight newspapers, twenty-eight hotels, a street railway, gas and electric lights, a water works, three grain elevators, 250 stores, and a giant brewery. Winser, *The Great Northwest*, 94–95.

the completion of the railroad. The city had arranged an exhibit of its wheat products, at which both Grant and Evarts spoke.[3]

Fargo is certainly the most important city in the Dakota Territory; but because of its position on the border it has been forced to forego the honor of becoming the capital city. The territory of Dakota is certainly one of the largest territories in the Union, and since 1879 its population has risen sharply to an estimated 325,000. By far the greatest number of people have settled on the fertile lands along the railroad.

The railroad cuts through the territory at the 46th parallel and the land north of the railroad has a very rich alluvial soil, level on the eastern border lands, rolling in the interior, and rather hilly in the west. The land is treeless, at least as far as we have come to know it; and they tell us the entire land-

[3] The first of the four special trains arrived at 11:00 in the morning, the last at 12:30. The inevitable speeches began with one by Henry Villard, followed by General Grant, Carl Schurz, H. M. Teller, the governors of Minnesota, Wisconsin, and Iowa, Senator John A. Kasson of Iowa, William M. Evarts again, and Mayor Carter Harrison of Chicago. "Fargo," wrote the correspondent of the *New York Times*, "is all alive to-day with enthusiasm, and the blare of martial music fills the air as I write. As usual there are speeches, triumphal arches, parades, and the multifarious devices with which the average American citizen manifests the exuberance of his joy." *New York Times*, September 9, 1883, p. 9; *Bismarck Tribune*, September 7, 1883. The speechmaking consumed a full two hours before the trains began to pull away at 2:30 in the afternoon.

scape up here is that way. Only in the river valleys does one see clusters of poplars, cottonwoods, and birches. The trees define the course of the rivers so they can be spotted from great distances.

The wheat has all been cut, but the grain is still standing in shocks out in the fields. Everywhere there is an activity in the fields as we have never seen before. The threshing machines are out there in full motion. The grain is put into sacks and hauled off to the elevators to be reloaded into railroad cars for shipment.[4]

Here and there on this endless prairie are the farmsteads, for the most part modest little wooden houses, but now and then a rather elegant set of farm buildings. In places where the prairie has not yet been broken and is still in grassland, there are areas that look like a carpet made from a thousand kinds of flowers.

Dakota is natural wheatland, but only through the railroad can its potential be realized. Prices for good land are skyrocketing. Out in these western

[4] As the trains sped westward that afternoon of September 4 across the level countryside they were greeted at every station by crowds that had gathered from miles around to cheer and hope that even a brief stop would allow them to see the distinguished visitors. Every building that was passed, a reporter noticed, was "more or less trimmed" with flags and bunting. At Sanborn, a brand new "city," where the train did stop briefly, Governor Jeremiah M. Rusk of Wisconsin demonstrated his prowess by taking over the operation of one of two threshing machines that were being run for the guests. *Chicago Tribune*, September 5, 1883, p. 3.

parts of the United States there are no highways at all. The railroad alone has the capacity to move the huge agricultural production cheaply and swiftly. Thus it is the first condition for a settlement and it is for this reason that the network of railways in the United States has developed at such a surprising speed, especially in the Northwest. We are learning a basic principle—a railroad is not built to service the existing traffic, but rather to create new traffic. In looking at a map on the cover of the railroad schedule, I counted no fewer than twelve railroads running from the west bank of the Mississippi to the shores of the Missouri River and in most cases extending beyond. One concludes that this territory holds incredible treasures.

In Dakota, not far from Fargo, are the colossal farms known as the Bonanza farms. They have been bought up by New York capitalists, who operate them like factories. On such establishments farming in our meaning of the term has ceased to exist. Perhaps I will be able to give you some idea of these farms from my own observations.[5] We are supposed

[5] "Bonanza Farming" was introduced in the Red River Valley in 1875 when two wealthy directors of the Northern Pacific Railroad purchased 12,000 acres about twenty miles west of Fargo and entered into a partnership with Oliver Dalrymple, an experienced wheat farmer, to grow grain by mass-production methods. Dalrymple imported gangs of workers and carloads of machinery; his large-scale techniques proved amazingly profitable, for they produced wheat at 35 cents a bushel which sold for 90 cents, with each acre yielding about twenty bushels. Hence eastern capital

to pay a short visit to Mr. Dalrymple's farm, but whether we will ever get there I do not know.

Tuesday evening, September 4, 1883

EVENTUALLY we were rescued from our forced stop this afternoon and we are well on our way again. It soon became dark and now we see only the lighted train depots and signal lights. For lack of outside observations to record, I will use the opportunity to comment on our Pullman sleeping car, where we already have spent four nights. I must admit that the very first evening I was rather skeptical about the metamorphosis of our car into a bedroom. But now I find it fascinating. Each evening at the retiring hour the Negro porter appears and applies his talents. It is possible for them to transform the car very rapidly since all the furnishings have been so meticulously put together. Pullman sleeping cars are occupied by both men and women, so passengers are advised to take the greatest caution in dressing and undressing. Since our party is entirely male, we are not so fussy; we just disappear behind the curtain and slip into our nightshirts.

flowed into the region, as Bonanza Farms of from 3,000 to 65,000 acres spread over the valley. Dalrymple's own profits on the 17,000 acres he operated by this time ran to $216,000 a year. This story is told in Hiram M. Drache, *The Day of the Bonanza; A History of Bonanza Farming in the Red River Valley of the North* (Fargo, 1964). Herr Mohr proved correct in his forebodings; the trains were so far behind schedule that they passed the Dalrymple farm in the night and did not stop.

In the darkness we have passed the Dalrymple Farm, Jamestown, and several other towns. We are informed that we will arrive in Bismarck early in the morning.

Beyond Bismarck
Wednesday, September 5, 1883

TODAY we laid the cornerstone for the Capitol in Bismarck on the Missouri River. I have never before taken part in such a unique ceremony.

Our train arrived sometime in the wee hours of the morning while we were still asleep. When we awoke, a number of vehicles were waiting for us on the open square in front of the depot. The depot itself was decorated with flags and wheat, and across the square there was a small display of agricultural and garden produce. We got into the carriages and in a procession moved through the streets that were spanned by arches decorated with pictures of Villard and Bismarck. At every street corner there was some sort of makeshift arrangement and the people had to climb over lumber and stones to get to the center of town. At the fringe of the city there is nothing but the endless stretch of prairie, and within there is a curious mixture of wooden huts and striking brick buildings.

Like a mob we moved forward, wagons, carriages, riders on horseback, and pedestrians, all headed uphill to the site of the Capitol, some foundation walls, a heap of bricks, and on top a scaffold. It was

Courtesy of Henry H. Villard

The four sections at Bismarck

a motley sight. In one direction there was a party of
Indians, in another a parade line, including figures
of Germania and Columbia, accompanied by a host
of people. Rising up from all of this activity was a
cloud of dust that gave the sun a reddish hue.[6]

[6] For an account of the joint celebration and cornerstone
laying at the new territorial capitol building, see "Historical
Introduction," pp. lvi–lviii. Preparations for the ceremony
are described in the *Bismarck Tribune*, August 31, 1883,
and the ceremony itself in *ibid.*, September 7, 1883. Accord-

In spite of the confusion the cornerstone actually was laid. Then a document was handed to Mr. von Eisendecher, German Ambassador to Washington. This document conferred on our great Imperial Chancellor an honorary citizenship of the city of Bismarck, named for him. Von Eisendecher accepted the document with a few thoughtful words, and said he was certain that Prince Otto von Bismarck would be happy to accept honorary citizenship in this city of the Far West. He then expressed his wish that the namesake, the city of Bismarck, would come to enjoy the same widespread and good reputation as the Chancellor.

We could not avoid the customary speech-making and well-wishing. Governor Ordway of Dakota expressed the boldest expectations for the future of Bismarck. He predicted that civilization would one day shift from the east to the west in America and that America would eventually find its heart in Bismarck. Then the crowd demanded some words from Evarts and he spoke well with good humor. Next they turned to Grant and he too gave a speech. Then Villard introduced Sitting Bull, the famous chief who has long been the terror of Dakota. The crowd chanted, "Give us a speech!" whereupon he

---

ing to local legend, one overenthusiastic citizen hung three bushels of apples purchased for the occasion on an apple tree which was shown the guests. They were astounded at seeing such luscious fruit in September. "Magnificent, magnificent," General Grant supposedly remarked. "I am surprised, surprised."

Courtesy of The Huntington Library

Laying the cornerstone of the territorial capitol
Bismarck, Dakota Territory

Taken from *Frank Leslie's Illustrated Newspaper*

mumbled a few words to himself, and then with-drew. Also by popular demand, Carl Schurz spoke.[7]

After the speeches I had a closer view of Sitting Bull. His face is wide and bony with a deep copper

---

[7] The speeches are summarized in the "Historical Intro-duction," p. lvii. They were printed in full in the *Bismarck Tribune*, September 7, 1883, pp. 1–6.

color and those rigid immobile features that are so
striking in all Indians. He wore a wide yellow band
around his brow, pulled tightly under his hairline.
In the back of his head was a piñon feather. He was
completely dressed with a shirt and pants and deco-
rative beads on his shoes. Sitting Bull caused the
Americans one of their most painful defeats, for he
played a decisive role in the annihilation of General
Custer and all his men at the Little Bighorn River.
Later he fled to Canada and then surrendered. Although he is treated well now, he is ever suspicious,
only trusting the agents of the United States Government with whom he lives. He has learned to
write well enough to sketch out his name and has
made a rather profitable business with his autograph. At the ceremony he sold each autograph for
one dollar, but after he found so many takers at that
price, he raised it by fifty percent.[8]

By chance I found a German in the crowd, but

[8] Chief Sitting Bull and his Sioux followers fled to Canada
after defeating General George A. Custer's forces at the Battle of the Little Bighorn. There he remained until 1881
when the increasing destitution of his people forced him to
return; with 187 of his fellow-tribesmen he surrendered at
Fort Buford that July. They were settled on the Standing
Rock Reservation where Sitting Bull remained bitterly un-
reconcilable until killed by military police in 1890. Correspondents on this occasion noted that he was completely
uninterested in the ceremonies, viewing all whites with sus-
picion, and he emerged from his lethargy only to admire the
red flannel shirt worn by the Chief Marshal of the Bismarck
Fire Department. *Frank Leslie's Illustrated Newspaper*,
LVII (September 22, 1883), 77.

most of the people were Americans who have immigrated from other states. They are the pioneers of civilization whereas the German immigrants tend to follow later. It is quite understandable that the techniques and experiences needed for the first settlers are lacking in the German immigrant.

Evidence that the settlers in this region are doing well is of course found in the growth of the cities. The hotels, restaurants, stores, and banks which make up a given town depend exclusively on the business they have with the settlers in their immediate vicinity. I visited a stationery store in Fargo to buy a lead pencil and found there a tremendous variety of articles, even the most expensive things. The success of the farmers must be good. They have acquired their land at a relatively cheap price and have had good harvests. Too, the wages are high.

The city of Bismarck obviously owes its existence to the Northern Pacific Railroad. In the year 1872 the decision was reached to build a railroad bridge across the Missouri River. The town that grew up at the construction site was originally named in honor of one of the railroad's engineers whose name was Edwin Johnson, hence, Edwinton. Later at the suggestion of the board of directors, the name was changed to Bismarck because they wanted to pay a compliment to the German Chancellor.[9]

[9] Bismarck was truly a child of the railroad. Its site on the Missouri River was selected by Northern Pacific engineers in 1872. First named Edwinton to honor the road's chief

Closely situated to the city is the military establishment Camp Hancock, a commissary for a line of forts throughout the Northwest. All provisions and war materials for Forts Lincoln, Yates, Stevenson, Buford and Assiniboine are supplied from here. From the top of Capitol Hill we could see Fort Lincoln on the other side of the Missouri.[10] On that side also are the hunting grounds of the Sioux Indians, generally feared by the people here.

A festival issue of the *Bismarck Daily Tribune*[11]

engineer, Edwin F. Johnson, it was renamed Bismarck early in 1873 in the hope of attracting German capital. Instead the Panic of that year soon ended construction, which was not resumed until 1879. By 1883 some 5,000 persons lived in the city, which had twelve hotels, five churches, four banks, and a theater. *Appleton's General Guide*, 437–438.

[10] Fort Hancock, built on the east bank of the Missouri River at Bismarck in 1872, was at this time used as a supply depot for goods destined for forts higher up the river: Fort Abraham Lincoln built five miles from Bismarck in 1872 to guard the Northern Pacific construction crews, Fort Yates established in 1874 at the Standing Rock Indian Agency, Fort Stevenson founded on the left bank of the Missouri in 1867 to protect a principal route to the Montana gold fields, Fort Buford near the mouth of the Yellowstone built in 1866 as one of a chain stretching from Kansas to the Columbia River, and Fort Assiniboine authorized in 1878 to protect Montana settlers from the Sioux and constructed a year later in the Milk River country. F. P. Prucha, *A Guide to the Military Posts of the United States, 1789–1895* (Madison, 1964), locates and maps all of these outposts.

[11] Six thousand copies of this special issue, each containing sixteen pages, were printed on September 5, 1883; it was, the editors boasted, the largest newspaper ever printed in Bismarck and contained more news than a dozen ordinary issues. Henry Villard purchased a thousand copies to dis-

has sixteen big pages filled with descriptions of the city, pictures, and dreams for the future. A tone of fanfare runs through the paper and this found its echoes in the nervous excitement of the events and scenes we experienced today.

Our stopover was very brief and our impressions superficial. How little we really saw of Bismarck and its beautiful sights! We returned to our train and presently were on the move again, crossing the Missouri River on a bridge that is one of the most significant and costly projects on the whole route of the Northern Pacific Railway.

On the far side of the river is Mandan, now two years old, with two thousand inhabitants.[12] The streets have been staked out and space has been reserved for a city park. Here too we stopped and took a look at the post office to get an idea of the heavy volume of mail here. Next to it is a bar where a waiter prepared us a "Sherry Cobbler" with an elegance one would expect only in New York. Already Mandan has two newspapers, a bank, and an excellent hotel, the Inter-Ocean Hotel. The town

tribute to his guests and friends. *Bismarck Tribune*, September 7, 1883.

[12] Mandan, lying directly across the Missouri River from Bismarck, was reached by a "graceful and substantial" iron bridge built by the Northern Pacific at a cost of a million dollars, and opened on October 1, 1882. Mandan was only two years old, but growing rapidly. At this time it boasted two newspapers, a bank, churches, a lavish hotel called the Inter-Ocean that had cost $60,000, and a block of red brick stores. Winser, *The Great Northwest*, 111–122.

stands in the center of good wheat land and claims to have cheap coal as well as good loam soil for making bricks. In the vicinity there is also a substantial amount of cattle business. Close by in the hills are the remains of a culture that even the Indians claim is strange to them. The bits of glass, arrow tips, cooking utensils, etc., that have been found are still awaiting some expert to solve their mystery.[13]

For a time we continued our trip through the monotonous, treeless area, crossing a number of creeks and rivers, all of which apparently empty into the Missouri. There, too, were long stretches of uncultivated land and the only traces of human habitation were the wooden snow fences built to prevent the roadbed from becoming blocked with snow. Severe storms blow down from the north and blanket the land under a layer of snow. Yet the inhabitants claim that one does not feel the cold so much and that the heavy snow eventually goes away by itself.

Among the towns we passed through, one was of extra special interest; it was Richardton, a German settlement.[14] The houses were all neat and clean,

[13] According to Mandan Indian legend, this was the spot where the first of their people ascended from underground caverns to begin life on earth. The heavily-sodded lodge rings there, some of them rectangularly shaped and filled with stone weapons, beautifully decorated dark pottery, and the bones of giant-sized men and animals, indicated the remains of an earlier culture that had thrived there. *Mandan Pioneer*, April 27, 1883.

[14] Richardton, lying eighty-six miles from Mandan, was

but they stood there like toy houses taken out of a box. One looked just like the next and we were not able to glean very much information about our countrymen there. It seems that whether a settler is satisfied or unsatisfied depends more or less on what he expected when he came to America. A new home must have a great deal to offer before a man is ready to reconcile himself to such a new way of life.

The Badlands
Late afternoon, September 5, 1883

As A CHANGE in our routine we were given a good opportunity to see a little of the Badlands.[15] Even before we came to the Little Missouri River, which forms the border between Dakota and Montana, the geological change was evident through the train windows. All sorts of beautiful formations—strange outcroppings of mountains, terraces, and knolls—

founded in 1882 as a colony for German immigrants by C. B. Richards, a passenger agent for the Hamburg Steamship Line. It failed to lure the numbers expected, and remained a tiny hamlet. Winser, *The Great Northwest*, 130–131.

[15] The Badlands of the Little Missouri River Valley, lying just north of the Northern Pacific tracks, were formed centuries ago when the area lay beneath the sea. "Hell with the fires out" was the way they were described by General Alfred Sully when in the 1860s he first saw the weird formations of buttes, domes, pyramids, hills, and cones, all in brown, red, grey, and yellow sandstone or hard clay. The town of Little Missouri where the train stopped had less than one hundred inhabitants in 1883, and no longer exists, although it was near present-day Medora. Winser, *The Great Northwest*, 131–133.

jutted up from the flat prairie land. At the town that bears the same name as the river, carriages were waiting to drive those who did not care to walk into the Badlands. The name simply means that this land is difficult to cross. The French explorers traversed this area long before the advent of the railroad and discovered that this was a *pays mauvais à traverser*. The phrase eventually was translated and shortened to "Badlands."

What from the train had seemed like isolated bits of grotesque rock suddenly appeared before us in their totality. As we hiked across the land we were surrounded by eroded land with holes and canyons, interlaced by many colorful ribbons of coal. All around us were mountains in curious forms—like military bastions or like castles with terraces and cupolas. After an hour of walking we finally arrived at our destination. From high on a plain we had a view into a deep valley, Cedar Canyon. The sun was already sinking low, a bluish mist drifted out across the magic landscape, and in the twilight the mountainous shapes took on a fantastic and moody quality.

For the return trip I accepted the offer of a seat in a carriage pulled by two gray-white horses. Only then did I become really aware of the meaning of the "Badlands." Truly they are difficult to cross! Either we were straining to hold back or we were climbing mountains; we were forever slipping and sliding. But how calmly and confidently our driver

Taken from Rudolf Cronau's *Von Wunderland zu Wunderland*

The Badlands of Dakota

guided the team! He accomplished as much with his words as with the reins. Just as we approached the exit, we caught sight of a woman on horseback; she flew past us at full gallop down the mountain. How self-assured, how boldly she rode! And right behind her came a pair of cowboys. All three were on their way to watch over the gigantic herds down below. We are told that sheep raising is very big business here. It is interesting that the Badlands provide such fine pasture land when the whole area has the character of a barren desert.

Now we are all settled back in our train and happy to be here although the exercise and diversion did us good. In the immediate vicinity of the town Little Missouri, the Marquis de Morès, a son-in-law of the New York banker von Hoffmann, has bought a large plot of land. He plans to give sheep to a number of farmers for raising. He will supply the necessary buildings and equipment for a slaughter house, ship the meat east in refrigerated cars, and then share his profits with the farmers.[16]

[16] The Marquis de Morès, a wealthy French nobleman, arrived at the town of Little Missouri in April, 1883, with a new wife and ambitious plans to build an empire in that thinly settled land. Buying giant ranches for cattle and sheep, he laid out the town of Medora, named after his wife, on the eastern side of the river and there built a packing plant designed to process 150 beeves a day for shipment east. Slaughtering began in October, but competition from eastern packers soon ended the enterprise. He did continue a profitable trade with both coasts, as well as raising sheep and cattle, and introducing irrigated farming on his 12,000

We are now in Montana, a land of mining, cattle raising, and wheat growing. Montana is also the home of the great buffalo herds though these have been shrinking fast. There is one herd grazing about twenty-five or thirty miles north of the railroad, which numbers in the hundreds of thousands.[17] Now and then animals stray into the vicinity of the train and those passengers who are enthusiastic about hunting take potshots at them.

The fact that in Montana millions of buffalo are able to find fodder both winter and summer indicates that Montana is destined by nature for cattle raising also. Apparently the cattle grow so well here that Montana cattle are usually one and a half times heavier than cattle from the states to the south. Cattle raising here seems to be as simple and as easy as can be. The ranchers simply turn the cattle out free to roam on the pasture lands; there are no barns

---

acre estate. Donald Dresden, *The Marquis de Morès: Emperor of the Badlands* (Norman, 1970), tells the fascinating story of his life.

[17] By this time the giant herds of buffalo that had roamed the plains were facing extinction, victims of the high prices paid for their hides and the ease with which they could be killed with repeating rifles. In 1881, 75,000 buffalo skins were shipped through Bismarck alone; a year later the Northern Pacific carried more than 200,000 hides eastward. By 1883 so few remained that only 40,000 skins were sent to market, and by 1884 only one carload. One observer on the Little Missouri River noted that "I saw buffalo lying dead on the prairie so thick that one could hardly see the ground. A man could have walked for twenty miles on their carcasses." Wayne Gard, *The Great Buffalo Hunt* (New York, 1959).

and of course nobody bothers with milking. When the drought arrives in late summer, the grass wilts and the coarse stems become hay; but it does not lose its quality as fodder. In the winter the cattle for the most part paw their fodder out from under the snow. They roam over huge areas and every head bears a brand. In the spring and fall the herdsmen, known as cowboys, go out after the herds and sort them out. In this operation, honesty is a rigid requirement. In the fall the cattle that are destined for market are sorted and driven to stations on the railroad. At the stations are large corrals in which the cattle are cared for until they can be shipped. At present the cattle business seems to be profitable, but as more settlers begin to arrive and narrow down the unclaimed lands, this primitive style of cattle raising will have to give way to much more organized methods.[18]

[18] Cattle ranching spread over western Dakota and Montana after 1878 when the Indians were forcefully evacuated. By 1880, 428,279 longhorns were pastured in Montana and 140,815 in western Dakota, all on government land, with only imaginary "range lines" separating the herds. The cattle, which drifted from one ranch to another while grazing, were separated in spring and fall "roundups" where newborn calves were branded and the beeves singled out for marketing or returned to their owners. Mohr was right when he predicted that this free-and-easy form of ranching would soon give way to more organized methods. By the middle 1880s the range was dangerously overstocked, with grass supplies inadequate to sustain the herds should any natural disaster strike. This came in 1886–1887 when a summer drought was followed by a bitterly cold winter. The thou-

But for the present the herds and their keepers—the bold young men known as cowboys—continue to thrive. In many ways these fellows can truly say of themselves, "We lead a free life." They have a streak of romanticism in them and are as free and easy with their money as they are with a revolver. They are extremely touchy, especially in matters that arouse their jealousy. And of course they are excellent horseback riders, highly skilled with the lasso. The cowboy plays a role in the fantasy of the West somewhat like the role ascribed to the famous countryside robbers in Italy and Spain.

Friday, September 7, 1883

LATE Wednesday we reached Glendive and since then have been traveling along the Yellowstone River.[19] Yesterday morning we crossed the Bighorn River and at that point were about 3,000 feet above sea level. We still have another 3,000 feet before we reach the Mullan Pass, which is the great divide between the Atlantic and the Pacific watersheds.

Today the trip along the Yellowstone was pleasantly interrupted by a stop at Billings. Here again

sands of cattle that died convinced ranchers that the open range was outmoded, and that only fencing and winter feeding would assure profits.

[19]Glendive, founded in 1881 on the Yellowstone River in Montana, was the junction point for the Missouri and Yellowstone divisions of the Northern Pacific. The 1,200 inhabitants worked in the shops of the railroad, or supplied the ranchers in the nearby countryside. *Appleton's General Guide*, 438.

we had a reception that included a display of the local products—home-brewed beer, an immense chunk of coal from the nearby mines, and a large crowd of people from the town and neighboring farms. Fort Custer, located up on the Bighorn River, sent a detachment of soldiers to play military music and shoot off some artillery. The cannons cracked so loud that they are still ringing in my ears. Billings is still a very young town, founded in 1882 I believe, but it hopes to become the capital city of Montana.[20] Here Mr. Billings gave a speech honoring his namesake. He was one of the earlier directors of the railroad, the man whose energy and talent saved the Northern Pacific undertaking from

[20] Billings, as Mohr noted, was a young town, established in 1882 on the west bank of the Yellowstone River, but already boasting some 2,000 inhabitants, three hotels, three newspapers, a bank, a church, and a street railway capitalized at $40,000 although its total equipment consisted of two fifteen-foot yellow cars drawn by Indian ponies. The Coulson Brewery was one of the town's principal enterprises. Fort Custer, built nearby at the confluence of the Bighorn and Little Bighorn rivers in 1877, played only a minor role in the Indian wars which were largely over when it was established. Frederick Billings, after whom the town was named, was one of the organizers of the Northern Pacific Railroad, serving as its president after 1879, and playing a leading role in reviving construction. He and Villard tangled over the degree of authority each should exercise, a struggle that ended in September, 1881, when Billings turned the presidency over to his rival, although remaining a director. Villard thought highly of Billings, feeling that he more than any other man deserved credit for completing the line. Villard, *Memoirs*, II, 291–300.

complete failure before Henry Villard took it over and brought it to completion. The city pins its hopes for the future on the development of mining. During our short stop a chain of wagons passed by, each pulled by twelve or fourteen oxen and loaded with silver ore.

One is not surprised to learn that the civilization here also has its dark and seamy side. The mining industry attracts the miners, who earn high wages and lead a wild life. As a group they are composed of the castaways from human society—tramps and criminals, shipwrecked human beings, and student dropouts. We were shown through the music hall in Billings, which out here is given the distinguished title of "Opera House." In places such as these one meets a type of society that is no better than the criminal element in our large cities. The revolver is always loaded and close at hand. In Billings and Livingston, as well as in Bozeman and Helena, Vigilance Committees have been formed to dispense justice and to protect human decency. They warn those of bad repute to leave town. If somebody does not heed the warning, then the vigilantes will render him harmless at the first opportunity. For the time being such committees are the law enforcers in this territory.

8

The Rocky Mountains
and a Visit with the Indians

Somewhere in the Rocky Mountains
At sunrise, September 8, 1883

THE LOCATION is somewhat inexact because no-where is there a human settlement to be seen. There are only the wooded peaks from which the fresh pine-scented morning breezes rush at us from all sides. The train has been standing here since the first glimpse of dawn. As it is the eighth of September, I presume we are not far from the spot where the last nail is to be driven, the symbol of the completion of the Northern Pacific Railroad.

This is a good place to expand a little on the purpose of the railroad and some general impressions gleaned so far. This railroad will open up these huge stretches of fertile land to civilization and make possible the production of unimaginable quantities of grain and cattle. Thus it will contribute to the solution of one of the most pressing problems of our time, namely the betterment of a large number of human beings. In this respect the construction of the Northern Pacific will go down as one of the great events of all human history. The increase in the world's food supply has momentarily surpassed the growth of population. And this rare event can be directly attributed to the construction of this railroad.

Out here nobody talks of the present. In all of the towns that have sprung up along the railroad the people talk only of what is to come. Every inhabitant has an enviable faith in the glowing future of his own town. Jealousy among these small new towns is revealed in the most naive ways. What is even worse here in the West is the feeling of superiority over the East. Every town has something to show that the citizens claim can be found nowhere else in the United States. In Billings, in Bismarck, and in Townsend—an infant city just six weeks old—the citizens could show some moderation in their self-image relative to the whole world. They speak in such boastful words when they have the chance to show their accomplishments to strangers from the Old World! Yet, we should take this in the right spirit. The men from the East who have been giving speeches out here miss no opportunity to tease their western brothers about their own shortcomings. Mr. Evarts, the former Secretary of State under Hayes, has a special knack of making these Westerners laugh with his barbs.[1] It is precisely this

[1] William M. Evarts, Secretary of State under President Rutherford B. Hayes between 1877 and 1881, took his duty as principal orator of the party so seriously that he spoke at virtually every whistle stop. His humorous remarks and sly digs at local customs seemed to amuse rather than annoy his listeners.

vigor, this urge to become something, that gives a special charm to the American West.

From the Hudson River to the Rocky Mountains we have covered a distance of two thousand miles and yet there has been a repetitious monotony about the whole stretch. Where are the oak-covered estates of northwestern Germany, or the stately farm houses with their thatched roofs, or the villages of Thuringia nestled down in a quiet valley next to a murmuring brook that drives a miller's waterwheel? And where are the villages huddled among the vineyards hanging from the cliffs along the Rhine? From our train we have seen no traffic moving from one farm to another, or from one town to the next. Only an occasional wooden house do we see—usually in its natural color instead of a brightly painted green. And it is impossible for us to know why each one stands where it does. We can only guess that the owner must have acquired some land at that spot, but no brook, no group of trees, nothing indicates that this is a human settlement.

In New York we got the impression that some settlements there are suffering from depopulation and neglect. The western part of the state has already been taken over by the waves of population growth, but land cultivation is on the decrease. The soil cannot compete with the Far West, so they are shifting from grains to fruits and vegetables. The farther west we come, the better the farming areas look. In Ohio the fields alternate among vineyards,

corn, and wheat. In Indiana there is evidence everywhere of a thriving agriculture. The same holds true
all the way to the Mississippi River. But only a
trained eye can discover much variation.

The prairie has a somewhat different character.
The endless flatlands vanish from view at the horizon. But even the prairie terrain is not so different
from what we have in northern Germany. As soon
as the settlers arrive and erect their buildings, it
begins to look much like what is found in the East.
Now and then one gets the impression that all civilization has ended. Then the sight of a fence, a hay-
stack, or a herd of cattle gives a clue that this is not
the end of the world.

The vigorous manner in which the West is being
won over to civilization carries an unusual fascina-
tion for us. Even the most desolate town holds the
promise of a great future. At home in Germany, a
poor rundown village would be so aware of its destiny that it would be without hope. Yet out here,
any one of these small towns—so stark, so unfriendly, so poor, so lacking even in the essentials—might
someday become a new St. Paul or Minneapolis.

But now I should continue with the exciting
events of the past two days. From Billings we continued along the Yellowstone River, with the jagged
mountain formations beyond. These step-like terraces run in long, parallel stretches. Generally there
are many steps, one above the next. The land on
these plateaus, generally called "bench lands," is

said to be very fertile if it can be irrigated. In this regard we see that nature has come to the aid of man and does half his work. The river valleys, apparently ancient lake bottoms, follow the same incline as the rivers. Thus a stream can be tapped far up the valley and rerouted as much as fifty or sixty miles to irrigate the land. Just outside Billings we saw one of these extended watering systems.[2]

Then suddenly there appeared a huge herd of ponies driven by Indians, making us aware that we were now on an Indian reservation. On this reservation dwell the Crow Indians, a completely unwarlike tribe, we were informed.[3] Even in ancient times, when the Indians were the sole inhabitants of this great Northwest, the Crow Indians were distinguished as peace-loving.

[2] This irrigation canal was known as Clark's Fork Bottom Ditch, and had been built in 1879 and 1880. Running for thirty-nine miles and terminating near Billings, it was designed to irrigate 100,000 acres of the rich bottom land of the Yellowstone River Valley. Another company, the Tongue River Irrigation Company, had just completed a ditch fourteen miles long at Miles City, near Billings. Winser, *The Great Northwest*, 169–170.

[3] The Crow Indian Reservation, two hundred miles long and seventy-five wide, extending from the Yellowstone River southward to the Montana border and from Livingston on the west to a line just beyond the Bighorn Mountains on the east, had been set aside by Congress in 1868 as a home for the 3,000 members of the tribe. Its sparse population, linked with its abundant water supply, good soil, and hidden mineral wealth meant that almost immediately would-be settlers began pressuring the Indians and government to open the region to settlement.

Carl Schurz told us about the trips he made to these regions as Secretary of the Interior in order to get a better understanding of their situation. Schurz took great pains to describe the Indians from their good side. He cited many examples of their persistence, their toughness, their endurance, and their genuine fidelity.

We had already seen Indians at the celebrations in St. Paul and in Bismarck, but this was the first time that we had seen them in the wild of their own environment. From the distance, these fantastic figures on their ponies lent the scene a singular charm. The main wealth of these Indians is in their ponies. Some chiefs are said to have as many as 10,000 head. Looking at the Indians, we were reminded once again just how really far we are from home.

Eventually we crossed the Yellowstone River but remained in its valley. We could see that we were approaching the Rocky Mountains, but the misty air prevented us from getting a long-range view of the higher mountain regions. Finally we could perceive some of the forests that clothe the slopes of the mountains with green, albeit a rather sparse green. The area lost its oddly grotesque character but signs of cultivation were few and far between. The herds of ponies belonging to the Indians gave evidence that the territory was not completely uninhabited.

Villard had arranged for us to meet with the Crow Indians and witness a war dance. In arranging for this drama, he was not thinking just of our idle curiosity. If we are to get the proper perspective of this country and its people, then we must also see the Indians. They were formerly the rulers of this country and they have played a significant role in the cultural development of the Northwest, right up to the present time. Until recently Dakota and Montana, even Minnesota, lived under a reign of terror from the Indians. The struggles between the first settlers and the Indians comprise the earliest known history of this region. It is not so long ago that frightened settlers flocked by the thousands to St. Paul and Minneapolis to escape the attacks of the Indians.

The Crow Indians have received a large tract of land on which they can live. In spite of the fact that they formerly ruled this region, they are now considered foreigners. They are not citizens of the United States and the whites deal with them as with a foreign people. The land which has been allotted to them belongs to the whole tribe. They receive food, clothing, blankets, guns, powder, and lead from the Government of the United States, whose wards they are. The reservations of the different tribes are far removed from one another in order to avoid continuing the bloody feuds between them. The present intentions of the United States Government are certainly well-meaning; the government is trying to make up for what the white men have done to the Indians in the past.

The reservation of the Crow Indians stretches along the right shore of the Yellowstone River from Forsyth westward to the Rocky Mountains, a distance of two hundred miles. To the south it extends to Wyoming, having an average width of seventy-five miles. The territory is approximately as large as the state of Massachusetts and takes in the most fertile valleys. Some three thousand Indians live on this great tract of land. In the summer they ride around on their reservation, hunt, and tend their huge pony herds; but during the winter they sit around at the government Indian agency and ask to be fed. Even Carl Schurz agrees that such a situation as this cannot continue. Schurz proved himself a warm and friendly administrator for the Indians and has always taken up the cause of this unfortunate people with great partiality and true human sensitivity.[4] When he was Secretary of the Interior, he did a great deal for them; but he agrees that when an industrious people arrives on the scene, it is impossible that huge tracts of fertile land should be abandoned as a hunting ground for a few thousand Indians.

[4] As Secretary of the Interior under President Rutherford B. Hayes, Carl Schurz became famous (and very unpopular) because of his enlightened attitude toward the Indians and his attempt to staff the Indian service with competent humanitarians rather than the political hacks usually employed there. His views are explained in Claude M. Fuess, *Carl Schurz, Reformer* (New York, 1932), and his own *Reminiscences of Carl Schurz* (3 v., New York, 1907–1908).

To be sure, the Crow Indians have already given up a strip of their territory. In return for some money they had to abandon the Clark's Fork area, which includes the gold and silver mines.[5] In like manner more will be taken from them if they do not settle down to a hard-working way of life. Already there are those who talk of dividing up the tribal property, which includes the whole reservation, and allotting to every family as much land as is necessary to sustain life. The question as to whether the Indian can be turned into a settler and whether he can be educated as a useful citizen is still widely argued. Schurz does not despair for them. He points to the wide-ranging success of the Catholic Indian missions and to the education of the Indian children in schools which the government has established for them. It is said there are Indian villages that have had outstanding success in cultivating their fields and have awakened the envy of their neighbors. On the other hand, some maintain that

[5] Gold discoveries in the Clark's Fork region, followed by the usual mining rush there, forced the United States to bring pressure on the Crows to return that portion of their reservation. In April, 1882, they were forced to re-cede an L-shaped tract lying between the Yellowstone and Clark's Fork, and extending from Livingston to the territorial border. This cession is mapped in Charles C. Royce, *Indian Land Cessions in the United States,* Bureau of American Ethnology, *Eighteenth Annual Report* (Washington, 1899), while the emerging belief that the Indian "problem" could be solved only by allotting each individual land is discussed in Henry E. Fritz, *The Movement for Indian Assimilation, 1860–1890* (Philadelphia, 1895).

even if an Indian works for a while, he will never do anything beyond what is necessary to stay alive. One thing is certain, namely that with very few exceptions, the Indian remains foreign and inimical to civilization.

Opinion regarding the Negroes is quite different. Many claim that if by some coincidence Negroes were to remain alone in this country, they would be able to preserve the culture of the white man and continue developing it on their own. The Negro has definitely become a useful member of society, but the Indian has not, at least not in the northwestern parts of the United States. In the South, especially in Mexico, the Indians of course have a recognized place in society. They are born horsemen, good messengers, and can do other things.

Schurz mentioned that a certain chief was talking with him about the position of the Indian, about Indian development, and about prospects for the Indians' future. It became clear that the old chief viewed the situation in a statesmanlike manner. He perceived that some adjustments would have to be made and he comprehended the opposing interests of the white man and of his fellow tribesmen. But as soon as he was left on his own, his judgment reverted to the old way. Nor had he the slightest grasp of national affairs and concerns.

As we approached the Greycliff station, we anxiously anticipated our meeting with the Indians. To the left of the train we could see the pony herds growing thicker and thicker. Then an entire camp of disorganized tents came into view. Everything was in a state of excitement and motion—horseback riders were milling about, women stood in front of the tents, and children were screaming and running up and down beside the train! The train slowed down and then stopped at a lonely station building. As far as I could tell, it was the only structure in the whole town called Greycliff.[6] We all ran outside. The scene before us was novel and lively in every respect. Everywhere there was activity: to one side the Indian camp; on the mountain slopes the ponies; and before us the Indians—men, women, and children—some on horseback with two or three to a horse and some on foot. In between were the snarling and barking dogs. Amidst all this an area had been cordoned off by posts and canvas, and as a result it looked something like a circus or a fair. Leaning against the canvas wall were many strange-looking figures—Indian dancers. The few white men who mingled with the Indians were the govern-

[6] Greycliff, so named for the grey-tinted cliffs three miles away, lying eighty-one miles west of Billings, was only a station-stop with no settlers at this time. By this time the party's schedule had been badly disrupted. The first and second sections arrived in the late morning and early afternoon, but the third reached Greycliff after dark, while the fourth, which suffered engine trouble, passed through late at night without stopping. Fortunately the Indians were accommodating enough to repeat their dances for each new group, with the last lighted by campfires. *New York Times*, September 8, 1883, p. 2.

ment agents and the reservation doctor. As we approached, a monotonous, but still exciting, music blared forth. Women and children squatted on the sidelines to watch the drama. With them were the dogs, who were forever biting and chewing at one another. Outside the canvas wall, but looking over it, the mounted Indians stood in close formation. In all of their ornaments we noticed a certain similarity. Hides, teeth, feathers, and grasses dyed with red and ochre lead were the primary objects in the costumes. In addition, they had items brought in by civilization—colored cloth, beads, and brass rings. With the exception of tomahawks, there were no weapons in evidence. We were told the possibility always exists that out of this play something serious could develop. These Crows of course are very peaceful and can in no way be compared to the Sioux. But once worked up for war, perhaps they could forget themselves, which would not have been too pleasant for the members of our Villard party. Several scalps were tied to the belts of the numerous dancing warriors. It appeared that these Crows either are or were quite skilled in this unsettling practice. But Villard assured us that the chiefs had taken an oath to suppress all warlike tendencies in their tribesmen.

These Indians are truly a fantastic race, gifted with a lively sense for color and certainly not without other fine artistic abilities. Their ornamentation gave evidence of that. The guiding idea seemed to be to create a frightening appearance. Each had followed his own inclination, for no two were alike. Some were completely dressed, with a heavy jacket and pants made of leather or cloth woven out here in the West. Others came close to being naked, the only clothing being a belt at the waist from which hung two pieces of loin cloth or an apron-like hide. But for all that, the body was so completely painted—black, olive, and brown—that one could almost forget the nakedness. Some of their faces and arms were painted with red and yellow drawn lines and one even had a marking "a la Grecque."

The head decorations were just as complicated. Some wore a kind of tassel made of dyed grass, which seemed to hold the hair together. Others wore feathers and bird wings. One outstanding headdress was formed by the skin of a large predatory bird. It was wound around the head in such a way that the beak covered the nape of the man's neck. His upper body was naked and he wore something like a collar studded with elk's teeth around his shoulders. Exceptionally effective were the wings and tail feathers that formed a train extending down from his neck.

The decorations on their shoes—called moccasins—had a notable effect on the overall appearance. The moccasins were covered with beads and the choice of colors gave evidence of the Indians' artistic sense. The basic color was white, but some also used blues, reds, and yellows. Their jackets also were adorned with needle work. The older ones used pieces of horn and colorful porcupine quills instead of beads. All wore bells on their ankles and knees and bright brass rings on their arms.

Had we expected the dances to be performances of real fights between individuals or pantomimes of group fights, we would have been disappointed. The dance was only a ceremony, a symbolic performance with a pointed reference to war. At least the progress of the dance appeared this way to me and I had no chance to inquire more into its nature.[7] Inside the ring six men sat around a tub

[7] The correspondent of the *New York Times* had this to say of the dance: "Around an Indian drum, about two feet in diameter, and shaped like the kettledrum of an orchestra, there squatted seven or eight Indians, each beating the drum head with one long stick. Nearby sat the impressario of the company, an aged and gaily bedizened old fellow, who gave the signal for the opening overture by chanting, in a mournful falsetto, what was said to be a narrative of the mighty deeds of the Crows. As if fired by these patriotic recollections, the singer raised his voice to a shrill cry, and then the drummers began their music, first with a low rumble of the drum-head, then growing more excited, rapidly rising to a tremendous crescendo, the roll of the drum being a continuous throbbing. As the music quickened and its volume increased, the sitting Indians around the fire-light leaped to their feet, and flourishing weapons, wands, or whatever they happened to have in their hands, began to dance. They kept accurate time with the music, the step being two motions with each foot, first with one and then with the other. And all the time the dancers and the drummers gave utterance to a monotonous ululation of four notes, rising and falling in a regular scale, with an occasional yell or high key interjected, as it were, by accident. Round and round the fire they went,

over which a skin had been tightly stretched and they hammered on it with clubs—first one man, then the second, then the third, and so on—in a rhythm that grew faster and faster and ever more intense. To this they added a nasal, lamenting song. Finally we seemed to hear a bagpipe player. As the music became louder and stormier, we ourselves felt passionately aroused.

Then all at once all of the fantastic figures jumped into the air. At first they were in a semi-circle, about one hundred men strong. Then they broke into rows of six and eight, moving with a rhythmic beat forward and sideways until they formed a long line with the other groups. Then they divided off again. How can I describe the wild sight—hopping, stamping, backward sliding, bowed upper body, eyes downcast to the earth, bells ringing on their ankles and knees? From time to time they would let out a loud scream. As their movements became more violent, their eyes glowed with rage and the screaming became still wilder. Then suddenly the music stopped as did the dancing.

The dancers all crouched down and it seemed to us that the excitement of the dance had exhausted them. They gratefully accepted our offers of cigars and tobacco. After the dance the warriors as well as the onlooking Indians and their squaws engaged in

_____

yelling, stamping, shaking their weapons, and burdening the night air with a mournful cadence." *New York Times*, September 17, 1883, p. 5.

some lively trading. The Indians surely knew how to do business. They demanded the most ridiculous prices and would not come down, at least not on the first offer. They seemed to have everything for sale. They sold the shoes right off their feet and the rings off their arms.

We noticed the well-nourished bodies, the bony faces, and the hooked noses of the men. In their faces was an expression either of greed and terror or of cold indifference. The women looked little less elegant. In their costumes and facial features they looked so much like the men that an inexperienced eye could hardly single them out. Thus it was difficult to tell whether we were dealing with a young man or a young woman. Without exception the married women were completely covered. Even the children did not leave a very cheerful impression. Only one of the girls, five or six years old and full of childish confidence, tried to tease and joke with the strange white men. But what an expression of fright she showed when I tried to tag her. Apparently the white man is an object of fear for these creatures.

After the intermission the music began again. The warriors jumped up again and the same pantomime was repeated. At least I could not discover any difference from the earlier performance. The more I looked at these dancers, the more interesting their costumes appeared to me. In their whole decoration there was a definite sense of design and meaning. This was not just a barbarian paint-smearing and donning of junk. One could observe that every piece had its planned effect and even in the wild colors there was a certain aesthetic harmony.

Beyond the dance area the entire plateau was alive with our coppertoned friends. In long processions, the herds of ponies trotted toward the tent camp. Driven with whips and lassos, they made a powerful impression. The dance was the point of attraction and there the mounted troops of Indians came to a halt.

Of course we also visited inside one of the tents at the camp, where we found a fireplace with camping equipment. It smelled considerably. Thus, for obvious reasons we got out of there in a hurry.

Gradually it began to grow dark. The music started up again and they performed a new dance. A kettle with dog meat was placed in the middle of the circle and five or six men danced around it. As I understand it, the dance was supposed to make the dog meat tasty for whoever wished to eat it. They jumped around the kettle, taking all kinds of positions and making faces. This kind of hocus pocus apparently is typical, but it did make a rather miserable impression.

An ailing, elderly Indian of considerable respect cordially greeted Carl Schurz, whom he had known earlier from negotiations in Washington.

Eventually the music and the dance ceased. Probably the participants had to save some of their strength for the other trains that were just arriving.

We learned that one train—the fourth—suffered some kind of engine breakdown and was far behind. Since there was no way to lift the locomotive off the tracks, they telegraphed ahead to the next station for ties and tracks, as well as workers. Tracks and ties were quickly provided by tearing up a side track at the depot and transporting the pieces out to where the train stood. They simply laid down an extra track leading around the disabled engine and the trains behind were able to pass around it and re-enter the trackway in front. All traffic will have to be detoured around this engine until it can be removed from the pathway. This is a good example of the Americans' ability to help themselves out of difficulty.

A few blasts on the whistles of the locomotive, a cry "all on board", and everyone rushed to board our train—no one wished to be left behind.

Not much consideration is given to the passengers. No one knows who actually controls the train out here, so everybody has to look out for himself. There is not the slightest evidence of a train watchman or of his little house. Somebody checks the entire stretch of track once each day, several times a day in danger areas, but other than that it is the duty of those who live along the tracks and who cross them to watch out for themselves. There is no such thing as a fenced right-of-way or closed gates at the railroad crossing nor is there any warning sign. In larger towns there is a traffic controller, but here in the West one can travel for many hundreds of miles without seeing one of those officials who are so commonplace in Germany. By now we have become so accustomed to this informal traffic pattern that we hardly think about it. Moreover, for our special trains they have made many extra preparations. There is only one track and so the normal traffic, passengers and freight, is being sidetracked at stations until we have passed. In some cases we cause them a half-day delay. This kind of inconvenience is possible only because of the great patience of the Americans. I have often marveled at how much self-control these supposedly inconsiderate people have. Often we arrive five or six hours late at a station where we are supposed to have a ceremonial welcome and yet I have never observed any sign of impatience.

Late Thursday evening we arrived in Livingston with floodlights, fireworks, and music. I was already in bed, but some of our more adventurous companions accepted an offer from the local citizens to tour the opera house and a few of the saloons.[8] Livingston is still an extremely young settlement, having

[8] Livingston's plans for a gala welcome were upset by the lateness of the hour. Despite this, most of the town's citizenry appeared at the station where a giant arch decorated with buffalo and elk heads awaited the guests. The *Livingston Tribune*, which was printed in a small shanty on old-fashioned hand presses, had prepared a special edition of 2,000 copies to be distributed to the Villard Party, a task that required a full eight days of hard labor. *New York Times*, September 17, 1883, p. 5.

sprung up entirely since the first of April.[9] Already it has streets and a considerable number of wooden buildings. There are even a number of brick houses completed. Yet until the first of June there was not a single brick out here! Naturally there already is a bank and shortly it will have a new brick building. In this short period of six months they have put up stores of all kinds, hotels, inns, baths, and barber-shops, as well as all the other services needed to make a city, including newspapers. The avenue which runs past the railroad station makes a stately impression. Of course on some of the other streets there are still big spaces for buildings. They have not yet given much thought to paving the streets, but along the houses are the well-known wooden sidewalks.

Livingston is a child of the Northern Pacific Rail-road. There the company has its workshops, its lo-comotive sheds, and car barns. The city can look forward to a good future for other reasons too. There is coal and other mining in the area; it is also the center of a large cattle raising district. More-

[9] Livingston, nestled at the foot of the Belt Range at a point where the Yellowstone River turns abruptly eastward, was founded on July 14, 1882, when surveyors for the Great Northern camped on the site. First known as Clark City, it was renamed when the tracks reached there in honor of Crawford Livingston, a director of the company. By this time, a year later, 1,500 persons lived there; Livingston also claimed five hotels, two banks, three newspapers, seventy-five stores, two churches, and a school. *Appleton's General Guide*, 439.

over, Livingston is the point of departure for tourists visiting Yellowstone Park. They have already laid a track to the famous national park with its geysers, its waterfalls, and its gorges.[10] From the train station we could see the gap in the mountain range, through which the Yellowstone River exits from the park. The panoramic view from the station was wonderful—in the south the long arch of the Yellowstone Mountains—in the north the Belt Range Mountains; and Livingston itself, enclosed on a plain in the middle of this fabulous mountain scenery.

At Livingston we left the Yellowstone River, crossing its valley for the last time. Now we were for the first time truly deep in the Rocky Mountains. Since the smoke from forest fires made the thin air cloudy and ruled out any view very far into the distance, we had to be reminded that we were in fact in these mountains.

Our next goal was Bozeman, a mining and agricultural city founded somewhat earlier. But first we had to pass over the Continental Divide. A tunnel is being constructed 5,572 feet up from sea level. Although the passageway has been bored—a length of

[10] The Yellowstone Park Branch of the Northern Pacific Railroad ran fifty-one miles from Livingston to the little hamlet of Cinnabar, six miles from the northern entrance to Yellowstone National Park. From there, carriages or wagons transported guests into the park itself. Herr Mohr, and other members of the Villard Party, were to visit the park on their return journey.

3,500 feet—the tunnel is not yet complete. In order not to hold up traffic, they have laid a track across the pass. The temporary track will remain for emergency use even after the tunnel is completed. The ascent to the pass was too steep for our heavy train of ten large cars. So with great caution they unhooked and pulled two cars at a time up over the dangerous roadbed. It was a long and tedious task, but one that we observed with great pleasure and excitement. Actually our trip profited from the uncompleted tunnel.[11] By climbing over the peak, we had the opportunity to see the skilled mountaineer parties working everywhere. We breathed a sigh of relief after crossing the wooden viaduct that took us up across a gorge, but this incident added to the

[11] By this time the four trains were running together again; the first left Livingston at eight that morning of September 7 and the other three followed at half-hour intervals. Just ahead lay an exciting part of the journey as the tracks climbed steeply on a gradient of 119 feet to the mile to the crest of the Belt Mountains twelve miles away. There, at an elevation of 5,572 feet, a tunnel was being pushed 3,500 feet through the mountain, but delays due to cave-ins and the necessity of heavy timbering slowed construction. In the interim, tracks were laid over the summit of Bozeman Pass, climbing for two and a half miles at a gradient of 220 feet to the mile, more than double that permitted by federal regulations. Over these, two cars at a time were pulled by the locomotives. On the western side the tracks descended steeply through the wild defile of Rock Canyon, then emerged in the broad valley of the Gallatin River. There a switchback ascending a hill had been laid to stop runaway trains. *New York Times*, September 8, 1883, p. 2, September 17, p. 5; Winser, *The Great Northwest*, 180–182.

adventure. We reached nearly 6,000 feet before beginning our descent.

Then the separated sections of the train were again coupled together and we rolled on down the canyon arriving in the Gallatin, a broad and fertile valley. We passed near Fort Ellis and then stopped in Bozeman. This city of several thousand inhabitants, is nearly twenty years old. It owes its name to the founder who brought a group of immigrants here and decided that this was a good spot to build up a settlement.[12] We had not seen such a developed city since we left St. Paul days ago. It appears, though, that it has come to a comfortable standstill. Only recently with the arrival of the railroad has new life been injected into this city. At the train station there was an unpretentious display of products that have been grown on the plains around Bozeman, mostly with the help of artificial irrigation. We had never seen such fine produce. But perhaps more significant for the town's future is the ore, displayed in large chunks: iron, rich gold ore, silver-laden lead, and plenty of coal.

[12] Bozeman was settled in 1864 by John M. Bozeman who had guided a party of immigrants over the trail westward he had blazed through the Gallatin Valley. By the end of its first year it contained six cabins and a two-story hotel, but grew so rapidly that by 1883 it supported two flourishing mills, three banks, two hotels, and a number of small industries, as well as a population of 3,000 persons. Fort Ellis, an army post on the left bank of the East Gallatin River, was established in 1867 to protect the town from Indians. Winser, *The Great Northwest*, 183–184.

We got out of the train and were driven through the city. A doctor picked up myself and two other travelers and he took care to tell us everything that reflected well on his adopted city. Since Bozeman is much more developed than the other cities along the train route, the inhabitants have had time to pay attention to the decoration in their town. We saw nice gardens and clean streets. We stopped at one of the beer saloons and met the German proprietor. Even here in the Rocky Mountains there is no shortage of German names.

Then we were on the move again. For several hours we traveled on the flat bottom of the Gallatin Valley. Everywhere there were signs of cultivation—quite surprising since the valley lies 4,000 feet above sea level. As we were driving along, we met a stagecoach. In the afternoon we arrived at an interesting spot where three rivers—the Gallatin, the Madison, and the Jefferson—flow together to form the Missouri River. For a considerable distance downstream the Missouri is little more than a mountain stream encased by rock walls. Frequently it plunges in splendid falls before finally reaching Fort Benton, where it at last becomes navigable. Ships can then sail all the way to the Mississippi River, a distance of nearly 3,000 miles.

Gallatin City, where the Missouri begins, is just a village.[13] We followed the infant river to Town-

[13] Gallatin City, thirty miles west of Bozeman at the Three Forks of the Missouri River, was at this time a hamlet

send, then crossed the river and almost immediately arrived at the station of Helena. The city itself was still some distance away, lying at the foot of the mountains, partly hidden from view by a depression. For a time it was not certain whether we would spend the night there or move on.

In the meantime on the platform we met several Germans who told us about Helena and expressed an ambivalent feeling about the new town. They described the winter and the dust as practically unbearable. Apparently Helena has plenty of Germans, so many that they have formed a German singing society. After some hesitation we finally decided to accept the rides they so graciously offered to us in order to see something of the city. Time was short, so we flew at a gallop across the open plain to the city itself. It was a desert-like, barren terrain, but that is where the gold lies buried!

Helena, formerly known by the less poetic name of Crab Town, lies on both sides of Last Chance Gulch, from which they have already taken out nuggets and dust valued at ten million dollars. It has libraries, high schools, a host of churches of every denomination, a theater, and several newspapers. Our guide and driver was publisher of one and he allowed no criticism of his city.

---

with a few stores and a flour mill serving the farms of the Gallatin Valley. The village was laid out in 1864 under the assumption that it was at the head of navigation on the Missouri. Winser, *The Great Northwest*, 185.

There was a bustling atmosphere and the city seems to be in the midst of a tremendous boom, lying in the center of a rich mining district.[14] We were taken to the bank and shown some gold nuggets that had been found on the very spot where the bank was constructed. The city is lighted by electricity and also has telephone service. It claims to have 10,000 inhabitants, but in reality there probably are not that many.

As is true for all these mining towns, Helena also has a rough element in its population. In addition to the normal law enforcement agency, there is a voluntary security force that is called Vigilance Committee.[15] This committee holds summary court

[14] Helena, the capital of Montana Territory, was founded in 1864 in Last Chance Gulch by an unsuccessful miner who decided to test one last site before returning to Georgia. When he "struck it rich" other miners flocked in, eventually taking $16,000,000 in gold from the area. Unlike many gold-rush towns, Helena continued its rapid growth, serving as the center for trade lines between Fort Benton and other mining areas. By 1883, when its population touched 7,000, a group of gold plutocrats was emerging, with ornate mansions on the west side, carriages driven by swallow-tailed coachmen, and boxes at Mong's Opera House. It also boasted schools, a library, six churches, four national banks, electric lights, a water works, an admirable fire department, and a telephone system that connected it with nearby mines. Germans there had formed not one but two societies, one a Turnverein, the other a singing society. *Appleton's General Guide*, 444–445; Winser, *The Great Northwest*, 189–190.

[15] Herr Mohr had apparently been listening to some western tall tales. That a Vigilance Committee operated in Helena in 1883 seems highly unlikely, for nearly all that had functioned in the territory disbanded when a territorial gov-

over any good-for-nothing characters, asks them to leave town and, if this does not work, then takes steps to bring them to justice.

After the hasty drive through the city we were again delivered back to the train and on our way to the Great Divide between the Atlantic and the Pacific oceans—and to the Mullan tunnel. Unfortunately again the air was so full of smoke that we had only a very vague idea of the surrounding area.

Like the Bozeman tunnel, the Mullan tunnel is still under construction. Similarly they have laid a provisional track up across the pass. It was very steep and the construction seemed indeed to be of a temporary nature. Unfortunately it was already dusk as we moved along through the Prickly Pear Valley. The scenery that we would have seen in crossing the pass was lost.

Again, the crossing required a great effort. The train was divided into two-car units for the steep climb to the summit. It was too dark to see, but we guessed that we were being pulled along terrifying cliffs. From time to time we caught sight of a light far down below us and by the sounds of creaking

---

ernment was established in 1864. The Helena committee did execute one accused murderer, James Daniels, in March, 1866, after he had been released by the courts by what was believed to be judicial chicanery. He was the thirteenth victim of the Helena Vigilantes, and the thirty-third to be executed in Montana. There is no evidence of another lynching in the territory after 1866. Hoffman Birney, *Vigilantes* (Philadelphia, 1929), 344–346.

wood we could tell we were creeping across deep chasms. The maneuver caused great excitement among us. We stood out on the platform and peered into the dark night, hoping to perceive something of the ground we had just covered. Occasionally the dim moonlight broke through; and, as if to add to the spectacle, lightning from a brewing thunderstorm illuminated the heavens. We all realized that even the slightest accident would be fatal. The conductor and the brakemen worked with the most intense caution.[16]

Finally we arrived at the Divide, 5,773 feet above sea level, according to a placard at the spot. For us this was quite a height, but the Northern Pacific people pointed out that they were able to make the crossing at a point several thousand feet lower than the builders of the Central Pacific Railroad farther south. We stopped at a station called Terra Firma,

[16] The first two sections of the Villard trains crossed Mullan Pass in the early evening of September 7, the other two during the night. The pass, lying nineteen miles west of Helena and crossing the main range of the Rockies, was named for John Mullan who in 1867 laid out a wagon road from Fort Benton on the Missouri to Fort Walla Walla in Washington Territory. The tunnel under the pass, still under construction after being delayed by a devastating flood earlier that year, had been begun in December, 1881. It eventually bored 3,850 feet through the mountains at an elevation of 5,547 feet. A steep-grade track had been laid over the pass to care for light traffic until the tunnel was completed, and it was this that the Villard trains took. *Chicago Tribune*, September 8, 1883, p. 7; Winser, *The Great Northwest*, 189–191.

so named as a kind of reassurance to those descending from the summit. Here we waited for the other cars to arrive. As the hours passed we grew tired and went to bed.

I was already asleep when suddenly I realized I was in motion, being swayed from one side to the other. I could tell by the sounds that my traveling companions were still getting undressed, but were falling and stumbling over each other. One asked another whether he was hurt; fortunately he was not. What had happened?

It turned out that we had just been telescoped— that is to say, the rear part of our train had run into the forward part and the train had been shoved together. As the train left the Terra Firma station and rolled downhill, the porter on the platform of the second car noticed that the next car suddenly stayed behind and then disappeared in the darkness. He pulled the alarm cord to give the locomotive engineer the signal to stop. The locomotive and its two cars came to a stop. Then suddenly, the larger disjointed section of the train—our dining car in the lead—came rolling down behind us and plowed right into the rear car of the standing train. It ripped off the roof, tore away a portion of the side wall, and crunched into the car's body until the body frame, on which the fore part of the car rests, forced it to halt.

Fortunately we all escaped with no more than a good scare. Even the Englishmen, who were in the second car, did not suffer the slightest injury. They were sitting forward in the center of their car. For Henry Villard, who with his wife and four children occupied the last car of the train, the moments were most terrifying until he was assured that nobody was injured. The ruins of the damaged cars lay alongside the train; but the Englishmen, with characteristic good humor, called to Villard that he should not worry, nobody was hurt. Thus ended the day before the Last Spike ceremony.

9

The Last Spike

Deer Lodge River
Saturday, September 8, 1883

AT long last, we arrived this morning at the spot of the great event—the event for which we had been transported thousands of miles across land and sea. The place is in Deer Lodge County, Montana, straight north of Deer Lodge City.[1]

A festive feeling came over us as we disembarked from the train and set foot on the ceremonial grounds. We were greeted with the thunder of cannon, music, and the cheers of a large crowd of people. Before us lay a large wooden amphitheater, the open end facing south, and a wooden platform, both constructed for the occasion. The many tiers

[1] Villard chose the spot for the "last spike" ceremony carefully with an eye to its beauty and availability; the valley of the Deer Lodge River at its junction with Independence Creek was gay with autumn foliage and rimmed with mountains. Not far to the south lay Deer Lodge City with its 1,200 inhabitants, most of whom were on hand when the special trains arrived. Reporters estimated the crowd at between 1,500 and 3,000, with the exuberant correspondent of the *Bismarck Tribune* guessing 5,000. "A motley gathering," the *New York Times'* reporter judged it, made up of miners, farmers, railroad laborers, ranchers, and newspaper men. *Bismarck Tribune*, September 14, 1883; *New York Times*, September 23, 1883, p. 6.

of seats, holding perhaps one thousand people, were decorated in green and richly ornamented with American, English, and German flags.

We were not the first to arrive at the spot. Those coming from the West had arrived earlier and were on hand to greet us. Also on hand for the event was the native population—if such an expression can be used in an area so recently opened up for settlement. There were farmers, miners, ranchers, and cowboys with their wives and children, from the neighboring country and more distant regions.[2]

A temporary track about one thousand yards long had been laid around the point at which the joining was to be consummated. Already through trains were running, but on the permanent roadbed the last quarter mile of track was to be laid before our very eyes.[3] One of the section gangs was coming from the West, the other from the East and the spot

[2] For a description of the ceremonies and the driving of the last spike see Historical Introduction, pp. lxi–lxv.

[3] As noted in the "Historical Introduction," the real "last spike" that completed the Northern Pacific Railroad had been driven two weeks before, at 3:00 in the afternoon of August 23, in Independence Gulch, not far from the site of the official ceremony. The crews had laid the last nine and one-half miles of track that day, working from east and west. A handful of the curious were on hand to cheer, and to listen to a brief speech by a company agent praising the workers and paying tribute to the contractors for finishing on time. When the "last spike" was driven by the foremen of the two construction crews, champagne provided by the company was opened, amidst more hilarity. *New York Times*, September 1, 1883, p. 2; *New York Herald*, August 24, 1883, p. 6.

Courtesy of Henry H. Villard

Crow Indians at last spike site

where they were to meet was marked by a placard with large letters:

> Lake Superior   1,198 miles
> Puget Sound   847 miles

Looking southward from the platform, we faced a wide open valley. The mountains were rather bare and not very appealing, but here and there we saw a cottonwood tree, similar to our poplar. Behind us flowed the Deer Lodge River through a wild and wooded valley. The air was heavy and foggy. A wide view into the distance was impossible and made the region seem somewhat oppressive for a celebration. Occasionally a shaft of sunlight penetrated the fog, but the air did not clear.

We were obliged to wait until the later trains arrived, each of which had to negotiate the difficult mountain stretch across the Mullan Pass. We found out last night how difficult the passage can be; and as we thought about our accident, we wished all the more to have our traveling companions safely with us. It took a long time for the second train to arrive and we simply had to practice patience. From the Americans one can learn much about patience. It is remarkable how these Americans, who strive so restlessly to move forward, can be so resigned to what is unavoidable. They certainly have more endurance than we have.

As we waited, we had some time to look around and become acquainted with our colleagues who had arrived by train from the West, also this morning. They were to remain only for the two-hour ceremonies, then turn around and head straight back. I met the mayor of Seattle, a man by the name of Mr. Struve, who was born in Oldenburg.[4] Al-

[4] Henry G. Struve, a native of Oldenburg, Germany, migrated to the United States when he was sixteen years old, read law, lived in California and Oregon, and finally in 1879 settled in Seattle. By this time he was a power in Republican circles, and in 1882 was elected mayor of the city. Struve

though I was well acquainted with the area of his birth, I was a complete stranger to the city he governs. He explained that it lies beyond Portland in the territory of Washington on Puget Sound.

Another man in the group was Mr. Oterendorp, a former captain for the North German Lloyd. More recently he had been a director of a Pacific Coast Steamship Company, and lived in Portland where he was employed as a harbor captain for the Oregon Railway and Navigation Company. I also became acquainted with a few governors from territories which we had passed through, with German Consul Rosenthal from San Francisco, and also with Dr. Lindau, a much-traveled Berliner.[5]

To provide the welcoming cannon salute, the United States Artillery had set up a half battery in front of the Last Spike pavilion.[6] I noticed a husky officer talking with members of our German party.

---

had been attorney for the Northern Pacific Railroad in Washington until 1883, personally conducting all litigation centered there. Clarence B. Bagley, *History of Seattle* (Chicago, 1916), II, pp. 750-753.

[5] Paul Lindau, a prominent German journalist and playwright, was the principal editor of the literary journal, *Nord und Süd*. Adolf Rosenthal was the German Consul-General in San Francisco at this time.

[6] The United States Fifth Army Infantry Band, together with a number of troops and a battery of cannon, had been sent from Fort Keogh for the occasion. The Fort, at the mouth of the Tongue River where Miles City stands today, was one of several established to guard the region after the Battle of Little Bighorn. It was named Fort Keogh in November, 1877. *New York Times*, September 10, 1883, p. 1.

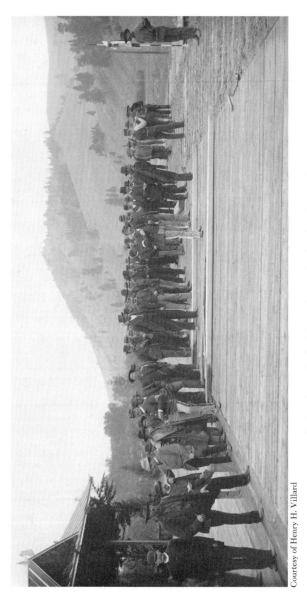

Before the arrival of the trains at the site of the last spike

They called me over and introduced me to this soldier from Bremen. Unfortunately my countryman no longer knew much about his former home. In fact he seemed completely indifferent to it, his entire interest being in his profession.

A number of Indians were invited to the celebration also. We understood that this spot is located on a reservation. Their chief was scheduled to take part in the ceremony by striking the last spike with the hammer, by which act he would give his approval to the presence of the railroad.

The ceremony was supposed to begin at 10:00, but it was not until 3:00 in the afternoon that the fourth train in our expedition arrived from the East. When we were at last all together, it was like a reunion—many of the people we had not seen since the day at Minnetonka. Finally the ceremonies could begin and appropriately they were introduced with music. At one end of the pavilion on the raised platform were the speakers and special guests. Mr. Villard with his family was the center of attention. He was surrounded by ambassadors and representatives of the United States, directors of the railroad, governors, the distinguished German and English guests, and others.

The speechmaking took an eternity—designed more for the American than the German ability to listen. The general public—all those who were not specifically invited—sat on the grass along the railroad bed in front of the grandstand. Henry Villard gave his speech of dedication in English, but an authorized German translation was distributed to us. His words were received with jubilation. Then Mr. Evarts spoke. This usually spirited speaker now had a task that did not lend itself to his usual humor and sarcasm. He talked about the Northwest, the history and exploration of this enormous land, and about the disputes with Spain and England—arguments that might be of some interest in an academic setting but that had no place in a speech to an audience already exhausted from many boring hours of waiting. Even so, Evarts did bring suspense and pathos to the closing words. He was followed by Mr. Billings, former president of the Northern Pacific Railroad.

Then Secretary of the Interior Teller, who represented the United States Government, talked about the significance of the railroad for the country. Next Henry Villard presented the English ambassador, who in turn introduced his countryman, Sir James Hannon. In a lengthy speech the latter thanked Villard for inviting the foreign guests and expressed the joy of his country over the magnificent undertaking achieved by her offspring.[7]

[7] The guests were forced to listen to Henry Villard; William M. Evarts, official orator of the party and former Secretary of State; Frederick Billings, former president of the Northern Pacific; Secretary of the Interior H. M. Teller; the British minister L. S. Sackville West; The Right Honorable Sir James Hannon; and even (by popular acclaim) General U. S. Grant. Most of the speeches are printed in the [St.

Mr. von Eisendecher also paid tribute to Henry Villard and pointed out that Germany could be proud that one of her sons had brought this great endeavor to completion. He then introduced Professor Gneist, who spoke on behalf of the German guests. Finally on the German side, Professor Hofmann stepped forward, elaborating on the theme that the age of miracles was not yet over, miracles wrought by the application of science. The row of speakers concluded with the governors of the states and territories through which we are passing—Rusk of Wisconsin, Ordway of Dakota, Crosby of Montana, Moody of Oregon, and finally Newell of Washington. They kept their words brief, simply noting the significance of the railroad for their specific regions. We all held up bravely.[8]

Paul] *Daily Pioneer Press*, September 9, 1883, p. 2; *Daily Minneapolis Tribune*, September 9, 1883; and *Chicago Tribune*, September 9, 1883, p. 6.

[8] The Germans paraded some of their brightest stars for the occasion: Baron von Eisendecher, Imperial Minister to the United States; Dr. Rudolf Gneist, a member of the German supreme court, professor of law at the University of Berlin, and a representative in both the Prussian and Imperial legislatures; and Dr. A. W. Hofmann, privy counselor, professor of chemistry at the University of Berlin, and the world's most eminent microscopist. After their oratory the governors of the states and territories crossed by the railroad had the good sense to be brief: Jeremiah M. Rusk of Wisconsin, Alexander Ramsey of Minnesota (who was omitted from Herr Mohr's list), N. G. Ordway of Dakota Territory, Colonel John S. Crosby of Montana Territory, Zenas F. Moody of Oregon, and William A. Newell of Washington. The governor of Idaho was unable to attend, due to illness. Most of

The sun was already setting when we broke up to witness the symbolic act that completed the railroad. The crowd flooded the area, the dignitaries and the local people mingling with each other. As I looked around in the milling crowd, with the exception of a few Indians, some Negroes, and several Chinese, there seemed to be little difference between this group and a similar gathering that one might find in North Germany. There were of course more of the romantic figures like the cowboys—those herdsmen who are blessed with independence and who truly lead a "free life." Such individuals would surely be exceptions back home, but generally one cannot really tell from the types of people that we are more than five thousand miles from home.

As part of the symbolic completion, a stretch of track was laid in front of the pavilion. To be sure, everything was ready in advance. The rails were loaded in carts, the ties on both sides had already been laid on the roadbed, and piece by piece the rails were thrown off the carts. The workers picked them up quickly, attached each to the end of the previous rail, and drove the spikes.

There was even time to pay special compliments to the four-footed guest of honor, "Nig", a husky

these notables, reported the correspondent of the *New York Times*, "had the good sense to 'cut it short', although some were so eager to improve their golden opportunity that they exhausted the patience of the weary audience." *New York Times*, September 23, 1883, p. 6.

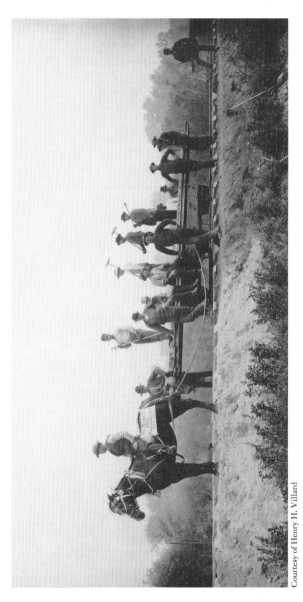

The famous "Nig" and track layers

horse decorated with flowers and ribbons. He played his role well by pulling the cart that carried the rails for the completion of the track. "Nig" has been in the service of the company for a long time. His claim to fame, though, is that he pulled carts all the way from Mandan, through the Badlands, along the Yellowstone, across the mountains right to the final spot—a distance of seven-hundred and fifty miles.

The contest between the workers from the East and those from the West caught our enthusiasm. However, the haste of those from the West caused their cart to tip over so that they lost the game.[9] Thus was the actual track finished; all that remained was for the last spike to be driven in on the last length of track. Photographers had their cameras in place and our painter had a good view of the scene, but in such moments as this the Americans have no consideration for others. Everybody was pushing his way into position around the towering figure of Henry Villard. Suddenly all dignity and ceremony was gone from the occasion as people were screaming: "The golden spike, the golden spike!"

[9] The ceremony is described in the "Historical Introduction," p. lx. When the crew working from the East, led by the popular old "Nig," was declared the winner, its leader, an obvious Missourian, drawled, "Wal, what do ye think of Old Massachusetts now?" *Frank Leslie's Illustrated Newspaper*, LVII (September 22, 1883), p. 70; *New York Times*, September 10, 1883, p. 1, September 23, p. 6.

Sketch by Farny of *Frank Leslie's Illustrated Newspaper*

Driving the last spike

As a matter of fact we had been told that a golden spike was to be the final one. From all precedents, a golden spike would have been appropriate. Deer Lodge County, where the festivities took place, is after all the gold district of Montana. The gold flakes in the river, flowing a few hundred steps from the place where the hammer was swung, are what lured the first settlers to Montana. So it would have been fitting to use a golden spike as a symbol.

Yet the iron spike that Henry Villard held up with his outstretched arm suited me much better. Indeed it had much more significance. "I have no golden spike but an iron one," cried Villard. "The spike which was driven at the beginning of the construction should now be as the last spike." Having located the man who drove the first spike, they brought him to drive in the last spike also. Amid the thundering of cannon fire and the fanfare of music, this man Davis hammered on the spike; then Villard gave it a blow as did Billings, Mrs. Villard, Evarts, Schurz, Grant, and even the three-month old Villard son. His father placed the hammer in his hand so that he too could strike the last spike.[10]

[10] The first blow was struck by H. C. Davis, who had been superintendent of construction and had driven the first spike when the building of the Northern Pacific began in 1870; he was now Assistant General Passenger Agent of the Manitoba Railroad. In addition to Frederick Billings, William M. Evarts, Carl Schurz, and General U. S. Grant listed by Herr Mohr as those helping drive the spike, blows were struck by Mayor Carter Harrison of Chicago ("without an invitation," noted the correspondent of the *Chicago Tribune*), ex-Sena-

Courtesy of Henry H. Villard

First train over the new tracks

Thus he concluded the work, through which his father had secured fame for the family name in the history of the Northwest.

tor James W. Nesmith of Oregon (who insisted on delivering an unwanted speech), Mrs. Billings, and a Crow chief who muttered a few words that no one could understand. Obviously Henry Villard's three-month old son did not strike a blow as Herr Mohr said; his father allowed him to touch the handle of the sledge. Wrote H. C. Davis to his son that night: "I can never expect to do anything so grand again." *Chicago Tribune*, September 18, 1883, p. 2; *New York Times*, September 23, 1883, p. 6.

Now trains decorated with wreaths and flags moved in from the East and the West to touch each other over the last spike. The locomotive engineers leaped from their machines and shook hands with each other—the festival was over.[11] The news was flashed by telegraph to all parts of the Union and to Europe. And the band played "Yankee Doodle," "God Save the Queen," "*Die Wacht am Rhein*", and then, out of respect for friends who were not present, the "*Marseillaise*."

The local people disappeared in various directions and a number of the guests returned by train to the East. Those from Portland, Washington Territory, and San Francisco joined our expedition. Finally our train pulled out, our next stop Lake Pend d' Oreille.

[11] The first locomotive to cross the junction point was Engine No. 154, driven by William Henderson and James Walsh, who had piloted the train of eleven cars from Portland. One of the five cars on the train from the East was "The Pioneer," which had been the first used on the Southern Pacific Railroad more than a dozen years before. All were elaborately decorated with flags and painted medallions, the gifts of the citizens of Sprague, a new town on the Columbia division of the Northern Pacific. *Frank Leslie's Illustrated Newspaper*, LVII (September 22, 1883), p. 7.

10

Lake Pend d'Oreille
and the Columbia River

On Lake Pend d'Oreille
September 9, 1883

THIS morning at dawn we slipped through Missoula, Montana, a neatly situated town of about one-thousand inhabitants, and headed into the valley of the Flathead River. We passed by some splendid mountain scenery and through some very deep cuts. The sides of the mountainous slopes were covered with tall fir trees. Somewhere beyond Missoula we crossed a viaduct built of wood, the highest of its kind in the world. It is two-hundred and twenty-six feet high and carries traffic across the Marent Gulch, a distance of more than eight-hundred and fifty feet.[1] With a certain pride Villard has repeatedly mentioned this bold and triumphant

[1] Missoula, a division point on the Northern Pacific Railroad, was a town of 1,200, situated at the mouth of Hell's Gate Canyon. The remarkable wooden trestle bridge over Marent Gulch, on which Herr Mohr commented, was 866 feet long and 226 feet high, and contained no less than a million board feet of timber. "As our train rumbled over its dizzy height," wrote a correspondent, "the pilgrims put their heads out of the car windows and eyed the verdurous depths below with real awe." *New York Times*, September 23, 1883, p. 6.

piece of construction. We were to stop in the middle of this towering viaduct in order to have a chance to marvel at its construction in leisure. But the unexpected delay of the last spike postponed our arrival time; we were already in bed, and it was only by coincidence that I looked out the window when the train seemed to be moving slowly and with exceptional caution.

It was in considerable terror that I peered out into the depths as we crossed over the wooden framework. The highest firs were far, far below our feet. But the tense anxiety lasted only for a moment, and soon the train was again winding its way along the side of the mountain. From pictures and descriptions we could get an idea of the structure. A small insignificant creek flows at the bottom of the chasm. However, the chasm itself is nearly nine-hundred feet wide, and a total of eight wooden pole towers were required to carry trains on the superstructure. In a short time we passed over another viaduct, this one a thousand feet long but only half as high.

The train passed into a deep cut, the Coriacan Defile, and then climbed across the watershed divide between the Jocko River and the Flathead River. Once again we were on an Indian reservation. This time it was the Flatheads after whom the river had been named. Through the efforts of Catholic missionaries many of these Indians have turned into settlers. Now and then we saw a group of Indians, but they were not in parade dress as were the Indians at Greycliff.[2]

Of much greater interest here were the Chinese. Entire tent colonies of these unchristianized guests with their long braids stretch along the railroad. Today being Sunday, they ought to be somewhere taking it easy, but here they stood massed together in front of the station. Without the Chinese railroad workers the Northern Pacific would probably not have been built for a long time, since manual labor out here is difficult to find.

Their tents or little huts are quite simple, but these people seem to keep themselves very clean; everywhere one looks their wash is waving in the breeze. For us they were really curious creatures, but their appearance as well as their bearing indicates that they are mentally gifted. Yet it is safe to assume that these sons of the empire represent the lowest classes of the Chinese people. We saw quite a few scrofulous, sick faces. They say that the Chinese have some kind of mange. One hardly sees any

[2] The Northern Pacific tracks followed the Jocko River Valley into the Flathead Indian Reservation, where 1,200 of the tribesmen lived on a million and a half acres of land. Neighbors were already eyeing the region covetously, pointing out that every family of four Flatheads had 5,000 acres of choice territory; the Indians, however, were angrily resisting all attempts to buy their holdings. Jesuit missionaries had by this time taught them to live in cabins, fence their fields, and grow their own grain, so that nine-tenths of them were self-supporting. E. V. Smalley, "The New North-West," *Century Magazine*, XXIV (October, 1882), 864–865.

brawny men, but even in the most sickly, one meets a sympathetic face. Their clothing consists mostly of pants and a cape or overcoat, usually made of blue cotton. The long braid on their otherwise shaved head, and the slanted eyes are very pronounced. In strength, they do not compare with either the Irish, the Yankee Americans, or the Germans; but they are persistent, diligent, and reliable souls, for they drink no liquor whatsoever. I have not been able to find out to what extent opium smoking goes on out here in the wilderness.

On this stretch they say there are also members of the Mormon sect working and they are supposed to be outstanding laborers. Unfortunately we were in such a haste as we passed through that we did not find out much about the relationships between the different races, about the different salaries they received, or about the way they are quartered for the winter. The Chinese understood too little English and the Caucasians have too many questions. All the Chinese did was inquire about this or that famous personality who happened to be in our midst. Grant and Schurz were most in demand.

Out here in the wilderness, far removed from the hard and fast rules of civilization, many a ruined man has again found his way. We were told of German officers who were "exiled" to work with these backwoodsmen, but out here the Germans have usually assumed the role of foremen and construction supervisors.

These railroad settlements are made up of curious mixtures. Especially in the town of Heron, where we passed at noon, we could view more closely the economy of these towns. Heron is now a permanent settlement and has all the signs of an embryonic city: saloons, restaurants, and a barber shop.

The large Negro barber was the Figaro of the village. He looked down on the lowly Chinese and gave us to understand how superior we both—that is, he the Negro and we the Europeans—were in comparison to the Chinese. In one regard, however, this barber was not one bit behind his white colleagues in New York. He demanded and got twenty-five cents from each customer for a haircut, whereas back in the East the highest one pays anywhere is twenty cents.

The unfinished look of the settlement is beyond comprehension. Of course it is only six months old now and, in addition, has to cope with this patchwork quilt of races.[3] There do not seem to be many women around yet. For all intents and purposes, Heron is still in the middle of the forest; in spots

[3] Heron, the junction point of the Rocky Mountain and Pend d'Oreille divisions of the railroad, was wholly the creation of the Northern Pacific; nearly all of its three hundred inhabitants worked in the company shops. Only a few months old, it displayed in exaggerated form the characteristics of most frontier communities, with high prices, few women, and the rough-and-ready masculine population that fascinated the visitors. Winser, *The Great Northwest*, 205.

the trees have been cleared, but everywhere the stumps are still jutting up out of the ground. But one should not picture a green thicket of forest as we are accustomed to seeing at home. The forest here is exclusively made up of pine trees, and to clear the railroad passage way, the wood was simply downed. The trunks of the trees were used for ties, but the branches and the rest of the wood that could not be used were simply cleared out of the way. As the easiest way they piled everything up close by the tracks and burned it. All too frequently the fires spread right into the forests and now the view from the train amounts to an uninterrupted panorama of barrenness and destruction. The half-burned, black trunks, ready to fall at any moment alternated with singed pine trees, whose needles have all turned brown. Apparently it never has occurred to anybody to clean up the mess.

But the mountain scenery is excellent. On our left the Bitter Root Range towered above us, forming the border between the territories of Montana and Idaho. We passed over from the Flathead River to the Clark River which flows into Pend d'Oreille Lake not far from Heron. The lake takes its name from the similarity of its shape to that of an ear lobe and the same name shows up again and again to designate certain mountains and rivers in this area. I am not sure whether the name owes its origin to the Frenchmen who immigrated here from Canada and left the name as a reminder of their former presence or whether the imagery derives from the Indian word, simply translated into French.[4]

At this point we were quite close to the Canadian border and at the point where the train touched the lake, it reached its most northerly position. The peaceful waters of the lake lay calmly before us as we came to a stop.[5] Lying at anchor was a very stately steamer called the "Sternwheeler", driven by a large waterwheel at the rear. Here too, as everywhere before, great care was taken in making preparations for our arrival. Leading from the station to the landing dock was a long plank boardwalk laid out over the flat, wet fringe of the lake. Unfortunately, the sky was overcast. Between the clouds and the smoke we found ourselves enveloped in blackness. Out in Oregon the long dry spells, together with man's negligence, have caused terrible forest fires. If you can recall the smoke of the occasional burning peat swamps in our country, then you have

[4] The origin of the name is still unknown. Pend d'Oreille is certainly not correct French, although it may have been contracted from Pendant d'Oreille by French traders. Scholars speculate that the term may have thus originated when applied to Indians wearing ear ornaments, or that it was simply a corruption of a now-forgotten Indian word. George R. Stewart, *Names on the Land* (New York, 1945), 224.

[5] Lake Pend d'Oreille, Idaho, is one of the nation's largest inland lakes, some sixty miles long and from three to fifteen wide, with a shore line of 125 miles and a depth of 1,800 feet. It is the outlet of the Pend d'Oreille River which flows from Flathead Lake. The Northern Pacific tracks skirted the lake's edge for nearly twenty miles. Winser, *The Great Northwest*, 208–209.

some idea of how the smoke from the forest fires blackens the air here.

There was no viewing the snow capped mountains here. Barely had we pushed out from shore, when thunder began to roll. As the thunderstorm developed, it started to rain and soon there was no view at all. Since our trip on the lake would be a waste of time now, our ship turned around. Our hosts offered us some consolation by stating that this rain would help filter out the smoke from the air in Oregon. As so often happens, we had no more than landed when the sky turned perfectly clear. But it was too late and we were loaded into the cars to move on through the territory of Idaho.[6]

I hope the name Idaho sounds just as alluring to you as it does to me. Idaho still has one great plus: nobody as yet has very much to say about it. At the point where we crossed through Idaho, the territory is very narrow but farther to the south it grows dramatically wider. According to Winser's Guidebook, *The Great Northwest*, Idaho is about 86,000 square miles in size and has less than fifty thousand inhabitants. Only about ten percent of the land is suitable for agriculture but eventually the mineral deposits should comprise the main source of wealth of the State.

[6]The correspondent of the *New York Times* made this journey, and was just as disappointed as Herr Mohr. He commented especially on the splendid isolation of Lake Pend d'Oreille, with no one but themselves to be seen. *New York Times*, September 23, 1883, p. 6.

After we crossed the western border of Idaho, we were in Washington Territory. By now it had become a rainy Sunday afternoon. The charcoaled tree trunks and all the sickly trees did not seem to benefit from the drenching rain. Now and then we noticed a few damp-looking Chinese. But toward evening it began to clear. As the train pulled into Spokane Falls, it was already growing dark and the people there had been waiting since eight o'clock in the morning. They had planned a program that had something novel for every hour of the day. Included in the afternoon was an opportunity to attend church, any one of a large choice of confessions. You see now what they expect of us here. On the program we noticed there was a German singing society, the "Concordia," that was supposed to entertain us with a concert.

But the people of Spokane did not show their disappointment. They received us warmly, assuming we were prepared to accept all the good things they had to offer us. Right out at the railroad station things began to happen. There was music, and a speech by Henry Villard. Several decorated coaches were waiting to drive us down to see the falls. In the background was a hotel brightly lit and regal in its appearance. However, I missed seeing either Spokane or the falls.[7] By accident, I was left behind,

[7] Herr Mohr missed a great deal by falling into conversation with his German friends. Spokane Falls was at this time one of the beauty-spots of the West. There the waters of the

caught in conversation with some German settlers who are very content here. A farmer, born in the Palatinate, had brought his American born son to the station to show him what some of his German countrymen looked like.

In the near vicinity along the Spokane River there is another Indian reservation called "Coeur d'Alene" and people tell me that the Indians there have come along so far in the art of agriculture that they bring wheat to market. In general the Indian cultivates and harvests exactly what he needs and no more.

The falls at Spokane are fabulous. So I am told by those who saw them. The wide Spokane River divides into three parts around two islands and the three arms waltz around the rim several times before tumbling over the edge into a basin. The water power is already being exploited and predictions are that with this gift of nature, great industries will someday blossom here. According to our guidebook, the city has large hotels, beautiful stores, good schools and churches, several newspapers, and the energy and know-how to take advantage of all opportunities. All this and a population of only one

---

Columbia River cascaded downward 150 feet within a half mile while basaltic islands, spanned by a series of bridges, caused the water to rush even more swiftly. As the streams converged into a seething basin, the guidebook reported, "eternal mist rises from the boiling abyss, the sunshine reveals a bow of promise spanning the chasm." Winser, *The Great Northwest*, 217.

thousand! At least that is what it says in Winser's *The Great Northwest.*[8]

Monday, September 10, 1883

AFTER the excitement of last evening and some early morning rest we rose to greet another day. From daybreak, however, we stood still in Ainsworth, where the Snake River empties into the Columbia. We had to cross the Snake River, known to the Indians as the Shoshone, but the bridge was not finished. A steamship ferry shuttled us across, each time taking four cars. Transporting the whole train took an endlessly long time, so long that one of my press colleagues picked up his gun and went out hunting.[9] But it looked to me as though he used his gun less skillfully than his pen. Our cook gave him instructions, but he still had no success.

[8] The city claimed 1,500 inhabitants, not 1,000, with four hotels, two banks, five churches, a grist mill, and machine shops. As one of the few major settlements established before the coming of the railroad, it served as a commercial center for a large area producing wheat and lumber. "Spokane," proclaimed the guidebook that Herr Mohr quoted so often, "is the most bustling and active place in all the region 'round. It has . . . a spirit of enterprise that will make the most of its opportunities." Winser, *The Great Northwest*, 217.

[9] The railroad was building a bridge across the Snake River just above its entrance into the Columbia, but this was still far from completed. The steam ferry boat was built especially to shuttle cars across the river, but still took an interminable time to move the five special trains. *New York Times*, September 23, 1883, p. 6.

The cook, incidentally, is also a German. He came from Frankfurt to America with his father who is now the owner of a well-established confectionery in New York. He astounded us as he related his experiences. In the Civil War he rose to the rank of lieutenant, then went back to Frankfurt, where he showed off his uniform to his friends. Eventually he returned to America again and to his profitable business. If I am not mistaken, he was hired specially for this Northern Pacific trip at a salary of four-hundred dollars.

In front of us is the mighty Columbia flowing past the mouth of the Snake River. On the right bank of the Columbia is a long chain of mountains, well eroded and worn down, in front of them a broad lowland. From the summer and fall drought, everything looks a brownish yellow, and on the opposite side of the Snake River and all about it doesn't look much better. Nothing but sagebrush on sandy soil. Lighted by the morning sun the entire area looks like a desert. On our side of the river the land slopes somewhat and they say there are lots of rabbits hiding out on the plain. But they are the same brownish yellow as the soil and the sage grass, so you would never notice them except for their transparent ears.

When it was our car's turn to board the ferry, two cars actually, we were shoved back and forth until we finally came to rest at the right spot on the sloping deck of the ship. Then two other cars were pushed on the tracks fastened to the other side of the boat. The ferry moved away from land, sailed for a time up river and then landed again in a position where we listed badly until the locomotive dragged us ashore. Everything worked smoothly. But it did not go so well for the Englishmen, the same ones who were thrown into such danger last Friday evening. Their car tore loose on deck as the ship pitched in the water under the lopsided weight. It rolled back on the deck, broke through the barrier, and would have fallen into the river had the tracks at the end not been bent up to prevent such an accident. This jolt caused Lord Carrington to cut his head.[10]

It was not until noon that we started out again, our cars once more hitched together. Eventually though we arrived in Wallula Junction, the terminal point of the Northern Pacific Railroad. Here it joins the line of a company that has been in existence for a long time, the Oregon Railroad and Navigation Company. This line runs from Portland to Wallula on the left bank of the Columbia River and then continues to Lewiston on the Idaho border. The Northern Pacific simply uses their track but does have plans eventually to build its own roadway on the right bank of the river.

[10] Sir Charles Robert Wynn-Carrington, first Earl Carrington, a member of the English party, was a man of very substantial wealth. He was serving at this time as captain of the Royal Body Guard.

In Wallula Junction the Northern Pacific has erected a large train station where we found a confusing bustle of human beings.[11] After a long wait we departed from this disruptive stopping point and headed down along the Columbia River, that mighty stream which is formed by the confluence of several rivers, some of them from far up in Canada. At Wallula these forks from the north and the south feed into one flow toward the west, the river thus formed eventually emptying into the wide Pacific Ocean at Astoria, Oregon.

The landscape along the Columbia River called to mind the description of the land formations in Colorado or the Badlands. But with the broad sandy flats along its banks, the view becomes more foreign, strange, and unusual. People keep telling us that farther back from the river the land is more fertile and that with artificial irrigation the earth becomes an extremely good benefactor. Off in the distance is a mountain range, the Klikitat Mountains. Farther down stream the mountains are closer to the banks and very steep. There was hardly a tree to be seen. Everything was brown, but I could not

[11] Wallula Junction was the meeting point of the tracks of the Northern Pacific, coming from the east, and the Oregon Railway and Navigation Company, coming from the west and Portland. A spur line of the latter also connected the city with Walla Walla, lying a few miles to the south. Save for a handsome combination hotel and railway station built by the railroad, Wallula Junction was an unattractive conglomeration of temporary shacks and eating houses. Winser, *The Great Northwest*, 220.

discern whether the color came from burned grass or weathered stone.

Once in a while we are surprised by signs of agricultural activity. For example, we passed a team of horses hitched to a farm wagon and later an agricultural machine, distinguishable by the red paint, parked back in a side valley. On the opposite shore was an Indian encampment, again on a reservation. On the whole the entire region has the character of isolation and sterility.

As the sun set over the horizon, the train stopped at "The Dalles." We all climbed out and down the railroad embankment onto a large expanse of alluvial rock. At certain seasons this rock forms part of the river bed but now the rock was completely dry. At this spot the mighty river was compressed from both sides by the rock cliffs and squeezed through a narrow channel 150 to 200 feet wide. The current rushed past the cement-like embankments with a surging force almost as if the water itself were compressed. The depth of these narrows has not been determined so far.

Along the river's edge lay a plateau of rock, polished by the water, and on top of this Indians had set up a camp. These inhabitants observed us cautiously from a distance. And as we stood there in awe of the river, the heavens were flooded by a gorgeous red sunset so that both the rocks and the sky glowed in all shades of red and purple. To the south the smoke and moisture clouds opened enough to bathe Mount Hood—that snowcapped giant of a mountain—in pink shades of light. The fleeting moment was so overwhelming in its strange beauty that it will never be forgotten.[12]

It was already dark when we pulled into the station of Dalles. Rather I should say "The Dalles"[13] because the name is never used without the article and apparently it is the French word for stone or rocky beds. Even though we were still under the spell of nature's solitude in these regions, we suddenly discovered that we were in the middle of a noisy crowd of people. Music, ear-shattering firecrackers, illuminated windows, red and white fires

[12] The Dalles, the narrow waterway through which the Columbia River pierced the Cascade Mountains, was some sixty yards wide and two miles long. The rushing waters provided a colorful spectacle that travelers long remembered. "The beholder," read the guidebook that was Herr Mohr's bible, "looks up from the sublimity of desolation around him, to see the same transformed into the ethereal and majestic, on a scale of grandeur that overawes as it impresses." Here Indians gathered by the thousands to catch the salmon that fought their way through the swift waters to their spawning grounds. By 1883, however, scores of canneries and a "salmon wheel" had been built along the banks to capture the fish in wholesale quantities. Only a few Indians remained to amuse tourists by waving at them. Winser, *The Great Northwest*, 233–235.

[13] Dalles City, which was second only to Portland as a commercial center, claimed 4,000 inhabitants at the time, with a waterworks, eight hotels, three banks, four public halls and theaters, three newspapers, and five churches. Boats of the Oregon Railway and Navigation Company could be boarded there for the trip to Portland. *Appleton's General Guide*, 448.

Taken from Rudolf Cronau's *Von Wunderland zu Wunderland*

Mount Hood and The Dalles of the Columbia

were all around us—a stirring salute for Henry Villard and his guests, way out where we thought there was nothing but wilderness. Like the people in Spokane, those in The Dalles had been waiting for a long time for us and for that reason their greeting was so thunderous.

But where in the world did all these people come from? What, for that matter, is The Dalles? Well, The Dalles is the home of the huge overhaul and repair stations for the Oregon Railway and Navigation Company. Furthermore, The Dalles is the main point for portaging the Columbia River, it is a place where all shipping has to be hauled over the narrows by land. We had only a confused look at The Dalles, then after the brief stopover were on our first lap to Portland.

11

Portland

Portland, Oregon
Tuesday, September 11, 1883

AT LAST we have arrived at the actual goal of our trip. Here in Portland they had expected us to arrive on Monday evening. But it was not until early Tuesday morning that our train pulled into the depot at Portland, rather East Portland on the right bank of the Willamette River, where the train tracks end. Thus our entrance to the city was a quiet affair. In describing this festival day, the Oregon German newspaper said, "There were no hundred-and-one cannon shots to be heard, no bells, and no train whistles." Reading these words, I realized that the whistling of locomotives and steamships on such occasions is the American form of bell-ringing at home.

Sunrise brought light to the Willamette River, on which were floating three-masted ships and several steamers. The river flows twelve miles from here into the Columbia River; thus we realized how very near we were to the Pacific Ocean. After all of our four trains had arrived, a ferry steamer took the entire party across to the other shore where the City of Portland is situated. It is built along the river on the slope of a hill covered with fir trees. What a pity that again a veil of smoke from the nearby burning forests prevented a view of the mountains, especially snow-capped Mount Hood.

Portland is the first large city we have seen since leaving Minneapolis and St. Paul. At the moment it is far behind those cities both in area and in population. But after being lost for so long in the loneliness of small towns, raw and unfinished, we were doubly pleased to be in the midst of an orderly city life again.[1]

Portland was wild with preparations for a festival. Once again a large number of splendid carriages were waiting in rows to take us to our quarters. Everywhere there were flags and pennants, many of them German flags.[2] After a brief rest we hurried

[1] Portland, situated twelve miles from the Columbia River at the head of navigation on the Willamette, had been commercially isolated save for its ocean connections with San Francisco. Hence the Northern Pacific Railroad, which opened direct rail access to the goods and markets of the East, promised to rejuvenate its economy and transform it into the trading center of the Pacific Northwest. It was already a progressive young city, with 23,000 inhabitants in 1880 and nearly 40,000 in 1883, ten banks, twenty commodious hotels, three public halls, a good theater, four street railway lines, and a fine water-and-gas works. In 1882 its commercial trade reached a figure of $40,000,000 and its manufacturing $7,000,000. Winser, *The Great Northwest*, pp. 243–244; *Appleton's General Guide*, p. 448.

[2] The *Portland Oregonian*, able to display more enthusiasm for flags and bunting than the jaded Herr Mohr, reported that never had the city "presented a more animated appearance." The most gorgeous displays were along First

over to the Court House to view the festival parade. Here again the parade gave us insight into the commerce and industry of this city. Portland is well on the way to occupying the dominant position on the Pacific Ocean. The incredible natural resources of Oregon find their natural center and outlet here. The city is becoming the great market place for the entire Northwest. It has another advantage in that it is comparatively far inland and yet has access to ocean-going traffic. Inasmuch as the railroad now offers connections to the East, Portland will no longer be dependent on San Francisco. It is this liberation, above all, that is being celebrated here, and with good reason.

Portland too had arranged a festival parade.[3] For

Street where a series of arches in various architectural styles charmed viewers: one at First and A Streets depicting a feudal castle "with such fidelity to nature that it elicited expressions of admiration from visitors and residents alike," another one at First and Adler, an example of "pure Gothic architecture . . . furnished and decorated in an elaborate manner," a third at First and Salmon in the Roman order, covered with flags and battle-axes. All were "elegantly adorned" with flowers, evergreens, streamers, flags, and bunting, and each bore a large "Welcome" sign. *Portland Oregonian*, September 11, 1883.

[3] If the local press can be believed, most of the state's inhabitants descended on Portland for the festivities, leaving farms and towns deserted. The weather was ideal, for a light rain had cleared the air and the sun shown brightly. "Not to be enthusiastic," wrote one reporter the next day, "the display yesterday was the grandest sight that Portland ever witnessed; not one of the grandest, but the very grandest of them all." *Portland Oregonian*, September 12, 1883.

the most part it was similar to the parades we had seen in St. Paul and Minneapolis, though hardly of comparable size. But with respect to the variety and taste of the displays, Portland was not a bit behind the other two cities. As a matter of fact there were some units in the Portland parade that were indigenous to this area and therefore added a distinctive touch to the procession.

On the other hand, the people of Portland cut out one section that would have added a very nice touch to the drama. We read in the program that the Chinese wanted to take part in the procession. They had planned to include a unit of one-thousand men and this would certainly have been a rich contribution, artistically as well as educationally. Their banners and costumes would certainly have been an interesting sight to behold.

But as you know, the Chinese are not recognized as having full citizenship even though they were a prerequisite for the development of the West Coast. To the Irish, they constitute a dangerous form of competition for jobs, and there is talk about deporting them. In this sense, the Irish have now won a victory because the Chinese were not allowed to take part in the parade. It seems the people here are more tolerant toward the Indians than the Chinese; at least the children from the Indian school of Forest Grove were in the parade. A unit of Negroes also marched along in the parade.

In every respect the parade captured our attention by its constantly changing scenes. There were many beautiful horses with fine, stately riders—these alone were enough to guarantee a successful show. It was obvious in all the participants that they enjoyed taking part in this affair and that every single one did his best to contribute to the overall impression. We were surprised at the love of the Americans for performances such as this. It is difficult for us to comprehend, because the American is otherwise such a modest individual concerned only with practical matters. Perhaps Americans sense a need to inject some form of cheer into the monotonous seriousness of their lives by such pageantry as these parades.

Several military companies from a regiment of regular army troops opened the parade, followed by the artillery.[4] In the second unit were the Negroes

[4]Stands for Villard's visiting dignitaries had been erected at the corner of Court House Square, but by the time their carriages arrived, the crowds were so dense that a passage had to be opened for them. The parade, as Herr Mohr noted, was not as long as those in Minneapolis and St. Paul, requiring only an hour and a half to pass a given point. It was opened by about a hundred pioneers who had followed the Oregon Trail westward in the 1840s, led by Medoram Crawford who made the journey in 1842, marching now though grey and bent with age. Then came the soldiers from Fort Vancouver, youthful Indians from the Indian Training School at Forest Grove clad in light blue uniforms, and the interminable industrial exhibits, lightened now by such novelties as salmon frozen in cakes of ice, a giant log eighty inches in diameter, and a stump of a forest giant with woodmen chopping at it. Interspersed with the wagons of dry goods, coal, and leather work were no less than eight compa-

and the children from the Indian school, for the most part half-breed Indians. They looked quite well disciplined and intelligent. By comparison to the Indians who performed the war dances in Greycliff, these seem like civilized people. One wonders what will happen to them once they leave school. Will they be able to sustain themselves in competition with the white population?

In all there were eight sections that passed by. The wagons or cars—I have also heard them referred to as floats—representing the business and industrial life of Portland took up considerable space in the parade. Once again we marveled at the complexity of businesses already in progress here— agriculture, the lumber trade, saw mills, and furniture factories all play a major role here.

The shipping and fishing industries were also represented. For example, there was a wagon hauling blocks of ice with fish frozen inside the blocks. The tanning and fur industry floats aroused our interest especially.

Interspersed among the industries were military units, veterans, and again a column of riders on splendid, sleek horses. One company was made up

nies of the state militia, units of the Mexican War Veterans and the Grand Army of the Republic, troops of cowboys, fire brigades, the various German displays that Herr Mohr noted with such pride, and the emigrant wagons with their Indian followers that ended the procession. *Portland Oregonian*, September 12, 1883; *New York Times*, September 23, 1883, p. 6.

exclusively of Germans led by members of the Schützenverein, or rifle club. They accompanied a float carrying the figures of Germania and Columbia. Certainly this unit was one of the finest ornaments in the procession! Eight knights high on their horses lent a wonderful foreign flavor out here in the Far West. The figures of Germania and Columbia sat hand in hand on thrones of rock—Germania sending forth her children and Columbia graciously receiving them. At the foot of the rock throne of Germania, the children dressed in their variegated old costumes of Germany present a colorful picture of our German peasant life, especially contrasted with the uniformity in the United States, despite the mixed backgrounds of the people.

Following the Germania-Columbia unit was a float covered entirely by flowers. It was arranged and built by a German, who placed a sample of every plant that grows in the state of Oregon on this float. Next came the German mutual aid society and the German gymnastic society with about sixty men and boys. And then Germania's most beloved offspring, Gambrinus. A huge beer barrel served as the throne for the inventor of that great drink, and all around the beer barrel sat the members of a beer drinking society.

Next came the Eintracht or Harmony singing society, and then several units representing the various German businesses, such as bakers and cabinet makers. The German section was concluded by a troop of Knights of Pythias of the Germania Lodge Number Twelve.

From the next section I must at least mention the three beautifully decorated young girls on horseback. Dressed in red, white, and blue, they represented the allegorical figures of Faith, Hope, and Charity. They were followed by children from the charitable institutions of this city.

Included also was a printing firm with the banner: "Germany gave us the art of printing, Germany gave us Villard, Villard gave us the railroad, and the railroad gave us freedom."

Closing the great procession was the dramatic display of an early immigrant train—that is, from about thirty years ago. Wagons and carts were of an earlier style and one could see that they had been traveling for six months, arriving here from the East after having crossed the prairies, the mountains and valleys, the rivers and swamps, pulled only by oxen. The men walked alongside. Their clothing betrayed the miserable conditions that existed along the route. Women and children were squatting inside the wagons, each of which was covered by a tightly stretched piece of cloth. Kettles and cooking utensils tied to the back end were clanking, making melancholy music for this display. "This is how we crossed the prairie in 1847," read the inscription. In order to present a more realistic picture of the dangers, the train was followed by a troop of Indians in their fantastic dress.

Portland is in the midst of its development. It still has plenty of room to spread out and when we turn our backs on the business district down near the Willamette, Portland looks more like a suburb than a city. You can see gardens and the wide straight streets with regular cross streets, and all of them have been planted with trees.

We were able to watch the parade from the large square at the Court House. There they had set up a large reviewing stand for Villard, the guests and the city and state officials, as well as their families. That is also where the speeches were given. Here also sat the families of the first fifty settlers. These pioneer men themselves rode at the head of the big parade. Everybody seemed to know them and paid them great respect on this day of honor.

Later the real festival ceremony took place in the Pavilion, a large building designed for exhibitions. It was very tastefully decorated. Opposite the main gallery is a podium set up for singers and musicians. The wall behind the podium was painted sky blue. With the right light effects, one might think he were looking out into the blue sky itself.

The hall and galleries were full. The ceremonies opened with a military march and then a song of praise by the three hundred school children of Portland.[5]

[5] The Mechanics' Pavilion on Third Street was, as Herr Mohr observed, "very gaudily, but tastefully decorated." Ceremonies began with a speech by Congressman M. C.

Henry Villard received a host of good wishes for the great service he has rendered to this part of the country. He then introduced Charles Russell, member of the English Parliament, who spoke on behalf of the English guests, and Senator Gröning, who spoke for the Germans. Considering that he had to speak in English, the senator did a very good job.

Words of praise were also delivered by Senators Kasson and Conger of Iowa and Michigan. Then Carl Schurz spoke on behalf of the Americans, particularly the German-Americans. Schurz hypnotized

---

George who awarded the builders of the Northern Pacific a place in the sun with those who had been responsible for the St. Gotthard Tunnel, the Biscay Canal, and the soon-to-be-built Panama Canal. Mr. Villard responded briefly before introducing the Lord Chief Justice of England, Charles Russell, "who followed in a line of ideas that seem to us something like platitudes"—or so the local reporter thought. Dr. Albert Gröning of Bremen, speaking for the German delegation, expressed his admiration for all the energy and sagacity of the city's inhabitants (a sentiment that the "inhabitants" heartily applauded). Then came the parade of American dignitaries: John A. Kasson, Representative (not Senator as Herr Mohr believed him) from Iowa, who closed with the fervent hope that "American civilization on the Pacific shores would not be forced back, but rolling across the Pacific, would bring the ancient millions of Asia into harmony with the civilization of our age, and with the religion to which we adhere;" Senator Omar D. Conger of Michigan who hoped that the West would not forget the religious teachings of the East; Carl Schurz who was delighted that Indians were in the parade and that they were being educated rather than slaughtered; and finally William M. Evarts who read a lecture on the wisdom of beating plowshares into swords and then back into plowshares again. *Portland Oregonian*, September 12, 1883.

his listeners, not only by his skill at oratory, but by the clarity of his arguments. It goes without saying that Schurz spoke in English, but one could tell that he is an honest politician who knows exactly how to approach an issue. The words flowed without the slightest stammer or stutter. Germany can be proud of having given Henry Villard and Carl Schurz to America. Today we realized this more than ever.

Mr. Evarts once again demonstrated his satirical skill in delivering a speech and then the crowd demanded Grant. But the brave general, contrary to his usual custom, had already slipped away. His popularity is still very great, but the politicians claim that the outbursts of public acclaim have no political implications. But for the fiery eyes and stern mouth, there is little about Grant to remind one of the old warrior. He became quite rotund and now has a red face; he looks more like a corpulent craftsman than a general or president.

The afternoon events ended somewhat in confusion, but in the evening the Pavilion was once again the center of festivities. This time it was a concert put on by the Orchestra Club of Portland in conjunction with the Apollo Club. Afterward there was an outdoor concert by the music corps of the 21st United States Infantry Regiment. This gave us a chance to get acquainted with some of the Portland women. The charming young women of this country, clothed in their finest evening dress, made an excellent impression on us. Unfortunately for us,

Park and Montgomery Streets, Portland

we had to leave early as we were invited by some of our countrymen to spend the rest of the evening at the Turner Club. There we were welcomed in a very warm manner.

The time in Portland is much too short, but so it has been everywhere. Tuesday slipped away too fast with the festival events and the late party afterward. Today our party is taking an excursion to Albany in the Willamette Valley.[6] However, I passed the opportunity by in order to get at my writing again, and more importantly, to find my trunk. This task was urgent since part of our group will be leaving for San Francisco and for a time it seemed that all of my belongings might go that way also.

We are staying either in hotels or with families. A number of the younger members of our party are staying on steamers lying at the pier. In this city the hotel industry has not kept pace with the general building boom. So many guests and visitors have congregated here for these significant days that the city simply does not have the means to take care of all of them.

I have the opportunity to stay at the home of Mr. Ewald,[7] who was born in Hamburg and who at one

---

[6] Albany, lying eighty-one miles from Portland, was an agricultural center for the upper Willamette Valley. There a college and several large mills brought home to the visitors the richness of the farm country about them. Winser, *The Great Northwest*, 249.

[7] Herr Mohr almost certainly was a guest at the home of Ferdinand G. Ewald at 226 Twelfth Street. Ewald, a clerk,

time lived in Bremen. Thus I have learned to know the residential area of Portland. The houses are predominantly made of wood, but somehow out here in the West one can overcome his prejudice against this kind of construction. According to the inhabitants, such houses are well-suited to the climate in terms of warmth and dryness. Of course Oregon does have a very mild climate. It is tempered by the currents of the Pacific Ocean, but these currents also bring in a great deal of moisture. From the end of fall to the end of spring hardly a day goes by without rain.

The architecture here includes attempts at every style possible with wood as the building material. Gothic and Renaissance dominate, but it seems that a style suited to wood construction has not yet been found. The houses are set rather far apart and often there are patches of virgin forest between them. Even the streets with their lines of trees give a friendly impression. At some points the forest begins where the city ends. From my window I have an excellent view and could easily imagine myself in the German Schwarzwald [Black Forest] if it were not for the dust.

Portland could be compared with Minneapolis. But as Portland is a seaport, one can see at a glance

secretary, and eventually assistant treasurer of the Oregon and California Railroad, one of Villard's subsidiary companies, had settled in Portland in 1879 or 1880 if the *Portland City Directories* for the period are accurate.

that much is different. There are large warehouses and big buildings belonging to the large rail and sea shipping companies which have a preferred status here. A long stretch of the water front is covered by ship docks made of pilings that stand very high out of the water. In the harbor the huge three-masters lie at anchor. Portland is the primary harbor for all the Northwest coast in spite of its being far inland.

The city of course does have rivals, both here in Oregon and in Washington territory—Astoria, which lies at the mouth of the Columbia River, and several others along Puget Sound, including restless Seattle. For the time being, however, Seattle does not have direct railroad connections. Portland has every reason to keep striving if she is to continue in her favored position.

Today Mr. Ewald took me to see the Chinese section of the city. Portland has a Chinese population of several thousand—as many as six thousand I've heard but in this part of the country one has to be a little cautious of these estimates. The Chinese occupy almost one whole street in the business section. They are all packed together like herring. They sleep together, dozens in one room, whereas according to our standards, not more than six men can spend the night in one room without danger to their health. As a pillow, the Chinese use a small block of wood the size of your hand, hollowed out on one side for their heads. They maintain their own way of life and their customs as far as possible.

Among all the other peoples and races living in the great Republic there is a wonderful melting process, yet the Chinese linger on as complete strangers. Even the Indians sometimes settle among the whites and eventually seem half European. Only Chinese refuse to be integrated or to give up a one of their national peculiarities. They come in contact with the whites only for business purposes.[8]

The thousands of years of Chinese culture have had a strong influence. The Chinese see and understand what the American needs and demands are but they still maintain a completely self-sufficient closed-off colony. It is a colony without women. Only a very few wealthy Chinese are married. The majority live a celibate life although a few no doubt have conquered the heart and won the hand of a German or Irish immigrant girl.

The Chinese remain as guests of the American nation and if times get hard they would have to pack their bags and return to their mother country. Native Americans reproach them, claiming that

[8] The Portland Chinese community grew rapidly during the early 1880s when anti-Chinese sentiment in San Francisco and Seattle drove many to seek homes elsewhere. By the end of the decade its "Chinatown" was second only to that of San Francisco in the United States, with at least 5,000 inhabitants, most of them living along Second Street between Pine and Taylor streets. As Herr Mohr observes, most clung to their traditional costumes, wearing "pigtails", loose flowing pantaloons, and blouses of cotton or silk. Percy Maddux, *City on the Willamette: The Story of Portland, Oregon* (Portland, 1952), 83–84.

they look on this country only as a source for getting rich. In fact, of course, this question of the immigration of the Chinese is not simple. A flood of Chinese could bring on severe problems for the United States, considering the huge population of China, the unlimited needs of its race, and their toughness and versatility.

The Chinese are organized into secret societies in which the rulers have tremendous power over the individuals of the group. No doubt they could form a state within the state. On the other hand, they are a very hard working people. They work for very low wages. In the framework of their standard of living, however, they do very well. In the American West, where there is an acute shortage of labor, they have been a useful and necessary component. The plan is to shut off the influx for the time being, but as soon as the number already here shrinks, immigration will once again be opened up to them.

The Americans are annoyed with the Chinese because they refuse to take part in American life, and because they toil at back breaking work until they have saved a little money and then return home with the money. But there are surely other reasons for this unfriendliness.[9] On the whole, Americans

[9] Only three years later the anti-Chinese sentiment exploded into violence when, in February, 1886, an "Anti-Chinese Congress" of various labor groups adopted several resolutions asking the expulsion of Orientals from the city by March 24, 1886. This was followed by a torch-light procession which marched through the downtown area shouting

should be glad that they can have these guests who have been so useful.

For us, these foreigners from Asia were a most interesting phenomenon. We visited their stores, their gaming houses and their opium dens. Unfortunately I cannot give you a description of their gambling and opium smoking. We went into their establishments with the protection of a husky constable and as soon as he appeared, everything that is forbidden disappeared immediately. Where we did go alone, we had the impossible situation of making ourselves understood. If the Chinese don't want to answer a question, they always have a lucky way out: they can simply say they do not understand. They are always sure that the person will not try to ask the same question in Chinese in order to clarify it.

It seems that a great population density in China has given these people the special instinct to make do with the smallest space. Their gambling rooms, their opium dens, their stores and their workshops are remarkably cramped for space. There is much that makes good sense in their nature and action. Besides workers, there are also merchants of all types and other business men among them. Certain specialized businesses have fallen into their hands.

"The Chinese must go," and urging all citizens to unite on the March 24 date. Violence increased over the next weeks, but sober heads came to the rescue of the aliens, preventing a wholesale assault although many individuals were brutally treated by mobs. Maddux, *City on the Willamette*, 80–82.

For example, all the laundries seem to belong to the Chinese. They are also quite adaptable as waiters, and they are praised for their cleanliness, their steadfastness, and their honesty.

An example of the handiness and skill of the Chinese is well demonstrated in the home where I am staying. The situation of maid service in America is always critical. The luckiest ones are those who know how to get along without any help. In the family I am living with during these pleasant days, a fifteen-year-old Chinese boy is the cook and the only maid in the house. He is truly the cook, not a cook's helper, and I must admit that I have seldom eaten better in this country. Once he has been shown how the food is prepared, he prepares it exactly as if from a recipe, and with machine-like perfection. The magical formula is "just like last time" and everything works out fine. In the evening they show him the menu that is to be served the next day, and then he goes off to his Chinese quarters where he stays with an uncle for the night. The next morning he arrives punctually, earlier or later, depending on how complicated the menu is for that day, does up his duties, waits on table, cleans up the kitchen and goes off again.

Postponed until this evening was the gorgeous illumination of Portland. All of the streets were brightly lighted with Chinese lanterns—tremendous numbers of them. They bathed the city in a magic light and outshone the gas lights, and even the stars.

For the most part, the lighting was concentrated on the business streets in the lower sections of the city. Downtown in the public squares were huge piles of logs on fire. The overall effect was unique.

In order to balance the festival's serious events, there was lighter fare. The Chinese community had invited Henry Villard and his distinguished guests to a gala performance at the Hong-Low Theater.[10] Naturally we accepted. On the surface the theater was little different from any other theater except that there was no curtain on the stage. In fact a curtain was unnecessary since the performance was not divided up into acts, but played continuously. In such a production there was no problem with scene changes.

The entire performance was accompanied by sounds which the sons of the middle empire would probably call music. To us Europeans, however, it sounded like plain noise. First there was a drumming, soft, then louder, then softer again. Secondly there was a banging on some instrument that I could not see very well. Thirdly there was a kind of

[10] The Hong-Low Theater, built in 1879, remained a cultural landmark until it was closed in 1904. Situated on the upper floor of a building at the corner of Second and Adler Streets, near the center of the city's "Chinatown," its auditorium was 100 by 95 feet, with a stage at one end rising five feet above the floor. No scenery, curtain, or footlights were used. Plays began at seven in the evening and continued until well after midnight. The orchestra usually included a flute, one-string fiddle, cymbal, gong, guitar, and trumpet. Maddux, *City on the Willamette*, 89–90.

plinking on a zither. Fourthly, somebody was playing on a very primitive violin. In addition, most of
the time there was singing—a high-pitched warbling
sing-song—such as one might occasionally hear in
this country from a group of babbling school girls.
These musicians either sat or stood in the middle
background of the stage and the actors performed in
front of them.

We entered the theater shortly after the performance began. On the stage stood a tall husky man
with a white beard and decked out in rich Chinese
clothes, basically red in color. For a long time he
did nothing but pick up his feet, one after the other,
and slowly move forward on the stage. Then he
leaned back on two poles which a servant held behind him in a horizontal position. They marched,
servant and master, the master always leaning back.
They moved with long, swinging steps, back and
forth. Several others, draped in parasols and flags
and under a kind of canopy, walked along behind
them. From what I could make out, this was a very
important part of the action, for the music became
stronger. As the intensity increased, the orchestra
added several brass instruments similar to our per-
cussion. These were smashed together with ferocious energy, letting forth a truly infernal blast of
noise. All the while the monotonous singing continued in one discordant screech.

After this group departed, another tall man appeared with a white mask. He had long black tufts

of hair on his upper lip, chin and cheeks, six in all. They looked a little like small horse tails.

Then the man with the beardy tails disappeared and several different male and female characters appeared. One of the women had a doll in her arms. Finally after some extended pantomiming, there was some talking—rather something between singing and talking—all accompanied by exaggerated gesticulating. Naturally we could not understand the words. Some of those on stage were strangely painted in their faces, others not.

Next appeared some figures dressed in white who climbed on a long table. There, to the accompaniment of a steady sing-song, they moved back and forth for a while, then jumped up and down. They threw open their garments to reveal blue, star-covered clothing, then turned their backs and buttoned up each other's clothing again.

Then there was another scene. A number of people were carrying swords and spears, waving them back and forth, up and down, apparently in no pattern at all. Every now and then they let loose a squealing scream, or they shouted in their high notes accompanied by the overall banging of the hollow brass plates. So violent was the drum beating that it was doubtful whether there would be any drum skins left.

Off to the side of the stage there was a canvas wall, above which two flags could be seen. This wall seemed to have some special significance, for several of the armed men swung their swords and lances into it with fierce expressions of pain. This action was accompanied by a loud crash and a fortissimo in the music.

Next came the gymnastic acts, something like our clowns perform at the circus. They did not show any special strength or skill in what they did.

At this point we had had enough and were glad to get out in the fresh air.

NOTE ADDED LATER:

I do not want to neglect giving you an interpretation that I learned a few days later from a reliable source.

The object of the piece was to show a war or an armed aggression. The man in the white beard and rich clothing was an emperor. When he leaned back on the poles held by his servant and walked in that position, it meant he was riding in a carriage. The man with the white mask was the usurping emperor. Anyone who was a bad man, or on the side of the illegitimate powers, was wearing a mask or his face was painted. (It certainly is a shame that a similar arrangement does not exist in real life.)

The man stroking his beard was showing his indetermination, or more especially, that he had no inclination to go to war. The scene with the small child meant that the soldiers were leaving their families and going off to war. The figures who were clothed at first in white, then in blue, were angels.

As long as they stayed on the table in their white garments, they were in the heavens, but as soon as they turned to blue, it meant they walked about visibly on this earth. The canvas wall with the flags was a fortress. The waving of weapons and the gymnastic exercises were the preparations for war.

Apparently all this was perfectly obvious to the countless Chinese in the audience. They followed the course of the play with great excitement and lots of applause. During the performance Chinese play-goers now and then got up and left. But that probably did not bother their understanding of the plot since the action seemed to move along very slowly and was already old and well known. Moreover, the same play ran for several days, often for a whole week. The action of a single evening corresponded to just one act in our theater.

The entire evening we had the feeling of being in a totally strange, and seemingly crazy world. On the other hand, what would a son of the Middle Empire say if he arrived from his homeland and went straight to see one of our European theatrical performances, for instance, a Wagnerian opera. Probably he would look down his nose at it just as we did at what was offered to us with best intentions here. So it is when two very different cultures suddenly confront one another.

12

To Victoria and Back by Boat

Portland
Saturday, September 16, 1883

AT THREE O'CLOCK this afternoon we arrived back from our excursion to British Columbia and we all agreed that these were the most beautiful days of our trip—which is what we have often said already. Each time Henry Villard assures us that we have even more exquisite things to look forward to. We hope that his prediction will again turn out to be correct.

Three days ago we left by boat for this beautiful trip on the Willamette River and the Columbia River, and Puget Sound, blessed by excellent weather the entire way. Our ship, *The Wide West*, is a so-called sternwheeler with a large paddle, like a waterwheel, in back. Such a ship can travel about twenty miles per hour. The view of the snow-covered mountains in the Cascade Range—Mount St. Helens, Mount Adams, and Mount Tacoma—complemented the attractive landscape and scenery surrounding the mighty Columbia. These are massive, isolated peaks, glowing like splinters of silver in the sun and soaring high above the rest of the mountain range at their feet. We got off the boat at Kalama,

Washington, a promising city of the future but one which at the moment has been severely reduced by a fire.[1] We then boarded a waiting train and traveled through virgin forests to Tacoma.

Virgin forests, yes, but sadly to say again we saw little but the destruction that the builders of the railroad have brought as a by-product. In order to clear a path for the tracks, they cut down the trees. To get rid of the trees they don't even bother to push them back into the woods; instead they heap them up along the roadbed to be burned. Then the fires rage to the right and left, laying bare a wide belt of land on both sides of the railroad tracks. All of these charcoaled trees provide stark witness to the negligence which is squandering this valuable raw material. Only occasionally did we get to look at a thick forest, usually a place where a brook or river is flowing from it.

A number of pretty settlements did interrupt the monotony of the black forest with their clearings,

[1] Kalama, thirty-eight miles west of Portland, lay on a flat just at the confluence of the Columbia and Kalama rivers. The town's growth began in 1873 when the Northern Pacific completed its Pacific Division from Kalama to Tacoma, 105 miles northward. When the Villard Party made the journey, the trip from Portland to Kalama was by boat, but later in 1883 the Northern Pacific finished laying track from Portland to a point opposite the city on the Columbia River. A giant ferry, capable of transporting a whole train, was put into operation at that time to carry the cars and engines across the river, thus connnecting Puget Sound with the East. Winser, *The Great Northwest*, 261–262.

fields, and meadows. If ever any one of us should be talked into turning our backs on Europe to settle somewhere in the Far West, it would rather be here than on the treeless prairies between the Mississippi and the Yellowstone. Here we feel so at home. For here the railroad was the herald of civilization.[2]

The mighty Mount Tacoma accompanied us all the way. Several of our party had left the group as soon as we arrived at Portland in order to climb the mountain under the guidance of Professor Zittel, a geologist for the State of Oregon. On the climb are the painter Dielitz, von Bunsen, von Schloss, and several others.[3] As we disembarked from our train at Tacoma, we caught sight of Puget Sound, over

[2] Leaving Kalama, the tracks of the Pacific Division of the Northern Pacific Railroad ran through the densely forested valley of the Cowlitz River, a region only recently opened to settlement and still scarcely occupied. From the Cowlitz Valley the road followed the Chehalis and Nisqually valleys to Tacoma. *Appleton's General Guide*, 448–449.

[3] Mount Tacoma, now known as Mount Rainier, was one of the Pacific Northwest's most majestic peaks. Its glacier-scarred walls challenged climbers and intrigued geologists. A long description of the mountain by Bailey Willis who had climbed it in 1882 was in the Winser guidebook used by the German party. Herr Mohr's pen slipped when he wrote of "Professor Zittel, a geologist from the state of Oregon." K. A. Zittel was a world-renowned geologist and explorer of note, but he was a professor at the University of Munich and a member of Villard's party from Germany. Konrad Dielitz was a German artist commissioned by Henry Villard to re-cord the journey, Baron Georg von Bunsen a member of the Imperial Reichstag, and Herr von Schloss a statesman and banker. Winser, *The Great Northwest*, 267–271.

which Mount Tacoma stands watch. This is a former volcano that now has a lake in its crater. Surrounding the rim are three sharp peaks. It glowed with a reddish color in the evening sunshine.

To the accompaniment of music we drove through the town. It is very unfinished in appearance and still has the look of deprivation, but everywhere there is evidence of its youth and growth. Most of the houses are built up on the hills. They stand in patterns that mark where streets will eventually be built rather than along well-defined streets. From the hills we drove down to the lower part where there is a landing dock for steamships, which the trains can reach directly.

The Sound itself seemed to widen into infinity, an unforgettable view. At the dock Henry Villard gave a speech and was enthusiastically cheered. Music played and the locomotives chimed in with their whistles as if they belonged to the orchestra.[4]

Then we boarded the *Queen of the Pacific*, a

[4] At Tacoma no parade had been planned, but Villard placed himself at the head of an impromptu procession, with a band blaring music behind him, and his guests falling into line as they walked from the train to the dock where they were to board a steamer for the voyage around Puget Sound. All were impressed, as was Herr Mohr, with the sunset over the mountain peaks. Even the cynical correspondent of the *New York Times*, who had found little good to say about anything from the food to the parades, wrote that "No such panorama of sea, sky, mountain and shore, I take it, can be found anywhere else upon the globe." *New York Times*, October 14, 1883, p. 5.

Tacoma and Mount Rainier

steamer belonging to the Oregon and California Navigation Company. To give you an idea of the activity of this steamer, I might mention that in the month of May alone it was dispatched twenty-seven times from San Francisco to coastal ports. Built in New York, she is the most beautiful ship on the Pacific Ocean. We were reminded of the *Elbe*.[5] Since this ship does not have to endure winter storms like those the Atlantic steamers encounter, her deck has been built up more. All across it are staterooms, and there is a freedom of movement for the passengers that makes sailing on her very pleasant. The first class saloon is elegant. It is located in the middle and runs all the way across the ship with a narrow extension running back to the stern. In the staterooms there are three bunks, one on top of the other, but with ample room for each of the three sleeping passengers who occupy the stateroom.

We glided out into the Sound by moonlight on water smooth as a mirror. Mount Tacoma became gray and ghostly as the fog and smoke rose up around it.

During the night we anchored in front of Esquimault.[6] The bay in which we anchored is divided off from the sea by a high ridge on which

[5] The *Elbe* was the North German Lloyd steamship that had carried the Villard Party across the Atlantic.

[6] Esquimault, a harbor and settlement three miles from Victoria, was the headquarters port of the English Pacific Squadron. Normally from three to five war vessels were anchored there. *Appleton's General Guide*, 448–449.

Victoria has been built. An English naval squadron was also lying at anchor in the bay, its largest ship being the *Swiftsure*.

A line-up of carriages was waiting to take us to Victoria, British Columbia. The beautiful landscape, rather dusty and burned now at the close of the dry season, did not show itself at its best. And with the sky overcast the view also was poor. Off in the distance was Mount Baker with its snow-capped peak, and in the West the mighty Olympia Range, an extension of the Cascade Mountain Range which is broken at The Dalles by the Columbia River. But all this scenery was hidden from our eyes. In fact, we could hardly distinguish at what point on the horizon the gray sky was separated from the gray and dismal sea.

The terrain in Victoria is hilly which gives the city a more interesting variety and breaks up the monotonous regularity that marks many American cities. Occasionally, though, is one reminded that he is no longer on the soil of the Republic but under the royal scepter of Queen Victoria. Victoria's population is very mixed. In addition to white men there are Chinese, black men, and Indians, who seem to have settled down here, some of them even donning European clothes. But according to reports they lead a rather lowly life. All of the stores were selling Indian handiwork to tourists, some of it genuine, some imitation, and all of it at high prices.

For about an hour and a half we drove around in

Victoria on its excellent streets. What a pity that we had to see the whole thing in such bad sunlight. It all looked so much like home—the houses out in the country with their lovely yards, the shade trees—mostly oaks—the hills, and the fields.[7] Though it lies quite a distance from the ocean, Victoria has become a summer resort for visitors from Portland. It certainly is not a bathing area; the cold polar currents that run along the coast during the summer make the water too cold for bathing. In winter, the situation is just the opposite because a southern current washes the coast and warms it. The prevailing winds are also greatly affected by these currents.

At ten o'clock in the morning we lifted anchor to begin our journey home.[8] At this point we were almost seven thousand miles from home. Even if we

[7] Victoria then claimed a population of 7,000, including many Indians. A water works and gas works gave it a modern touch, while a garrison of British troops stationed there added to the colorful Old World appearance for which it was to become famous. *Appleton's General Guide*, 449.

[8] A second contingent of the Villard Party, traveling on the steamer *North Pacific* and following an opposite course around Puget Sound, had a less pleasant time when it arrived a short time later. At a luncheon given for Victoria officials, the provincial prime minister, William Smith, predicted that someday the western United States would rebel against domination by the East and suggested that it might join Canada. These half-facetious remarks seriously offended the American guests who took their patriotism seriously. OUTRAGEOUS SPEECH, headlined the *Chicago Tribune*, September 19, 1883, p. 1.

were to travel continuously, day and night, with perfect ship connections in New York, it would still take more than three weeks to get home. Such a thought can make the heart full. We had just had mail from home, but even this was not much consolation. We need to remind ourselves that it has been only one month since we left German soil. This continual pressure to move on and ever-changing impressions alternating with terrible monotony are unavoidable when covering such colossal distances. But they have distorted all concepts of time. Have we been gone for weeks or has it been for months? Just how long has it been since we have left our families and friends in Germany? One has to stop and think.

You see, there was a somewhat melancholy mood in our party. We have been together through rain and shine, over land and sea, always held together faithfully under the banner of Henry Villard, but tomorrow part of our group will depart for San Francisco, on board the steamer *Columbia* . . . . We can truly say that we have kept a good fellowship among us all the way.

Probably if we had experienced common dangers, or had struggled for our survival or even if we had been forced to make our own arrangements, we might have become a more closely knit group. It is possible we would have become better acquainted with each other and with our friends who joined us in New York. But all our cares and troubles in life

were taken care of. We never had to think at all
about where we would get food and drink, or when
we were supposed to travel to the next stop, or even
how we were going to travel, what time we were to
depart, when were we expected to arrive, where we
could sleep, and how we could find lodging. Thus
everyone could ride along in a completely self-cen-
tered fashion without even thinking about the man
next to him.

Only after experiencing this in all its details is it
possible to realize just how much thought and planning went into it, and what mental and material
means were needed to carry out this expedition. By
looking into the face of Henry Villard, steady as the
Olympian calm, one could not possibly believe that
the effort behind this trip was any more difficult
than the enjoyment. I only hope that this extraordinary experience has not had any ill effects on our
character. Göethe has said that one can stand anything, except a continuous row of beautiful days. In
this case, I think he is wrong.

I have not noticed any evidence of bad moods,
irritability, grouchiness, pugnacity, or any sort of
unpleasantness. All of us have always gotten along
excellently with each other. The small incidents of
selfishness were of a strictly harmless nature. If, in
the close quarters of our Pullman sleeping cars,
someone figured out that by getting up early he
could enjoy an undisturbed quarter hour in the
washroom, it usually happened to him as it did to

Bismarck with Windthorst: somebody had gotten there just a little bit earlier.[9]

Even when it came down to the matter of giving speeches, there was no evidence of personal ambition on anybody's part. A committee had been set up to settle these matters and on the whole there were not very many speeches, either from the Germans or from the Englishmen.

On the way home!

The *Queen of the Pacific* carried us south again. On this return trip we could see what was hidden in darkness when we came north. The islands in the Sound were covered with trees, with a house here and there on one of them. We also see the island that caused the seemingly endless squabble over the San Juan Question. The island belongs to the Haro or San Juan Archipelago. On its west side it is divided from Vancouver Island by the Haro Strait and on its east side it is divided from the American mainland by the Rosario Strait. In which strait was the channel whose middle, according to the treaty

[9] Ludwig Windthorst, leader of the German Center Party, was principally responsible for Bismarck's failure to extend national authority over the Catholic Church. In the parliamentary debates over the Chancellor's moves to counteract the Church's newly announced doctrine of Papal Infallibility, he used his superior skills as a tactician to out-maneuver and out-argue Bismarck and force the withdrawal of some of the decrees. Windthorst was known as the only man in Germany who had won a personal victory over the Chancellor. Emil Ludwig, *Bismarck: the Story of a Fighter* (Boston, 1927), 416-419.

of 1846, was to form the boundary between the two countries? The island was claimed for both countries by squatters. The squatters fought among each other and the two countries could come to no agreement. Then Kaiser Wilhelm was called in to arbitrate the dispute. In 1872 he ruled that the island belonged to the Americans. Professor Gneist took part in the studies leading to this verdict and now he could see it with his own eyes—something he would never have dreamed of at the time he was working out the agreement.[10]

By noon we reached the newly established town of Port Townsend where everything points to a great enterprising spirit. Several hours later we approached Seattle, nestled along a slope on the right side of the Sound. Before long a flag-waving steamer

[10] The Oregon Treaty of 1846 stipulated that the boundary follow the main channel between the mainland and Vancouver Island. A dispute arose at once whether that "main channel" was the Canal de Haro or the Strait of Rosario; the acceptance of the former would give the United States the strategically important San Juan Islands while the latter would award them to England. In the Treaty of Washington, 1871, the matter was referred to the German Emperor for arbitration. He in turn referred the dispute to two jurists and a geographer who solicited help from other experts. One called upon for aid was Dr. Rudolf Gneist, himself an eminent jurist and professor of law at the University of Berlin. After studying water depth and the ebb-and-flow of the tides, as well as needed documents, the commissioners finally favored the Canal de Haro, thus placing the San Juan archipelago within the United States. Today's steamers confirm the wisdom of the Emperor's report by using the Haro Channel. Keith A. Murray, *The Pig War* (Tacoma, 1968).

moved toward us, and then another, blaring with music. Enthusiastic greetings were exchanged as one steamer after the other, large and small, plied back and forth, each filled with flags and people. In the background was plenty of cannon fire, and best of all, glorious sunshine. The steamers maneuvered into two columns to form an escort for us. The view became more and more interesting.[11] We could make out some stately buildings, but scattered between them were the familiar wooden houses, built in varying styles and surrounded by the tree stumps remaining from the virgin forests.

Amidst thunderous cannon fire we glided up to the landing dock, swamped by a crowd of people waiting patiently and orderly until the ship could finally be securely tied up. As a matter of fact we arrived too early and all the preparations had not yet been completed. We were to arrive a day later in order to take part in a local fair. But we missed all that because the program of our excursion had been advanced by one day. So everything had to be done in a rush; but if the citizens of Seattle were disturbed by this, they surely did not show it.

[11] Port Townsend, on the west side of Townsend Bay, was the port of entry for the Puget Sound customs district and seemed destined to become the region's leading city. Instead its boom collapsed in 1889-1890, as Seattle forged into a dominant position. At this time some 4,000 persons lived in Seattle, many of them engaged in the lumber trade. Villard was greatly pleased by the enthusiasm with which his party was greeted, and the parade of vessels that was formed to escort his ship to the dock. Villard, *Memoirs*, II, 312.

The celebration occurred on a plain in front of a beautiful building, the Academy, an institution of higher learning. We found our way there, some by carriage and some on foot. By way of comparison Seattle goes beyond anything we have seen so far of the growing, thriving American cities. A long broad street parallel to the Sound is rimmed by store after store. Here and there are beautiful buildings made of brick with large show windows and architectural ornamentation. For the most part, however, the houses are of wood and the streets unpaved.

The wooden buildings seem to have been thrown up overnight. In the course of time no doubt all the wooden houses will be replaced with stone, the streets will be paved, and the plank sidewalks will give way to asphalt or cinders.

This fall Seattle will finally be linked in with the American railroad system by a track leading to Portland via Tacoma. For some time the people of this city have felt discriminated against and since their warmest desires are now to be fulfilled, our visit turned out to be a kind of celebration of reconciliation on the festival square.

Henry Villard spoke good-humoredly, making excuses on behalf of the Northern Pacific for its neglect of Seattle and praising the Seattle people for their incomparable energy. Next a young lady stepped up to the podium. She was the daughter of the president of the Academy, or University as the higher education institutions are called here. Both

Courtesy of the Washington State Historical Society

Seattle, Washington Territory

Taken from Bagley's *History of Seattle*

in delivery and in content she gave a masterful speech of thanks to Henry Villard for his concern about culture, the sciences, education, and for the large amount of financial support he had contributed to the University.[12] Everybody agreed that this

[12] The University of Washington, struggling to overcome official indifference since its founding in 1861, seemed beyond hope in 1882 when a hostile legislature refused to appropriate any funds for its support. In this emergency Henry Villard gave the school $4,000, thus allowing it to operate

speech from one of the fair sex deserved the first prize in a speechmaking contest arranged for that occasion. On demand from the crowd, Carl Schurz spoke briefly, optimistically, and to the point as usual. He warned against a truly barbarian destruction of the American forests. Anybody who through careless neglect wreaks any destruction on the rich natural resources of this land must be brought to justice.

Both land and sea were aglow with the evening hues of red as the speeches concluded. Beef and mutton were roasting on a spit to be served at the public festival following later. As for us, a lightweight carriage drawn by two lively horses whisked us through the crowds down the steep slopes, over the sandy streets, and to our ship. It is something to behold the way Americans in the West know how to ride and to drive. An American's relationship to his horse is one of complete trust. Whenever things threaten to go wrong, the driver just whispers a few soft and friendly words—"Now boys, get on there," or something like that—and everything turns out all right. Nobody ever thinks of using a whip.

It was already dark as we boarded our steamer, now illuminated by electric lights. On board I once again met Mayor Struve of Seattle, whom I first met

until the legislature reconsidered its decision. He later recorded that the address of the young lady which so impressed Herr Mohr was "the most eloquent and the most moving" of any he heard on the entire trip. Villard, *Memoirs*, II, 312.

at the ceremony of the last spike. He was somewhat unhappy about the total vanity of Seattle's preparations for receiving us. But Henry Villard and all the rest of us assured him that in no other place had we received such a splendid welcome as here in Seattle. A major contributing factor, of course, was the location and natural beauty of his city.

As our ship left the harbor, we sat down to dinner on board. Following the meal, Mr. Salomon, the former Governor of the State of Wisconsin, spoke on behalf of the Germans and German-Americans in the group, expressing our gratitude to our host Henry Villard.

Professor Gneist handed the written tribute to Henry Villard with fitting remarks.[13]

Then Henry Villard thanked us in a moving commentary, warmly praising his German origin. He stated that the cultivation of things German lay very close to his heart but said it was the American nation as none other in the world that offered a man the opportunity to realize his full potential.

The gratitude which we expressed here did indeed come from the bottom of our hearts. Many of

[13] All speakers at the final banquet were already known to Herr Mohr. Henry G. Struve, mayor of Seattle and former attorney for the Northern Pacific, he had met at the "last spike" ceremony. Edward Salomon, German-born Civil War governor of Wisconsin and currently a leader of New York's German community, he had seen when he first arrived in New York. Dr. Rudolf Gneist had been a member of the Villard Party since it left Bremen.

us were in the United States for the first time, and most were greatly surprised by what we saw. And even though we have seen it in tremendous haste, we have seen enough of this New World to form a good idea about the peculiarities of its nature and its people as contrasted to Europe.

The undertaking which Henry Villard heads, or rather the complex of undertakings which he heads, is certainly one of the most extensive anywhere, even in this vast, bustling land. Surely his activity will always remain one of the significant accomplishments in the history of the American Northwest. It is quite impossible in one month to judge the future ramifications of his accomplishment. About one thing, however, there can be no doubt: a great future for vast territories has been unlocked here by Henry Villard's railroad.

13

On the Way Home

Walla Walla
Tuesday morning, September 18, 1883

As you may have gathered by now, we are truly on our way home, traveling back eastward. Once again, a railroad car is our home and in our cramped quarters the line *"Mein Vaterland könnt grösser sein"* [my fatherland could be larger] becomes our theme. But experienced as we now are, even in the swaying railroad car we are able to dress and undress in the smallest places.

At first we were overcome by a feeling of imprisonment as we settled down once more in our Pullman Sleeping Car. But then we do have access to the dining car, which also serves as kitchen and storeroom. By German standards our accommodations are luxurious. We follow the American pattern of eating. This means meat, fish, and eggs with morning coffee or tea; light lunch at one o'clock; and dinner not until seven o'clock in the evening. Every day we get fresh, hot bread. But although the Americans mean well, we who care about our stomachs would really prefer what they call "stale bread." Our car has a very good wine cellar, with Bordeaux, Rhine wine, Moselle, and Champagne.

Then too Milwaukee beer and mineral water are available.

So we are again living as one big happy family. We are careful never to talk about politics. Anyway the scattered reports we have received from Europe by telegraph are often incomprehensible. In Portland we at least were able to fill in a little by reading the newspapers. There we read that the stock of the Northern Pacific Railroad has fallen sharply on Wall Street in New York and that our trip is being termed a mockery by the press.[1] On the whole we are so preoccupied by the new experiences that such news has little effect on us. We have learned, though, that Henry Villard will be leaving us at Helena to return directly to New York, where he is desperately needed at this time.

But I should begin this return trip back where it started—at Portland. We left Portland on the *Wide West*, which carried us down the Willamette River and on to the Columbia. At first the shores were flat and the river valley very wide. We passed by Vancouver, one of the oldest settlements and a former fort.[2] But then the mountains closed in—wide ridges

[1] For the Northern Pacific's financial troubles at this time see the "Historical Introduction," pp. lxvi–lxx. The *New York World* was particularly critical of the Villard Party, charging that the railroad was spending $250,000 to entertain the visitors, when the money could have been better spent on its workers and stockholders.

[2] Fort Vancouver, one of the historic sights encountered by the party as it began its water journey on the *Wide West*, a vessel owned by the Oregon Railway and Steam Naviga-

alternating with hanging cliffs. We were tempted to compare this river with our own Rhine, but here everything is so much larger, both the river and the mountains. The Columbia flowed along in complete solitude. Occasionally we saw a steamer or a small boat, or maybe a canoe, but hardly a settlement along the banks.

Very suddenly the scenery changed; the heights receded from the waterline and were replaced by strange terraces, almost artificial in appearance, built up and back from the river. Eons ago this great river bored its way through the Cascade Mountains, creating wild and foaming rapids and powerful whirlpools below. Since a ship cannot cross these, we were taken by rail around the rapids. From the bank high above we could get a wonderful view of the enormous tides of raging water. Involuntarily we were reminded of Niagara Falls. Above the rapids we once more boarded a steamer. A canal is now being built around the cascades so that this hindrance to ship traffic will soon be surmounted.[3] We continued on the river until dark, to a point up-

tion Company, had served between 1825 and 1845 as the western headquarters of the Hudson's Bay Company. At this time the city of Vancouver was emerging about it.

[3] At the point where the Columbia River cut through the Cascade Mountains the water fell rapidly, creating what a guidebook called "a seething caldron of foam." A portage railroad conveyed goods and passengers around the falls, but was destined to be replaced by a canal, known as the Cascade Locks, then under construction. *Appleton's General Guide*, 448.

stream just below The Dalles, which we had earlier
visited by train. At this point the railroad picked us
up. Then we took leave of the river that had filled
us with such magnificent memories.

Take a look on the map where Walla Walla lies
and you will know from where these lines are written this morning. The depot is some distance from
town and I must say that from this distance the
town looks like a frightfully desolate spot, but a
crowd of well-dressed people is waiting here to welcome us. A musical band is playing to wake Henry
Villard from his sleep. And on the platform awaiting us is a row of beautiful carriages, some of the
four-in-hand type, that would not be out of place at
any royal palace in the world.

In the Rocky Mountains
Wednesday, September 19, 1883

YESTERDAY MORNING we were driven into Walla
Walla in handsome carriages, with a local citizen as
our guide.[4] He performed his job zealously, always
in the best interests of his town. "It is a wonderful
country, Sir." He assured us that on the Pacific
Coast there is no other region like this one. Accord-

[4] Walla Walla, founded just after the Indian wars of 1855-
1858, was in the center of a rich farming valley beneath the
Blue Mountains. Although it lay in an arid plain, the town
was shaded by trees and was notable for its orchards and
gardens. Its population was 5,500 at this time, and business
booming as the agricultural regions in the vicinity were
brought into production. Winser, *The Great Northwest*, 223.

ing to him, everything grows here even without rain. Potatoes come so-o-o big and yet no drop of rain has ever fallen on them. As a matter of fact this area has indeed been without rain for some time. We viewed a small exhibit of local agricultural products above which a sign read: "180 days no rain."

Walla Walla is much nicer than it appeared from the depot. It is a town of 5,000 inhabitants with a main street wider than one would find in all of Bremen. We saw a few brick houses, some with architectural decorations, and amongst them wooden houses that looked no better than booths at a fair.

The official reception took place in the Court House, but by the time we arrived the hall of this large building was already filled. So I wandered about on the street in search of a barbershop. Suddenly I caught sight of a troop of mounted Indians, two hundred strong, men and women, all on horses, painted and adorned, screaming and shouting. These were the Umatilla Indians from a reservation nearby. Even though we had earlier seen the Crow Indian performances in Greycliff, this sight still made a deep impression on me.

At the barbershop I fell into the hands of another German. He came from the vicinity of Hamburg and has been here for three years. Besides being a barber he also farms some land and has two houses in town which bring him ten dollars a month in rent. He owns lots to build two more. So he is doing well and has written to his relatives that they should come over and join him since there is still good land to be bought cheaply. There are many other Germans here also. In my opinion they do very well out here. They are hard workers and save their money—far better than the Americans.

Back at the Court House, Schurz spoke about the Indian question, which is very close to his heart. Senator Chapeaurouge spoke for the foreign visitors and his contribution was well applauded.[5] "We are now heading for home," he said. "We will tell our friends that just as the wealth of America is infinite, so too is the hospitality of her people. If we tell them how well we were received here, our listeners will think of the tales of *One Thousand and One Nights*. But this analogy does not fit because in America there is no darkness, no night, no dream. Everything is bright daylight and everybody is awake and lively." He closed then with thanks to Henry Villard for having offered us the opportunity to see something of America with the assurance that this trip has brought out the warmest feelings for the land and for her cities.

At noon we left Walla Walla and rode back to Wallula Junction where we again picked up the main railroad line. In the afternoon we crossed the

[5] Senator Charles de Chapeaurouge was the official representative of the city of Hamburg in the Villard Party. Carl Schurz obviously used this occasion, as he had others on the trip, to plead for a humanitarian policy toward the Indians and for forest conservation.

sandy flats on our way to Ainsworth. The town is located at the mouth of the Snake River, which drains hinterlands reaching back to the great Salt Lake. Here we crossed back to the northern side of the river on ferry steamboats, a long and tedious operation.[6]

The train stopped on the barren prairie and we got out to walk to the crossing point on the river. A few of our comrades made use of the opportunity to go swimming in the cold Snake River. One of the Englishmen has made it a point to take a swim, if possible, in every river we cross. He has twenty-six in his log at this time. The ferry had to make several trips before it had transported all of the cars in our train. So we climbed aboard the upper deck of the ferry and rode back and forth across the river. From our spot high up in the fresh air above the river we had a nice view over these strange surroundings and time passed fairly quickly. It was already late in the afternoon and the sun lingered as it slowly set. The yellowish brown sand flats and sage grass, which had earlier looked so unbearable in the bright sunshine, were now bathed in a softer light. The hills reminded one of Italy, the entire region bearing characteristics of that land. On one side of the river

[6] A branch line of the Oregon Railway and Navigation Company connected Walla Walla with Wallula on the Columbia River. Here the travelers transferred to the Northern Pacific Railroad. At Ainsworth, where the line crossed the Snake River, the slow ferrying of the cars that had delayed the outward trip was duplicated.

stood a desolate Indian tent with half-dressed, dirty human beings inside. Beyond, an Indian riding his pony was chasing a herd of cattle. Also in view was Ainsworth with its miserable colony of workers encamped to build the bridge.[7]

Finally, by evening, all of our cars had been brought over and we continued on our way to the Rocky Mountains.

This morning we awoke at Sandpoint, right on Lake Pend d'Oreille, and after breakfast we sailed forth on a steamer to take our cruise, refreshed by the splendid weather and the cool morning air. The lake is completely enclosed by mountains. Along its shores are several saw mills indicating that the great wealth of its forests is being used. After our return we paid our respects to Henry Villard, who was not feeling very well and did not make the excursion.

Our train climbed higher and higher into the Rocky Mountains until we reached Clark's Fork, whose banks we had found so charming on our trip out. The stream, flowing back and forth between walls of stone, is so enchanting that it ought to be

[7] Ainsworth was at this time little more than a construction camp. Situated on a sandy plateau in a sage-brush desert, with not a single green tree or bush to relieve the grey landscape, it was composed largely of temporary shacks housing the workers who were building the railroad bridge across the Snake. Even the guidebook author could describe it as nothing but "uninteresting." Winser, *The Great Northwest*, 220.

decorated by some old fortresses, castle ruins, and mysterious old towns. The river here is perfectly suited to such a fairy-tale setting. On both sides of the river the mighty, towering mountains enhance the charm of the river itself.

After dark we arrived at Ravali, on the Flathead reservation. From here we will make an excursion tomorrow to Mount MacDonald.[8]

Ravali
Thursday evening, September 20, 1883

THAT WAS a strenuous day, a complete disappointment, and yet I am happy that we made the trip to Mount MacDonald. We did not find what we were looking for, but we did have a chance to observe the scenery of the Rocky Mountains, which I would not have wanted to miss. According to the report of Director Pumpelly, there was supposed to be a marvelous view from Mount MacDonald in the Mission Range just fifteen miles from the depot at Ravali.[9]

[8] Villard planned this stop at the tiny hamlet of Ravali (spelled "Ravalli" today) because he had been told that the view from the summit of nearby Mt. MacDonald, 9,800 feet tall and the highest peak in the Mission Range, provided a superb view of the entire Rocky Mountain area. He had been misled, for as his guests were to find, the journey was hardly worth the effort.

[9] Raphael Pumpelly, a well-known geologist who had served as director of the United States Geological Survey, was between 1881 and 1884 in charge of the government's Northern Transcontinental Survey which was making a detailed examination of the northern portions of the trans-Mississippi West.

Henry Villard wanted to offer something spectacular to those of his guests who chose not to take the San Francisco route home. He thought he could provide them with one more pleasure and in addition bring to the attention of the world one more attraction of the Northern Pacific route. Thus he had a pathway cut through the forest so that we could climb Mount MacDonald on the backs of Indian ponies.

We arrived last evening at the Ravali depot, situated in a pleasant virgin forest. In fact the railroad depot is Ravali. We soon discovered a bonfire off in the distance, evidence of other inhabitants. At first we could not make out who they were or what they were doing. We sent out a reconnaissance party and they discovered a gathering of Indians encamped around a fire and gambling passionately. The Indians became somewhat angry at the idea of having uninvited guests. Our party then inquired of them where the wagons were that were to meet us and take us on the excursion. At least a dozen teams were needed to take us out and we had not been able to find a trace of them.

In the morning when it was time to go, we climbed down from the railroad embankment to the hard dusty ground below. Before we had taken twenty steps we were all full of dust, but then we noticed our wagons and their teams trotting toward us. We climbed aboard and galloped off across the sticks and stones. The road was miserable, and our wagon was tilted at an impossible angle. At such a moment one was lucky to be sitting on the upper side. We passed through a hollow and climbed a series of hills. Finally we reached a plateau. The dust, fear, and skidding were now over. A wide plain sprawled before us, forming a prairie between the two mountain ranges. Down beyond the plain the mountains rose proudly to the heavens—gigantic mountains of 10,000 feet, some with snow covered peaks.

Then we headed for Mount MacDonald. All of our wagons appeared to be in a race and we marveled once again at the care and skill of American drivers. They are the owners and well acquainted with the frightening terrain, but in this confusion they also had to look out for other wagons. Axles, spokes and wheels, everything seemed so thin and fragile, and the harnesses seemed so patched together; yet nothing broke or tore.

A big building[10] which attracted our curiosity

[10] St. Ignatius Mission, founded by the Society of Jesus in 1854 in the valley of Flathead Lake, was a thriving institution and one of the foremost purveyors of Christianity and the white-man's culture to the Indians of the Northwest. Over the years a sizeable village had taken shape, with a school, flour mills, homes for workers, and an imposing array of church structures. These were partly supported by the federal government, which paid the mission $100 yearly for each of the hundred or more children in its school. Its activities received much favorable publicity that summer when it was visited by a congressional committee under Senator George G. Vest of Missouri. William L. Davis, *A History of St. Ignatius Mission* (Spokane, 1954).

St. Ignatius Mission, Montana Territory

stood up on the hill in the middle of the prairie. As we came closer, we discovered that it was a church and that another large building stood next to it with several log cabins clustered about it. These made up an Indian mission, St. Ignatius. Besides the church, there was a home for the fathers, the school, and several huts. We rode right past this village, but what we could see made a good impression. One is struck by the great power of the Catholic Church in working effectively with these wild men.

We hastened on farther. The wagons were now spread out into a mile-long line. Scattered far and wide out on the prairie was a herd of cattle. Even though the prairie looked so natural and untouched, in fact it was cut up by a network of irrigation ditches built for artificial watering. Not far from the mission we waded through a good-sized stream that is tapped for irrigation purposes.

Suddenly we discovered in the distance a herd of horses driven by half-breed Indians. The paths of these Indian ponies and our wagons inclined closer and closer together until finally we met at the bank of a creek. Everybody got off and grabbed a pony to mount. All who were willing to ride in a saddle could ride up the spur, as the English call it, which Mount MacDonald sends out. A freshly cut roadway followed along the backbone of the spur, through the woods, and as we ascended we gained a nice view of the prairie behind us. It stretched like a sea below us, yellowish brown, the grass was all dried up though still usable as fodder for the cattle.

We rode for several hours in a long line up the mountain. The forest was stately, without underbrush, producing splendid pine trees. At one point two of the ponies slid off the road when their riders grabbed them too tightly on the bridles. Gradually the forest grew thinner and we could tell that we were several thousand feet higher up than the spot where we got on our horses. The landscape was similar to all high mountain regions, here a small dark green lake, there the remains of a snow drift. Then we dismounted and began our journey on foot, supplied with climbing sticks. The path was quite steep and meandered past a chasm with deep deposits of snow.

We still did not have a good comprehensive view down into this "valley of incomparable beauty." Our geologist, Professor Zittel,[11] was very near the front, a long way ahead of me; but before long several of our more adventuresome fellows came strolling back down, maintaining that there was no more to see a thousand feet higher than right here. I decided not to climb farther just to find out whether they were right or not, and decided instead to begin the descent on foot from that point.

Still it was a long hike. The hope of getting a

[11] Professor K. A. Zittel of the University of Munich, a famed geographer, was capitalizing on the opportunity provided him by Henry Villard to learn more about American land forms. He had already visited Mount Rainier.

good lunch for all this strenuous activity kept up my spirits for some of the time. Finally a party of picnickers waved me over. Indeed they did provide a lunch, but it was parceled out in tiny little portions. By some mixup they brought the food and drink from only one of the dining cars. So the rule was, go easy on the provisions and starve if you must! Go hungry at the very time when we had earned the right to eat a good meal. All each one got was a sandwich, an orange, and a teaspoonful of cognac to save us from slow death by starvation.

I continued down the mountain. Sometimes I had company; sometimes I was alone; the entire way was very tedious. At long last the forest came to an end, revealing a hazy afternoon. Off in the distance were forest fires, which accounted for the illusion when we mistook some waving grass for a lake. Finally I reached the spot where our wagons were standing and discovered that part of our group had already left. Some of the Englishmen, as well as a representative of the Austro-Hungarian embassy, were still waiting for the rest of the tourists. They had refreshed themselves by taking a bath in the creek, but they had had nothing to eat or drink.

As the sun was setting, we hastened off across the plain. Our only hope was that the mission would not refuse us a drink of water. So we drove up to the priest's house to be greeted by one of the brothers. He already had guessed our difficulty and brought along a pitcher of water and a glass. We gratefully accepted his offer. The brother was an appealing person, probably French or Belgian, but he spoke perfect English. The mission had a fine house and the church and school were also well kept up. The garden was neat and circling around this center were about twenty or thirty log cabins inhabited by the Indians. Their children went to school and received instruction in the Catholic religion. The conversation was brief.

Several of the men who were afraid of the strenuous climb up Mount MacDonald had driven over from Ravali, where our train stopped, to visit the school and the whole mission. One of the gentlemen brought back a notebook from the school with examples of writing by these Indian children. Some of them were done with extraordinary skill. The St. Ignatius Mission must be a significant place because I found it entered on the map in my Stieler Atlas, which has won the reputation of being the best map available and is used by everybody.[12]

We moved on and except for the anticipation of the miserable trip through that hollow, our drive was pleasant and refreshing. But even through that portion we made it safely and were heartily welcomed by our colleagues who had arrived back at the train earlier. Night had fallen, but one of the

[12] Apparently Herr Mohr carried with him the large, and very heavy, *Händ Atlas Über Alle Theile der Erde und Über das Weltgebäude* (Gotha, 1881 edn.) prepared by Adolf Stieler. This was a standard atlas in Germany, and did show the mission on its plate of the Montana area.

wagons was still missing. Eventually, however, our missing comrades arrived unharmed.

Our food had never tasted so good as this evening and tonight we surely had the right to make some heavy demands on our wine cellar. Our mood was not even dimmed by the report of our friends who were late in returning. They should have seen the "most magnificent scenery," which we less enterprising individuals had missed. But apparently they did not see much of anything, not even Flathead Lake. How the illusion about Mount MacDonald ever got started is a mystery. Anyway we can be grateful for an interesting day. After enjoying a comfortable life with no physical strain at all, the minor strains of today were good for us. Also, our party became better mixed socially.

We are rolling toward Yellowstone Park, have passed Helena and Bozeman and crossed those rugged mountain passes.

14

Yellowstone National Park

Mammoth Hot Springs, Wyoming Territory
National Hotel
Saturday, September 22, 1883

HERE we are in Yellowstone Park! Actually we are only at the entrance near Mammoth Hot Springs and you will notice from the letter heading that civilization has now reached the site of these wondrous, natural phenomena. We are in a wooden hotel, only half finished, but of colossal dimensions. It has a bar, parlors, and the beginnings of hot baths, all of first class caliber. It stands all alone in the wilderness, a few hundred feet from the hot springs.[1]

Yesterday at Livingston we first saw the natural cut through the mountain range where the Yellowstone River flows out of a narrow mountain valley. This cut is also the route of the Northern Pacific

[1] Earlier that year, in March, 1883, the Secretary of the Interior had leased six ten-acre plots within the park to the Yellowstone Park Improvement Company which agreed to build and operate hotels on each site. That at Mammoth Hot Springs was the first—and last—to be built by the company. It cost $150,000 and at the time the Villard Party arrived had just opened its doors, even though far from completed. Henry J. Winser, *The Yellowstone National Park. A Manual for Tourists* (New York, 1883), 91-92.

branch line that follows the river for some fifty miles. On our right was the Gallatin Range and on the left the Yellowstone Range. The final stop of the train was some eight miles from the hotel.[2]

This morning we were driven the last distance through the valley of the Gardiner River. The only town along the way was Gardiner City, which has just come into being. There a number of log cabins have been built as well as wooden buildings of the style now so familiar to us. Otherwise the scene was one of loneliness. Finally coming down a steep hill, we arrived at the hotel here, which stands 6,500 feet above sea level. Here also is the residence of the Park Inspector and a contingent of soldiers. Earlier their job was to keep the Indians in check, but now they keep the park free of tramps and vagabonds. It is said that when President Arthur was visiting the park recently,[3] some cowboys planned to take him

[2] Visitors to the park entering from the north left the main line of the Northern Pacific Railroad at Livingston and took special cars on the road's Park Branch Line fifty-one miles through the Yellowstone Valley to Cinnabar, where the tracks ended. From there carriages or wagons transported them an additional six miles to the entrance of the park at the newly founded hamlet of Gardiner.

[3] President Chester A. Arthur had spent several days fishing in the Yellowstone National Park in late August, during a six-week tour of the West. While he was there a correspondent reported from Ogden, Utah, that August 24 a gang of some sixty-five tough-looking men who had been camped on nearby Willow Creek left for the Yellowstone country. They planned, an informant revealed, to kidnap the President, conceal him in a cave in the park, and hold him for

captive and hold him for ransom. Apparently their plan withered as nothing came of it.

Our party has now been reduced to about fifty guests, including the German ambassador von Eisendecher and his wife and the English ambassador and his daughter.

This morning we were given our hotel accommodations. We then split into groups to prepare for the trip to the Upper Geyser Basin, where we will be spending several nights in tents. We had the choice whether we wanted to ride on horseback or in buggies. The horseback riders departed today and the rest of us will wait until tomorrow. This arrangement was necessary because of lack of adequate sleeping places, beds and bedding. It was not just the younger men who chose to go by saddle. Privy Councillor Hofmann rode a pony and our cook accompanied him as an aide because they wanted to collect water from the spouting geysers to take back home for analysis.[4] Carl Schurz, von Bun-

$500,000 ransom. The gang's leader, it was rumored, was a Texas badman with a price on his head, and most of the remainder were renegade cowboys or outlaws. General Philip H. Sheridan, who commanded the three hundred troops in the park, took immediate steps to intercept the kidnappers, but they never appeared. *New York Times*, August 26, 27, 30, September 1, 1883; *Chicago Tribune*, August 30, 1883, p. 1.

[4] Professor A. W. Hofmann of the University of Berlin, the world's best-known microscopist, was obviously using the opportunity to broaden his scientific knowledge, just as had Professor Zittel. The others mentioned were all, with the exception of Carl Schurz, German members of the

sen, City Councilman Weber, von Eisendecher,
Colonel von Xylander, Lieutenant Pertz, Senator
Gröning, and a majority of the Englishmen climbed
on horseback. Even several of the ladies were not a
bit afraid of the fifty mile horseback ride each way.
The others of us held back for the buggies. After
the others had taken off and we had had lunch, we
were able to spend some time at Mammoth Hot
Springs.

These springs rest like a Sphinx at the entrance
of a mysterious valley, 1,000 feet above the Gardiner River. They still excite the same questions that
have long been asked about them: How did this
wonder come about and how long will it last? One
soon gets the impression that the Mammoth Hot
Springs are in the process of dying. The formations
are among the most splendid and yet the most curious phenomena in the whole park. They consist of
three or four terraces formed on contoured lines
equally distant from the Gardiner River and running for several hundred feet along the sandstone of
the mountain. Such a heavy flow and such beautiful
formations do not exist in the other geyser areas of
the park.

Villard Party: Georg von Bunsen of the Prussian legislature and German Reichstag, Max Weber who also served
in the Reichstag, ambassador to the United States Baron
von Eisendecher, Colonel Emil Ritter von Xylander of the
Bavarian army, Lieutenant Pertz who was representing
the *Norddeutsche Allgemeine Zeitung*, and Albert Gröning
from Bremen.

Taken from Rudolf Cronau's *Von Wunderland zu Wunderland*

The Mammoth Hot Springs in Yellowstone Park

Yellowstone National Park was discovered only about a decade ago. It is true that since the beginning of the century there had been vague information about a land of marvelous phenomena, but this report seemed to be in the realm of fantasy. Only in the 1860s was there any reliable information. In 1870, the United States geologist Hayden was sent on an expedition to confirm these reports.[5] It is interesting to note that when the expeditionary team saw the first sign of steam from the geysers, they cried, "The Geysers, the Geysers!" Just as when Columbus cried "Land! Land!" as he caught sight of the New World and found his confidence confirmed by reality.

The name "National Park" could lead one to believe that the landscape surrounding the volcanic wonders has been artificially constructed to give it the look of a park. Nothing could be farther from the truth. Except for a few very primitive paths, a few dikes through the gulleys, and some timber

[5] Although the Yellowstone area had been visited by fur trappers in the 1830s, little was known of the region until three expeditions—in 1869, 1870, and 1871—disclosed its wonder to the world. The last and most important of these, led by Professor F. V. Hayden, reported so convincingly on the uniqueness of its attractions that Congress responded in 1872 by creating the first of the nation's national parks, the Yellowstone National Park. Its more than two million acres of land, Congress decreed, should be set aside "as a public park or pleasuring ground for the benefit and enjoyment of the people." Hiram M. Chittenden, *Yellowstone National Park* (Stanford, 1933 edn.), 57–67.

trestle bridges, not a thing has been touched. Being entirely on a high elevation—at least 6,000 feet and on the average 7,000 feet—Yellowstone Park is really a raised plateau.

The vegetation is, considering the high altitude, very well developed, especially in comparison to the Alps. The landscape is covered with huge fir forests and the trees are rarely crippled or stunted. But man has done devastating damage. Thousands of acres of forest land have already been burned and charcoaled tree trunks follow the railroad for miles and miles. Winter storms have subsequently broken down the rotting tree trunks all along the mountain ridges, and of course nobody can clear them away.

Tomorrow morning, Sunday, we will move out in the carriages.

Cinnabar on the Yellowstone
Wednesday, September 26, 1883

FOUR DAYS AGO I reported from the National Hotel of Yellowstone Park, telling about my joyful arrival at the gates of this wonderland. Today I am again back at the train and you won't believe how much dust and dirt we have swallowed, or how many bumps and bangs we have endured in the buggies, or what dubious and dangerous paths we have crossed in order to reach the Upper Geyser Basin and to return. If I ever felt like recommending the National Park to anyone, I would definitely tell him to wait a few years until the Improvement Company for the park has had time to do more work on this project. The plan is to equip the park with tramways, starting from the railroad.[6]

The National Hotel has been under construction since the twenty-sixth of May. Since the hotel will accommodate hundreds of people at one time, the owner is very interested in seeing the tram system completed. When that is accomplished, the strain and sweat needed to pay a visit to this wonder of nature will no longer be so great. For the time being we had to be satisfied with the buggies and riding horses. As you can imagine that did not increase the comfort of the trip any. But perhaps our appreciation was enhanced by the knowledge that to date only a very few people have had the opportunity to see the geysers of Yellowstone Park. This will soon change. Ever since the completion of the Northern

[6] The park narrowly escaped that fate. Patrick A. Conger of Iowa, who became its third superintendent in 1882, was disinterested in his task and a willing tool for self-seekers. His attitude encouraged a group of speculators organized as the Yellowstone Park Improvement Company to seek control of the choice scenic spots to be used for private gain, as well as to plan the hotels mentioned above. Congress, in March, 1883, frustrated these designs by ruling that no site of more than ten acres be leased to a single party, that troops patrol the park to prevent vandalism and the slaughter of game, and that ten assistant superintendents be employed as a police force. Corruption among these employees threatened these conservation efforts for a time, but at least the Improvement Company's plan to scar the countryside with tramways was blocked. Carriages and coaches were used exclusively in the park until the age of the motor car. Chittenden, *Yellowstone National Park*, 104–109.

Pacific to Livingston, the number of visitors has risen sharply. The Americans have great patience and endurance. And even when it is only for pleasure, a thousand mile ride on the railroad is for them no insuperable problem.

The leader of our expedition was Mr. Winser, information bureau chief of the Northern Pacific Railroad and the author of several valuable guide-books and manuals on the railroad and the park.[7] Mr. Winser was formerly the American consul in Coburg, Germany, so he speaks our language and in his own likeable and winning manner has often assisted us inexperienced travelers on our expedition.

Sunday we left the hotel in buggies. First we followed a path along the Hot Springs, then up a steep mountain.[8] From the top of the heights we could see the distant peaks of the Rocky Mountains. At our feet lay the broad plain, generally covered with

[7] Henry J. Winser had been commissioned by Henry Villard to prepare two guidebooks specifically for the visiting dignitaries, but with the understanding that they be sold to tourists thereafter: *The Great Northwest. A Guide-Book and Itinerary for the use of Tourists and Travellers over the Lines of the Northern Pacific Railroad* (New York, 1883), and *The Yellowstone National Park. A Manual for Tourists* (New York, 1883). Herr Mohr relied on both for much of his information.

[8] The route to the Upper Geyser Basin being followed by the visitors first ascended the face of Terrace Mountain over a road so steep that a half-day was required to traverse the two miles, as the horses had to stop and breathe at each new terrace. Winser, *Yellowstone National Park*, 25–26.

pines, but at one place well covered by deciduous trees. In their beautiful fall colors, they offered a sharp contrast to the dark pines. We moved on and again arrived in fir forests. The trunks had hardly any branches. The region had been devastated by fire; and charcoaled, dying forests truly created a melancholic, depressing mood.

Soon we discovered what bad roads and dirt are really all about. We were shaken up, covered with dirt, harried by danger, and even dumped out of the buggy.[9] On the road there was little to draw our attention and distract us from the miseries of the trip. On the whole, though, we maintained our good humor, or better said, it turned into a kind of gallows humor. Whenever we came to a spot where there was likelihood of slipping off the edge, somebody would begin to tell a horror story, or some grizzly joke. As we moved across each critical point, which often took more than a quarter of an hour, there was always some joking. At times we nearly fainted with laughter.[10]

---

[9] Herr Mohr expressed a general discontent when he complained of the wretched roads in the park. With a total congressional appropriation of $15,000, from which salaries and all other expenses had to be paid, little remained to build highways. "Considering the small amount that is annually appropriated by Congress for the maintenance of the National Park," wrote the author of the park's guidebook feelingly, "the roads between the principal points are kept in passable condition, but there is much room for improvement in this respect." Winser, *Yellowstone National Park*, 23.

[10] Having reached the summit of Terrace Mountain, the

Along the way we also started yelling back and forth between carriages and even got a scolding for it. But we endured this punishment as well as the miserable dust and dirt, the stale puns, and the rough road. Finally we did arrive at the geysers. I believe they were named "Norris Geyser Basin" in honor of the man who discovered them.[11] On a high spot not far away stood some tents with wash basins and towels as well as a pool of water. We got our instructions for spending the night there and then headed for the geysers.

From a distance we could see the clouds of mist rising from the basin. After a short walk through the woods we arrived at the edge of a sink hole and looked out over the basin. A wondrously strange sight!—a blinding white flat, in size such that it would take about ten minutes to walk around it. Everywhere there was boiling, cooking, hissing, croaking, steaming, and smoking. One hesitated to

road followed by the German party ran along the foot of vertical cliffs to the Middle Fork of the Gardiner River, then past the famed Obsidian Cliffs where the blocks of obsidian that littered the landscape had been splintered to form a glass-like highway surface. Beyond the cliffs the trail skirted Beaver Lake, ascended a pass over the highlands separating the Gallatin and Gibbon rivers, wandered through seven miles of open park land, and finally emerged at the Norris Geyser Basin. Winser, *Yellowstone National Park*, 27–29.

[11] The Norris Geyser Basin was named for P. W. Norris, the second superintendent of the park. Its entire surface was a mass of hot springs and small geysers, the most famous being the Monarch Geyser and the Minute Man Geyser. Chittenden, *Yellowstone National Park*, 93 note.

go forward and climb down to its very edge. All over, the hot water was oozing out of the earth. It spouted, sprinkled, and trickled; smoke billowed from every crack, and every minute a little geyser shot up. In one place the earth actually thundered as steam escaped from its depths. It sounded something like a locomotive when it blows off excess steam. Close by was a mud volcano. A thick gray brew was slowly bubbling and boiling. Then suddenly, as if it were a bad-humored trickster who wanted to play a joke on his visitors, it flung its mud water ten feet into the air and belched forth a hot, stinking smoke.

At the other end of the basin we climbed out to the upper rim and walked to a second basin which looked like a lovely park. Here we discovered other little geysers, all cooking and spurting with snow-white steam rising everywhere. The entire region was interlaced with these geysers.[12]

Having worked up a good appetite, we took our meal in the tent by the light of a single candle. This time we all practiced temperance because they had forgotten to bring the wine and beer along. From

[12] The party probably camped at Elk Park, a grassy meadow near the Norris Geyser Basin that was recommended as an overnight stopping-place by the guidebook. Konrad Dielitz, the German artist who accompanied the German group, was then thirty-eight years old. Gustav Schwab, head of the shipping firm of Oelrichs & Company that served as agents for the North German Lloyd Steamship Company, had joined the delegation in New York and been with them since.

outside came the light and the warmth of a huge campfire. Our entire party gathered around it, even the ladies who arrived after we did. The mood of the party got more and more exciting. Somebody started singing a German song and soon our painter, Dielitz, and Gustav Schwab formed the nucleus of a chorus, which sent out one German song after another into the dark night.

Opposite us around the fire were the drivers and their assistants, all adventurous looking fellows. Behind them stood the wagons to complete the perfect picture of an encampment. The daughter of the British Ambassador asked for *"Die Wacht am Rhein,"* and of course her request was fulfilled. Such a cheerful chord was struck and the mood lasted till quite late in the night. Then everyone went off in search of his bed. The older gentlemen were provided with portable beds, the others stretched out on mattresses laid on the ground. There were plenty of blankets for everybody.

We slept rather well, at least as well as possible considering the many who snored, the barking dogs, and the horses that kept trotting back and forth past the tent. (They had been turned loose to graze on the meadow.) The cold was less of a problem than we had expected at such a high altitude during this time of the year.

Monday morning before dawn we were dragged out of bed. One by one we crawled out of the tents, looked for a washbasin and towel, went to fetch our

own water from the brook, and then scurried to get
ourselves ready. We all helped each other, passing
around a whisk broom to brush off our clothes. Nobody bothered to polish and clean too much. We
were served breakfast and then all piled into the
buggies to continue our awful journey. The romantic atmosphere of the evening before, the morning
toilet, breakfast—everything taken together put us
in a good mood, which made the worst traveling
conditions seem like nothing. Soon we were working our way up a divide, then under terrifying conditions back down again. We forded rivers and
passed over newly broken roadways with their hor-
rendous dust. After an hour and a half we came to a
nicely built wooden building, an inn erected for the
use of travelers in the park. Here we found the
group that had left earlier on horseback. Now on
their return from the Upper Geyser Basin, they had
stopped here for a rest. Some of them appeared to
be quite exhausted. One or two others had decided
to continue their trip on foot. In so doing they felt
they would suffer less from the dust and the rough
roadway.

For a time we followed the Gibbon River, which
eventually flows into the Madison, which in turn is
one of the sources of the Missouri. Then we had to
climb back over a divide again, the one which separates this river from the Firehole River. So again we
slid down the mountain, crossed the river and followed along a tributary of the Firehole, passing sev-

eral of the main geysers of the Lower Basin. The geysers covered the ground with a blanket of gravel-like stone spewed out with the water. Here the route branched off to the lake and the famous Yellowstone Falls.[13] Unfortunately for us, this route was not to be taken.

Finally we reached the goal, the Upper Basin, the spot where the tents had been set up in the middle of the geyser field. In this area were some forested mountains, which were covered with a white layer, something like plaster. Here and there were mighty outcroppings of basalt rock. And in the middle of the scene sat Old Faithful. All around this geyser were small knolls created by the water from the geysers. Clouds of steam continuously escaped from

[13] The most spectacular geysers in the park were concentrated in either the Lower Basin, a thirty mile area in the Firehole River Valley with seven hundred hot springs and seventeen geysers, or the Upper Basin eight miles away which was only four miles square but contained a number of the principal geysers within a half-mile radius. To reach the Upper Basin from their camping spot near the Norris Geyser Basin the pilgrims followed Gibbon Canyon where 2,000-foot cliffs pressed so tightly that the carriages were forced to drive along a river bed at spots, climbed over a high divide where they looked down on the Falls of the Gibbon, and wound through eight miles of forested countryside to the Forks of the Firehole River where a crude hotel had been built. Here the road forked, one branch leading to the Falls of the Yellowstone, the other to the Lower and Upper Geyser Basins. The trail to the Lower Basin ran first through open portions of the Firehole Valley, then through marshy land to the basin itself. Winser, *Yellowstone National Park*, 33–40; *Appleton's General Guide*, 439–444.

them. We walked right up to the opening of Old Faithful, which had an irregularly-formed throat several feet in diameter. One could see the water rising up and down with a violent, boiling motion.

Suddenly it rose, the steam emission grew more active, the water at first tumbled over the rim, and then Old Faithful did his duty. The column of water rocketed splendidly into the air, became lost in a cloud of steam, and fell precipitously to the ground. The magnificent drama took several minutes. The subterranean forces cast the water higher and higher. It almost seemed as if there were some competitive race involved, for smaller water columns developed alongside the main thrust, forming together a beautiful canopy of spray and steam. At a cautious distance we stood stunned, looking into the workings of such volcanic forces.[14]

The eruption lasted for several moments at its peak, then gradually sank back until the water had receded to its earlier level again. Old Faithful has the lovely characteristic that it goes off at a regular interval, about once every hour. If it ever does get a little late, as it did in our presence, then it excuses itself by producing an even more majestic eruption.

[14] Old Faithful at this time stood on a mound of geyserite of its own making eleven feet tall, with a base that measured 215 by 145 feet. Each eruption was preceded by a few preliminary spurts, then a series of rapid jets that sent a column of water from 106 to 135 feet in the air. Eruptions occurred at intervals of from 54 to 80 minutes, and lasted four or five minutes. Winser, *Yellowstone National Park*, 46.

Winser's guidebook informed us that "the temperature inside the crater immediately before the eruption is 200 degrees Fahrenheit. The boiling point here at this elevation is 199 degrees. Old Faithful can also do the laundry. Soiled pieces of clothing thrown into the throat will usually be returned clean."[15]

In this respect, however, Old Faithful was not too reliable. Of the numerous handkerchiefs we threw in, the geyser kept quite a few. The amazing thing was that the woolen material came out completely shredded up, recognizable only as a bunch of little rags. One of our group who is a strong supporter of the wool industry made this experiment and had to accept the sad results.

Old Faithful has the place of honor in the Upper Geyser Basin. But it is not the biggest geyser. Opposite our tents, which were located a ten-minute walk from Old Faithful, was a whole colony of geysers. We could hardly walk ten steps without encountering an opening where the water was boiling, cooking, and at times making attempts to spout up. We had to be careful because these geysers are totally unpredictable. It can take days, even weeks, before some of the water-spewing geysers decide to go off and show what they can do. But if they feel like it,

---

[15] The guidebook went on to say: "Old Faithful is sometimes degraded by being made a laundry. Garments placed in the crater are ejected thoroughly washed when the eruption takes place." Winser, *Yellowstone National Park*, 46.

they thunder forth several times on the same day.

Following the instructions of our friendly guidebook, we walked around to see the other famous
geysers, at least to see their waters: the "Giantess",
the "Grand Geyser", the "Turban", etc. Then we
walked back to the other bank of the Firehole River. Up on a hill we met a party that consisted of an
entire family and most of their relatives, wandering
like nomads through the park. They came out here
on the Northern Pacific and were now slowly working their way back to the railroad. The people had a
well-equipped farm wagon, their tent was erected,
and a cook stove had been set up. They insisted
that it was only their "wanderlust" that inclined
them to take up such a nomadic existence.

Several thousand feet farther westward we came
upon a small geyser plateau. In the middle of it was
the geyser called "Splendid," surrounded by several
smaller springs. Our guidebook promised an eruption about then and sure enough, it did not take
long until "Splendid" began to spew forth.[16] It became more and more blustering, then shot up into
the air, scattering the water gorgeously in all directions. We ran quickly around to the other side to
see the water in the golden hue of the sunshine. A
little geyser next to "Splendid" then took off, try-

[16] The "Splendid" erupted every three hours, according
to the guidebook that Herr Mohr was reading, throwing a
column of water and steam as high as did Old Faithful.
Eruptions lasted from five to ten minutes. Winser, *Yellowstone National Park*, 52.

ing to mimic his big brother. He was cooking and brewing for a time and all of a sudden he shot out long, slanted squirts of water over on "Splendid". "Splendid" reached a height of about 200 feet. Then immediately afterward we saw in the distance down the valley another geyser flinging a pillar of water and steam into the air.

The number of springs and geysers is legion and every one of them would be a natural wonder of the first class anywhere else in the world. But at Yellowstone Park they are as plentiful as blackberries and therefore their magnificence sinks into the realm of the ordinary. The subterranean workshop that creates these wonders is continually busy. But the laws of its machinations are not always clear as yet. A geological explanation of this region is still awaited. The layman gets carried away by his dreams when thinking about this phenomenon, which is so rare on this earth. Hekla in Iceland has long enjoyed the privilege of having geysers and claimed to be the only one to have them; but that claim can no longer be made. The geysers of New Zealand are also said to be much smaller than those in Yellowstone Park.

The natural wonders of Yellowstone Park are a great attraction for all the Americans. America's national sense of vanity is strengthened by having something besides Niagara Falls that can be found nowhere else in the world. Out of a sense of flattery, the people in the United States honor and respect

The Castle Geyser of the Yellowstone

Taken from Rudolf Cronau's *Von Wunderland zu Wunderland*

this gift of nature and make pilgrimages to it as to a Mecca.

Stories about the geysers are listened to with great respect. The National Park Improvement Company has ambitious dreams of building nine monstrous hotels and a tramway through the whole park, all the way to Yellowstone Lake and to the canyons of the Yellowstone River. Mr. Hobart, the director, believes not only that these will be built but that they will be paid for from the revenue.[17]

Americans can spend a long time enjoying something and a long trip by railroad does not frighten them at all. It would, however, be a great improvement if the trip into the park could be shortened for the hurried visitor. The person who cannot stay very long could then see the drama often and at different times of the day and could enjoy it in its many aspects. The total impression made by the park will improve immensely if the visitor does not have to endure the time-consuming and tedious trip by horse and buggy.

We spent a third night in the tents of Yellowstone Park and then covered the entire distance back to the hotel in one day.

[17] Hobart was director of the Yellowstone Park Improvement Company and was conniving with Patrick A. Conger, the park's unscrupulous superintendent, to mar the countryside with tramways and hotels. See above and Footnote 6.

15

Cities on the Mississippi:
St. Paul and St. Louis

St. Paul
The last of September, 1883

AFTER leaving Yellowstone Park, we traveled un-
interruptedly for almost sixty hours before we
arrived here in St. Paul. We first came here some
four weeks ago, to be welcomed at the festivities for
the opening of the Northern Pacific Railroad. At
that time everything had a look of celebration. Now
I am seeing the city in its everyday clothes. Festival
decorations have long since disappeared, but the
city does not look any worse for that.

Anybody who comes from the Far West has seen
all he wants to see of the prairie and the wheat
fields of Dakota. As he steps out onto the terrace of
Grote's Tivoli in St. Paul, near the bridge over the
Mississippi River, his heart must skip a beat.[1] It is a

[1]On the westward journey the Germans of St. Paul had
planned a "commers" at Grote's famed beer garden, the
"Tivoli," which stood on the banks of the Mississippi, high
above the water, and provided a fine view of the valley. The
crowded schedule forced the cancellation of that bit of the
entertainment. Now Herr Mohr was back to see what he had
missed, and to mingle with the large German-born colony in
the city. Of St. Paul's 41,473 inhabitants in 1880, 4,965 had
been born in Germany.

sight filled with splendor. One tries to compare this river with one of those in Germany, perhaps the Rhine or the Elbe. It looks so familiar and yet there is something so foreign about it, which makes it all the more alluring.

At this point still quite near its source, the mighty river arrives flowing in a northerly direction from the south; it swings into a sharp curve against the heights on which St. Paul is situated, and turns again toward the south, its normal direction.

On the left bank at St. Paul, the plateau drops precipitously to the river. After the Mississippi has flowed through the city, it expands onto a broad plain, on which both the left and the right banks ascend gradually. At a most dizzying height the bridge, supported by cables, leads across the river to the other side. The heights are covered with deciduous trees and the plain is pleasantly interspersed with houses, woods, and fields. The river is filled with countless islands, some grown over with foliage, others only sandbars that disappear when the river achieves its normal flow of water.

This charming view is indeed exquisite! It can best be enjoyed from the Mississippi River bridge. But we who enjoy a "gemütlich" atmosphere and a glass of beer while looking at such a scene went down to the Tivoli, a covered terrace located on a ledge next to the river. Down in the beer garden we heard much German spoken. As a matter of fact, it was possible to imagine that we had been suddenly lifted from the shores of the Mississippi and transported back to a German tavern. The decorations and furnishings were strange though. The head of an elk or a mountain goat reminded us that we were still near the wild, virgin forests. Hermann Grote himself qualifies as a German saloon keeper and from a distance of ten steps one can already tell he is a North German. This he does not deny, for his home is at Kloster Zeven, in Bremen, nor has he forgotten his homeland.

St. Paul is growing into a giant. It now has about 90,000 inhabitants, at least that is the estimate given. The last census taken in 1880 placed the population at 42,000, but it is said to be completely unreliable.[2]

When one considers that in 1855 St. Paul was a tiny city of four to five thousand people, then the boldest expectations of growth come as no surprise. A local German immigrant who has spent these past thirty years here explained that back then St. Paul was entirely dependent on river traffic. When the winter closed off shipping because the Mississippi had frozen over, it sometimes became a matter of life or death whether shipping would start again a

---

[2] The 1880 census figures, showing 41,473 inhabitants, were certainly far less "unreliable" than the estimates made in 1883. These were arrived at by multiplying the 1880 figure by any number between two and three-and-one-half, depending on the optimism of the multiplier. They ranged between 88,378 and 123,728. Hanson, comp., *Grand Opening of the Northern Pacific Railroad*, 65.

couple of weeks earlier or later in spring. When the
first ship would arrive from the south, the entire
city of St. Paul would crowd down by the river's
edge to rejoice at the ship's arrival. It became a
symbol that the long winter's frost had at last been
broken.

The founding and rapid growth of St. Paul was
not the result of pure accident. Nature had created
a perfect spot here for a settlement. The vertical
rock banks along the left side of the Mississippi
mark the spot where the center of business lies in
St. Paul. The banks form a kind of bowl and the
streets from both sides run down into it. In that way
the city has a varied terrain and does not have the
deadly monotony that characterizes most other
American cities. To be sure the city was laid out
with regular, square streets but the circumstances
have occasioned an irregular corner or hideaway
here and there.

The wooden structures have disappeared from
the center of the city. Many of the buildings that
were first erected to replace them are quite modest,
but just as the city is growing the style of building is
also taking on a new character. Some of the business
blocks have brick buildings rising six stories and
although they are simple, they look functional.

Store after store lines the streets. But brick apparently is not adequate because they are now using
sandstone as the building material for the very new-
est structures. Everybody in St. Paul has the wildest

dreams and expectations for a continuing boom. The city has excellent railroad connections. More than 150 trains arrive and depart daily. The older lines link the city to the East.[3] One can choose among several routes to get to the Great Lakes and the same holds true for the southerly direction. Then there are the smaller towns and the wide open West with its need for foodstuffs and industrial products. St. Paul is the funneling point for all of the land produce originating here in the North, especially for cattle and wheat.

Even now the merchants of St. Paul are casting their eyes all the way to the Pacific Ocean. They not only entertain the hope that a significant percentage of the American trade will find its way via St. Paul and the Northern Pacific Railroad to Asia, but that the United States will now be in a position to take away some of England's enormous export trade with China, Japan, and India.

There is a very large element of Germans in St. Paul. The number is not quite as great as it is in St. Louis or Chicago, but they do account for a high percentage of the total population and would have to be reckoned in the thousands. Among them are some who have been in St. Paul for decades. I also talked to a number of natives from Bremen. Several

---

[3] Herr Mohr was once more reading his guidebook, which told him that five railroads served St. Paul, and that 150 trains arrived or departed daily. Winser, *The Great Northwest*, 20.

have very important positions in the banks. The younger ones have taken up positions as clerks, or in similar types of employment. Those I have talked to are happy to be in St. Paul and they like the comfortable life here. A very fine German newspaper keeps up on happenings in the Fatherland. Its editor is Dr. Albert Wolff, formerly of Braunschweig, who was expelled during the revolutions of 1848.[4]

The roads leading out of the city are lined with many beautiful houses which are surrounded by gardens and beautiful shade trees. In these areas the wooden structures have by no means been done away with, but they are no longer the only construction material in use. They are also more pleasantly built, so that one learns to like them a little. By making air spaces in the walls and stuffing them up very tightly, these homes do hold out the cold in the winter, even the grim cold of a winter in Minnesota. Likewise, in the summer they do offer rather good shelter from the heat. Understandably, it is much less trouble to build with wood than with mortar and stone.

High up on the hill, the Germans with some means have built their houses and to a certain ex-

[4] Albert Wolff, born in Germany in 1825, reached the United States as a political exile, and in 1853 settled in Minnesota. There he rose rapidly in the newspaper world, becoming editor of the *Volkszeitung* in 1877. Warren Upham, comp., *Minnesota Biographies, 1655–1912* (St. Paul, 1912), 874.

tent, their construction is reminiscent of home. I enjoyed a marvelous Sunday in several of these homes on the heights above the Mississippi. The party was made up of a mixture of Germans from every imaginable part of Germany, with the pleasant addition of German-American ladies and young misses. We enjoyed both serious and light German music. Everything indicated how close all of our hearts still were to our good old Fatherland even though it had been decades since many of the older generation had been back home. A longing to see home just once more was very much alive in all of them, but circumstances often have compelled them to postpone a visit from year to year. In some cases, the people have been away so long that they have grown somewhat afraid of going back in search of home. So much of what was once near and dear to them probably would no longer exist. In cases of those who left when they were young, all the older people will have died off and a new and totally strange generation will have taken their places.

The young people who left Europe only a few years ago have generally had good experiences. Assimilation of Germans with native Americans seems to be accomplished very easily. And the German seems to work better among the Americans than when he stays isolated with his countrymen. The energetic and fomenting quality seems to come from the Americans. Many times it has been remarked that the cities which have a predominantly

German population do not keep pace with their rivals which are made up of a mixed population.

Of course not all have found their fortunes in America. If a man does not know how to use all of his ability to fit in, and does not discipline himself to take on great responsibility, he will not get ahead either in the East or in the West.

As we sat and drank our beer in this friendly company, an officer of the law walked by. He looked quite romantic in his blue uniform and felt hat with a golden band and tassel. He turned out to be a man from Bremen. "Willi Bremer, come on in," called someone and so he did, temporarily disregarding his official position. Indeed, William G. Bremer did come from Bremen. He had helped build our drainage canals and after a fight with a fellow worker decided to skip out and come to America. He took part in the war and later got this job in St. Paul. He had just completed his watch on the beat and would not let us go to bed without first taking us over to his house for refreshments. We even had the honor of taking a midnight drive in his patrol buggy through the streets of St. Paul to pick up an arrested suspect. On the streets there was plenty of life and activity.

What is really astonishing is the number of vehicles constantly out and about in every city. The American of the West is a born rider and driver. Whenever conditions permit, he takes a buggy with one horse or a team to get wherever he wants to go.

There is a countless number of attractive little carriages. They whisk through the streets with the greatest of skill and despite their delicate construction, they withstand all the frightful conditions of the American streets without any trouble.

The streets, the streets! The streets are a sore point in every American city. Dirty, muddy, or dusty, it all depends on the weather. Rough, full of holes, hilly, in every city almost without exception they are the object of cursing and swearing. But in spite of all the complaining, it seems that nothing can be done to improve them.

In St. Paul the sidewalks are entirely made of wood. So long as the planks are nailed down, the understructure solid, and the holes not too large or too frequent, then it goes all right. They say these are only temporary until they can lay a sidewalk of stone slabs or cinders.

We took a drive out to a region where there are only country homes. Everywhere they were working and building so that peace and solitude could not be found anywhere. Then we crossed the bridge and turned right upstream and past a sawmill and some lowland forest and pastureland. At this spot one could still get lost in his dreams. At the edge of the river, tree covered islands divided and restricted the view. High on the rocky cliffs of the opposite shore stood Fort Snelling. Everything was so mysteriously beautiful in that afternoon autumn sunlight.

Then we passed Mendota, the oldest settlement

in the area and eventually arrived at the Minnesota River, where it flows into the Mississippi. A ferry took us across and we landed right at the foot of Fort Snelling, a very imposing sight on top of the rock.[5] Undoubtedly the fort served as protection for the early settlers against Indians and there was still evidence of many a rough and bloody engagement in these regions.

Fort Snelling is now more or less a military station or rendezvous point for troops being sent to the frontiers. Around the actual fort, with its gun slots and pinnacles, is a row of cottages built to serve as living quarters for the fort's officers. At the moment they have artillery companies and there are several Negro regiments.

A bridge high above the river brought us onto our highway leading to St. Paul. The view was very beautiful. Down below, the river makes a sharp bend as it flows between steep and narrow cliffs. Unfortunately our time was too short to pay a visit to the oft-sung waterfalls of the Minnehaha.[6] Instead

[5] Fort Snelling, built in 1819 at the confluence of the Mississippi and Minnesota rivers, was at this time a picturesque edifice, its white walls rising abruptly above the almost vertical wall of the bluff on which it was situated. Its commander in 1883 was Brigadier General Alfred H. Terry. Evan Jones, *Citadel in the Wilderness: The Story of Fort Snelling and the Old Northwest Frontier* (New York, 1966).

[6] The famed Minnehaha Falls, immortalized by Henry Wadsworth Longfellow in his "The Song of Hiawatha," were reached by a pleasant drive beyond Fort Snelling. They were, however, something of an anticlimax for those

we drove along on a fine country road toward the city and were soon enveloped in the ferocious business traffic once again.

As night began to fall the electric lights were turned on. Stores, businesses, hotels, and houses—everywhere they profusely squander the light. The stars were already shining when we said goodbye; such pleasant days we spent here.

St. Louis
The first days of October, 1883

WE LEFT St. Paul, where nightly frosts were already announcing winter, and arrived here in St. Louis to find summer temperatures still prevailing. On the way we passed through Milwaukee, the most German city in the United States. Unfortunately we rode right through and I only saw the view from the depot. I regard my failure to see Milwaukee as one of the sins committed during my journey through the Northwest. Similarly, we spent only a few hours in Chicago on this return trip. By the second morning we were again riding along the Mississippi and continued close beside it until we reached East St. Louis where we crossed the suspension bridge into the city of St. Louis.

As in New York, it is a suspension bridge de-

---

who had read the poet's description. "The falls," admitted one guidebook, "are picturesquely situated, but they hardly merit the prominence that Mr. Longfellow's poem has obtained for them." *Appleton's General Guide*, 356.

Courtesy of the Missouri Historical Society

The levee and the Eads bridge, St. Louis

signed by Roebling.[7] It is built in three long arches
spanning the river and is the only structure of this

[7] Herr Mohr erred when he attributed the St. Louis bridge
to John A. Roebling, a designer of the Brooklyn Bridge.
The 6,220-foot structure bridging the Mississippi from the
foot of Washington Street to East St. Louis was planned and
built by James B. Eads, and was known locally as the "Eads
Bridge." Suspended on four piers holding three spans, and
built on two levels, it was begun in 1869 and opened in 1874
at a cost of $10,000,000. J. T. Scharf, *History of St. Louis,
City and County, from the Earliest Periods to the Present Day*
(2 v., Philadelphia, 1883), II, 1075.

unusual design. It is stunning in every respect. The bridge has a twofold purpose: on the lower deck it carries trains and on the upper deck provides for pedestrian and wagon traffic. From the bridge we continued to the depot in the middle of the city. The immediate surroundings were ugly and the pavement terrible. St. Louis freely admits that it has never had a reputation for good streets. When it rains, they are covered with mud and during dry spells one can lose his way in the dust.

The city is filled with excitement and festivities. The fair week has just begun and all the hotels are swamped. From far and near the population of Missouri and the neighboring states has flooded into St. Louis. After hard and bitter summer work, everyone is ready for a festival.

We arrived at the risk of not finding overnight accommodations, but my luck held up and in no time I was settled at "Kötter's Hotel," a German inn opposite the famous Southern Hotel.[8] Everything in this hotel is German, but with an American veneer. It is, in fact, astonishing how very little German customs have influenced the exterior form of life in America. Take any American city and you

[8] The guidebooks of the time fail to mention Kötter's Hotel, but they make much of the Southern Hotel, formally opened in May, 1881, and generally reputed to be the finest hostelry in the city. It occupied the entire block between Walnut, Elm, Fourth, and Fifth Streets, and was six stories high, and was completely fireproof. Scharf, *History of St. Louis*, II, 1447-1448.

cannot tell whether it has a large, small, or no German settlement in it. Whether it is the style of building, the platting of the streets, the public buildings, the stores, the restaurants, right down to the signs and inscriptions on the business places and in the display windows, every single detail is American, modeled largely after English patterns of living that are strange to us. Likewise the hotels are peculiarly American, even the hotel belonging to Mr. Kötter. Though its owner is a German and its staff as well as customers are all German, nevertheless its style of construction and its furnishings are completely and totally in the American style.

I do not mean to say that the interior arrangements in private dwellings and in hotels are less comfortable than in Germany. The total uniformity of life in the United States has its good side. What develops as a fine practice is immediately recognized and accepted everywhere. Thus the need for certain things is easily satisfied, for it is so universal that it can be accomplished by mass production. On the other hand, in Germany so much consideration is made for individual preferences that too much attention is paid to variations and efforts are scattered. But here I go, digressing into observations which I wanted to save for another time.

Barely had I registered in the hotel when a waiter walked up to announce that for many years he had been a teacher not far from Bremen. Fate had brought him to St. Louis, where he temporarily found a job and lodging in the hotel, but he hoped some day to return to his profession by getting a job in Mexico. At breakfast I bumped into an old schoolmate, who has spent many years here in a small town in Missouri. He operates a fine dry goods business and was in St. Louis both for business and for pleasure. That is, he was making use of the fair week to visit with people and keep up his business contacts while also injecting a little diversion into his routine life.

As you can see, the Germans are not scarce in St. Louis. In fact, to say that a quarter of the population of St. Louis is German is not too high an estimate. In St. Louis the Germans also have political significance. They proudly proclaim that it was their determined stance that broke the wave of rebellion which threatened to erupt in Missouri. They feel St. Louis performed a heroic service in defense of the Union even though this meant going against its own immediate interests, for St. Louis had very close ties with the slave-holding South. If Missouri had seceded from the Union, St. Louis would have found an excellent position within the Confederacy. More important to the citizens of St. Louis, however, was their loyalty to the Union and the preservation of the United States. It was the Germans of St. Louis who made a major contribution to this patriotic outburst of public opinion.

Today, not even two decades have passed since the conclusion of the terrible four-year war. It ended

only with the enforced disappearance of a great social evil. Yet how wonderful it is that the deep
wounds caused by that conflict seem to be completely healed. Admittedly, there is probably still
some silent sympathy for the South among the former soldiers and those who suffered heavy losses,
but there is no present threat to the Union of any
plots to restore the former status in the South. The
black men have become citizens of the Republic,
while prejudice has subsided and hate against the
black race is no longer expressed in brutal ways.

St. Louis was compelled to make great sacrifices
as a result of the war. Through the economic collapse of the plantation owners, the city also suffered. One notices even today that St. Louis was
formerly frequented by a rich, aristocratic class of
people, although perhaps these reminders derive
from a former French influence here.

Nature has not been particularly favorable to St.
Louis. One exception of course is the river. Fifteen
miles north of St. Louis the waters of the Missouri
flow into the Mississippi. From the bridge that rises
majestically over the river one has a view over the
whole city and its environs.

Seeing the river and its banks inside the city was
a great disappointment. I had imagined that the water would be covered with Mississippi steamboats,
one next to the other, for miles. So I had read and
heard earlier. Such was the picture I had from my
earlier reading. But these exciting days have passed

and today the river is no longer so important. It is the railroads that count.

Here the banks of the Mississippi are flat. Presently, in the fall of the year before the rainy season, the water is so low that some of the steamboats have stopped running. I was thinking about taking a ride on the river, but I was advised against this because I could be stuck somewhere for days. During November and December the Mississippi usually also has a low flow. In December of 1882, for example, it dropped to a depth of two feet and six inches, while in July it stood at thirty-two feet and five inches.

It was somewhat surprising to learn that for a rather long time in the winter, the river south of St. Louis can become closed by ice. There are, of course, years in which shipping is not stopped for a single day, but in other years the river can remain shut for as much as two and a half months.

St. Louis is among the top commercial cities of the heartland. Thanks to the excellent railroad system, and also to the water route, St. Louis is the focal point for immense masses of products from the interior of the country. From here these items find their way to the sea ports. On the other hand, St. Louis is in an excellent position to be a distributor through which major portions of the neighboring states are supplied with industrial materials from the East and from Europe. In every way it has the characteristics of a large city. According to the census of 1880, St. Louis had a population of

350,000. Today this figure probably stands more nearly at 400,000.

The streets are wide and naturally straight as a bullet. The city layout is just as regular as we have come to expect in every American city. Likewise the building style is not exactly outstanding for its originality, but there are some nice structures. The streets that run down toward the river have been selected by businesses such as banks and insurance companies. Characteristically this is the area of heaviest traffic. The Germans are well represented among the firms in this section as well as in a wide range of positions. On the whole they all do very well. They work much harder here than they did back in Germany. The strong competition demands a larger input of effort and strength. But since people here live decidedly better and become much richer than in our country, even the lower classes are willing to put forth greater effort. The secret of success for the immigrants seems to be this: they have been freed from the former social restraints that hampered their energies and thus feel themselves driven to a more liberated, more energetic use of their strengths and abilities.

A fellow German who was a pleasant and informative traveling companion to all during our trip on the steamer *Elbe* is the owner of a large wholesale hat house in St. Louis and we were pleased to accept his invitation to tour his business. The entire five-floored building was filled from top to bottom with hats, caps, gloves, etc. All the styles of head-gear that we have seen during our travels—on the cowboys, the mountaineers, the farmers, and the city folks—could be seen again here. Only here there was not just one of each, but crates of every imaginable kind. On each crate was a model of the contents. In addition to all kinds of hats, there were gloves and mittens for men and women. We saw some built for the cold in certain regions that were so heavy we could only think of Siberia, certainly not of dressy clothes.

Just as large are the wholesale houses for luxury and art items—bronze, chinaware, gold and silver products, as well as wide selections of jewelry, frequently imported from Paris. I would like to pick out one characteristic incident to illustrate how wide the gulf is that separates America from Europe and how difficult it is for ideas and cultural refinement to make their way across the ocean. This remains true despite the fact that every week thirty steamers make their way between the continents. The statue of Hermes of Praxiteles, an incomparable treasure which has become such an everyday item in Germany that no cultured home is without one, is an art object which now is completely unknown in America. I have looked everywhere, in art stores, in plaster reproduction shops, in chinaware stores, but nowhere have I seen a reproduction of this bust. I even checked in different stocks of reproductions retained by antique dealers but Hermes was always missing. Among the most cultured Germans in this country, at least, one finds someone who has a fleeting knowledge that this work of art, one of the finest in the world, exists.

St. Louis is having its fair, what we Europeans call a *Jahrmarkt* or *Kirmes.*[9] To be sure the fair and the *Jahrmarkt* do have certain things in common, but judging by the way they celebrate a fair here, one must admit that it represents a step forward from its sister custom back in the Old World. On the one hand a fair is a folk festival, but it has a serious side to it as well. The St. Louis fair consists primarily of an agricultural exhibit, with displays coming from the entire Mississippi Valley. Simultaneously the fair has the quality of a *Messe* or general market because after being shown, the machinery, cattle, and other products are offered for sale. I must admit I have never seen a finer agricultural display nor a larger accumulation of rural products and animals.

[9] The St. Louis Fair, launched in 1856 and growing more elaborate yearly thereafter, attracted customers from all of Missouri and from much of the Mississippi Valley. "Fair Week," usually the first week in October, was a gala occasion, with the streets decorated and illuminated, a "Night Pageant" staged Tuesday evening, and a city holiday proclaimed Thursday. Its center was the "Fair Grounds" of the St. Louis Agricultural and Mechanical Association in the northwest section of the city, where handsome buildings, an amphitheater seating 40,000 persons, and a permanent zoological garden occupied eighty-five landscaped acres. Walter B. Stevens, *St. Louis the Fourth City, 1764-1909* (2 v., St. Louis, 1909), I, 955-959.

In addition to this business aspect of the fair, there are many other things to be seen: illumination displays, stage performances, military balls, even a festival in the stock exchange.

A theatrical group called the "Veiled Prophets," from Moore's Lalla Rookh, is producing acts for the embellishment of fair week. Accordingly, the veiled prophet, who lives in his water grotto on the river, is honoring the city with his visits. He is surrounded by his fantastic household, including Queen Mab who has been freed from a five-hundred-year captivity and is now introducing her fairies and elves to the New World.

Around this general theme, new and old fairy tales and elf narratives are dramatized and presented to the public from large wagons.[10]

The streets have been wonderfully illuminated. For miles, arches with gas lights have been hung

[10] The "Veiled Prophet" celebration originated in 1878 when St. Louis businessmen and social leaders decided to sponsor a festival to rival New Orleans' "Mardi Gras." This was to be arranged by a secret society known as the "Lalla Rookh,"—a name borrowed from Thomas Moore's *Lalla Rookh: An Oriental Romance*, first published in London in 1817. Membership in this society had by 1883 become so prized that it was passed from father to son. The members of Lalla Rookh annually selected a "Veiled Prophet," supervised preparations for a parade to honor him, and staged a ball during "Fair Week" that climaxed the city's social season. The parade, always built upon some theme such as "Fairyland," was led by the Veiled Prophet resplendent in satin robes, and wound through St. Louis streets over a five-mile route. Stevens, *St. Louis the Fourth City*, 958–959.

Courtesy of the Missouri Historical Society

The Veiled Prophet Parade, St. Louis

Taken from *Harper's Weekly*

under white or red cupolas all along the route taken by the parade on the first day of the fair. Interspersed with the arches are gas lanterns fastened to poles. These endlessly long streets and avenues so gloriously lighted are really a sight to behold. Admittedly, I missed the first night but the streets have been lit again each evening. They have also made extensive use of electric lighting. Individual business establishments have hung dozens of arc lamps from extensions in their store fronts.

The second major parade was postponed because of rain.[11] It was sponsored and arranged by the merchants and businessmen and was to present some idea about the commerce and trade of the city. All of the significant businesses of St. Louis were represented either realistically or in allegory. A parade was of course nothing new for me after the parades in St. Paul, Minneapolis, and Portland. But here the exhibitors had more time to prepare, and established traditions probably helped them in certain aspects. Here, as in other parades, it was apparent that Americans have a strong liking for satire and that they can well appreciate a joke. In their wit they display a fresh bold spirit and confidence in the further growth and development of the country. No less interesting than the floats was the accompaniment. There were different military companies which have taken the patterns for their uniforms from the armies of Europe. The fire brigade presented its steam sprayer and entertained our ears with the shrieking sounds from the steam whistles.

To throw light on the individual units, Negroes with torches frequently walked beside the floats. There was a large silk firm which has branches in

[11] The first parade, held annually during "Fair Week" Tuesday night, honored the "Veiled Prophet"; the second, Thursday night, allowed the merchants and industrialists to display their wares.

many cities of the Union, called the Nonotock Silk Company. On its float twenty or more knights in armor held rolls of silk cloth on their lances, with the inscription of the company printed on it. One of the import houses offered a float carrying a little steamship covered with the merchandise which the importer has for sale. The brewers brought out their King Gambrinus on four floats. The Missouri Bicycle Company loaded its float with velocipedes and behind it there rode a troupe of riders using the velocipedes.

Thus followed float after float. Each funny float was received with applause and cheering. For me, the attitudes of the observers were just as interesting as the drama itself. There were perhaps a hundred thousand people lined up along the streets through which the parade moved. The many, many buggies and wagons parked in the side streets brought in curiosity-seekers from the suburbs and surrounding areas. Nowhere did I observe any rough pushing and shoving by young or old as sometimes happens when ruffians take pleasure in making themselves as burdensome and unpleasant as possible to the majority of the audience. And when the performance was over, very few policemen were needed to untangle this crush of buggies and get everybody on the way home. I was amazed at the orderliness and patience of all who took part. It never occurred to anyone to push or rush.

All the taverns and evening spots are crowded

Courtesy of the Missouri Historical Society

The Fairgrounds, St. Louis

during the evenings, and scenes are lively, but nowhere do the police have to be called to restore
order. When the festivities are over, everyone leaves
peacefully. I do not think we Europeans have any
reason to believe that we are superior to the people
of the United States. Certainly in times of political
turmoil the large masses of people in Europe will
not disperse so harmlessly.

St. Louis has its own special place for the fair,

called the fairgrounds, which is a park west of the city large enough for cattle and agricultural machinery. The streetcar system in St. Louis is well developed so one can easily get there and at a minimum expense. It is a large area that includes also parks and a zoo. For the different displays, large but simple buildings have been erected. The short time that I had available to spend during the afternoon was entirely insufficient to cover the extraordinarily large fair.

Most intriguing to me was the farm machinery. Here was inventiveness at work trying to solve difficult mechanical problems. The Americans possess a precision of workmanship in carrying through the inventions they have brought to light. A great need for such machines is coupled with the capability to create them. The guiding principle in all of this agricultural machinery is to save on human labor. Indeed, the most diverse branches of technology cooperate to solve the needs of agriculture.

The only thing that could be compared in size to this gigantic display was the wagon and carriage exhibit. There were hundreds of vehicles of every kind. Driving in this country is no luxury; rather it is an everyday necessity. The great distances demand it and, as my fellow Germans who now live here assure me, the climate in America is not suitable for very much walking. After a few years here immigrants break away from their old habits and go to horseback riding or driving a team. Even in those areas of the United States where there are adequate hotels and inns, nobody travels on foot.

The light American carriages with their spider-web frames are extremely practical in their construction. They have all kinds of clever devices to make them open or covered, to turn the seats for ease in getting in and out, etc. Yet I have not come to really fall in love with them. Getting in and out is not very easy. Since the step is between the wheels, I do not see how ladies get in and out without dirtying their dresses. The little, thin wheels are also quite unsteady and when one drives along on those awful streets and roads, he bounces and jumps hither and thither. But the demand for such buggies is enormous.

In the middle of the fairgrounds is an area of animal exhibitions, races, and demonstrations of operational farm machinery. It appears that 10,000 or more people could assemble there. Between the arches that support the grandstand are concessions and restaurants as well as stores and booths, something like the arrangement of our traditional *Jahrmarkt*.

With the beautiful weather which has followed a day of rain, an incredible number of people have crowded into these spaces. It is crowded everywhere, but especially in the restaurants and taverns. Pilsener Beer is presently very popular, but one does not have much trouble getting a glass of good wine in St. Louis either. Just head for the "Bremen

Ratskeller." Our offspring in the West is certainly no disgrace to its old namesake. Here too is a cellar with large and mighty arches where the noble liquid is stored in barrels and bottles. And it was a pleasant surprise to find that the Germans on the Mississippi still drink the blessed wines of the Rhine, believing in their hearts that in all the world there is no better wine. It has been great fun during these few days. Drunkenness, loudness, and excesses, if they do occur, are kept quiet and hidden from the light of day . . . .

In addition to the fair the Germans have had their own historic celebration. In this week it has been two hundred years since the first German settlers—Mennonites from the Rhine regions—left their homes to find a new life in America. These were the founders of Germantown, Pennsylvania.[12] Germans in many cities of the United States have taken notice of this event. Here in St. Louis, the German clubs arranged a festival in the great hall of the Stock Exchange and despite the many and great

[12] Strictly speaking, the founders of Germantown were neither Germans nor Mennonites. The first arrivals, who reached Philadelphia October 6, 1683, came from Krefeld in the Rhineland and Krisheim in the lower Palatinate, and hence were Rhinelanders rather than Germans. They were also Quaker converts, although coming from Mennonite villages. They had been financed by a society of merchants in Frankfurt am Main, whose agent, Francis D. Pastorius, is generally credited with being the founder of Germantown. Charles M. Andreus, *The Colonial Period of American History* (4 v., New Haven, 1934-1938), III, 302-303.

distractions at the fair, some two thousand Germans attended.[13]

The program was simple but dignified. None of the ordinary attractions normally used to get people to come were used. The fact that two thousand countrymen nevertheless chose to come together for the event shows how alive are the feelings of cohesiveness among the Germans. It shows also that they remember the Fatherland by honoring the pioneers of German origin who first broke the path on which millions were to follow.

After a musical introduction came a speech by the festival president, Dr. Storkloff, who concluded with a poetic tribute to the founders of Germantown. A young German lady, with beautiful diction and enthusiasm, recited a poem: "Vergesst die Deutsche Sprache nicht." (Do not forget the German language.) There were also patriotic songs by the combined male singing societies of the city.

Carl Lüedeking of the *Westliche Post* newspaper gave the festival address. He recounted many historical facts about the Germans who emigrated for the sake of their beliefs. He pointed out why they set-

[13] The celebration was held in the "Exchange", or main hall, of the Merchants Exchange Building, an imposing structure on Third Street between Pine and Chestnut built in 1875, and claimed by St. Louisans to be "the finest edifice of the kind in the country." The "Exchange" was 221 feet long, 100 wide, and 70 tall, and was used during the day for the city's stock exchange. *Appleton's General Guide*, 238–240.

tled in Pennsylvania, a state which gave the impetus to a chain of developments that had consequences for all of mankind: "For the first time in history a society came into being which in its very constitutional law included the principles of complete freedom of religion. It offered equality on grounds other than religious principles, singling out only freedom of conscience as its basic law. This fundamental principle, independent from any religious faith, resting solely on a secular political society, was later transferred from Pennsylvania to the Constitution of the United States in Philadelphia. This sturdy tree of wisdom, this great principle of freedom of thought and conscience, is rooted back in Germantown. William Penn laid the cornerstone, for he was the immortal building master. But the German Land Company of Frankfurt delivered to him the material with which to build, namely the Germans who from 1683 onward became his apprentices."[14]

[14] Dr. Carl Luedeking, a prominent writer, teacher, and member of the school board, was also an editor of the *Westliche Post*, which was generally ranked as one of the better German-language newspapers then published in the United States. Its market was large; of the 350,518 people living in St. Louis in 1880, 54,901 were from Germany. W. W. Kelsoe, *St. Louis Reference Record* (St. Louis, n.d.) 66; Stevens, *St. Louis the Fourth City*, I, 222.

16

Cities on the Ohio:
Louisville and Cincinnati

A NIGHT train carried our party from St. Louis to Louisville on the Ohio River. Dawn was just breaking as we crossed the long bridge over the river bed to enter the city. "Bed" is the right word, for the river is now just a small stream between large sandbars. But in the autumn after heavy rains and in the spring when there is a sudden thaw after heavy snowfalls, water can fill the entire river bed.

Not so surprisingly I found the city to be laid out in a regular pattern with wide streets that suffer from the congenital disease of all American cities, namely, very poor pavement. As a result the streets are lacking in cleanliness. Not that the people are not concerned about their dirty streets—they are making extraordinary efforts. Not only do they employ brooms and conventional sweepers, they have a steam-powered sweeper in operation.

In Louisville it soon becomes apparent that tobacco is king.[1] In fact I was told that the city holds

[1] Louisville's tobacco market was in the 1880s one of the largest in the world, with sales of over $5,000,000 yearly. The city claimed 125,000 inhabitants, and was the commercial center for the state of Kentucky. *Appleton's General Guide*, 324–328.

Southern Exposition Building, Louisville

first place as a tobacco market. I visited one of the tobacco sheds and found myself amidst a group of German countrymen who were following the auctioneer from barrel to barrel. The auctioneer called out the offers and bids with a tongue so quick and skillful that it defies description. One would almost think he had some kind of clock mechanism in his throat. Barrels were opened, samples taken from three different places and officially certified, and then the bids were taken. It was obvious that buying this product is a much trickier business than buying ordinary products that are sold at a fixed price. Here, every barrel was an individual item to be judged in each case by the quality of the leaves.

The great Southern Exposition is taking place in Louisville now.[2] The exposition building has been erected in a beautiful park and includes displays of art, commerce, and agriculture. Even though I was able to attend it only briefly, I must say that again I

[2] The "Southern Exposition," a miniature world's fair, was held in a giant building erected for the occasion on a forty-acre plot on the west side of Fourth Street, built at a cost of $300,000, and described by the local paper as "in point of immensity, among the foremost in the world's catalogue of big structures of the kind." The Exposition, opened August 1, 1883, with elaborate ceremonies attended by President Arthur and any number of distinguished guests, attracted 770,048 visitors during the hundred days it operated. These viewers could gape at 1,500 industrial exhibits while the display of art works, most of them borrowed from eastern collectors, was acclaimed as "the most valuable loan exhibition ever displayed in the West." *Louisville Courier-Journal*, August 2, 1883.

was impressed by the complexity of the machinery on display. The arrangements were all very practical; there was plenty of space and light; and the exhibitors took the time and the money necessary to show their products to the viewers from the most desirable side.

Quite a distance from the large exhibition building in a pavilion by itself was an impressive exhibit of paintings and sculptures. In Chicago we had already seen an art exhibit, though of a purely local character, and it was there that I first made acquaintance with American painters. It is obvious that they have received their training and apprenticeship with the impressionists in Paris . . . .

The trip from Louisville to Cincinnati on a beautiful sunny afternoon will be among the fondest of my memories. The entire region is under cultivation and we passed through cities and towns that are no longer in a rough or unfinished stage. Almost everywhere the fruits of men's labors were visible. We flew past lovely villas and could see the farmers driving home from their fields. These rural scenes filled me with wonderful memories of home.

It was already quite dark as we arrived at the great bridge over the Ohio River, leading from Kentucky into the state of Ohio. It was a sight filled with fantasy to look from the heights of the bridge down at the lights on the boats and steamers and the long rows of lamps on the docks, in the streets, and high on the hills that encircle the city. Electric

Courtesy of The Public Library of Cincinnati and Hamilton County

Riverfront from Central Bridge, Cincinnati

lights glowed in the buildings giving them a castle-like appearance. Through the fog and darkness I tried in vain to get a view of the city and its environs as we moved on the viaduct deep into the heart of the city, eventually descending to the street level.

I spent the night at St. Michele's Hotel.[3] It is run

[3] The list of better Cincinnati hotels printed in *Appleton's General Guide*, 315–316, fails to list the St. Michele.

on the European system—that is, you pay for your room and take your meals à la carte. In contrast, under the American system you pay a fixed price for room and board, between three and five dollars, without wine, depending on the class of the hotel. Wine on the menu in an American hotel is a rare item. The menu usually offers ice water, coffee, milk, or buttermilk.

Cincinnati is full of Germans.[4] Entire sections of the city, house after house, have nothing but Germans, at least residents with German names. But even here, how little the Germans have externally influenced the streets and buildings of the city. Fountain Square is one exception; it does have a European flavor and reminds me of Frankfurt. The square takes its name from the famous fountain, the largest bronze art work in the United States. A wealthy donor, Mr. Probasco, gave it to the city. The fountain was originally designed for the Hanseatic city of Riga . . . .[5]

[4] According to the census of 1880, 46,157 of the city's 255,139 inhabitants were born in Germany.

[5] The bronze Tyler-Davidson Fountain, which dominated Fountain Square in the heart of the city's shopping district, rested on a bronze base twelve feet square ornamented with bas-relief figures showing the uses of water; four giant bronze basins rose from the base, and in the center a column supporting the heroic figure of a woman with outstretched hands, water raining from her fingers. The fountain was designed by August von Kreling of Nürnberg and cast in the royal foundry of München. It was erected in 1871 at a cost of some $200,000, the gift of Henry Probasco, a wholesale hardware tycoon. *Appleton's General Guide*, 315–320.

The bowl in which the main portion of Cincinnati lies is filled with the smoke of many factories and is unbearably hot in summer. To the northwest and the east the city is hemmed in by very steep heights, on which the elegant suburbs have grown up. High on top, the people are not tormented by the smoke, and there cooler breezes temper the heat. Ascending the hills is made easy by the use of so-called elevators that are like mountain-climbing railway cars. To reach the villas on the hills one takes a horse drawn streetcar to the foot of the hills, then transfers to the cars of the elevator. Mighty machines power the cars up to the heights and at the stops on top large entertainment areas have been built.[6] They are mostly beer gardens in the mammoth style characteristic of America and here the inhabitants can catch a breath of fresh air. The suburb of Mount Auburn, the aristocratic town of Clifton, and the zoological gardens are all well worth a visit to get a better idea of the wealth of this city and the charming geographic position . . . .

[6] At this time, four inclined-plane railroads left from the business section of the city and ran to the tops of the surrounding hills. At the top of each was an extensive beer garden. *Appleton's General Guide*, 322–323.

17

Cities of the East: Boston, Philadelphia, and Washington

NEW YORKERS tend to say that whoever has seen New York has seen all the cities of America. This may be correct, but only with great reservations. It is true that New York ranks first in many things: as a center of shipping and trade, as a seaport, as the focal point of wealth, as a city of splendor, as the hub of world traffic, and as the nerve center of pleasure and enjoyment. In reality, all American cities are only segments of New York, located somewhere else. So much is the same everywhere—layout, architecture, buses, horse-drawn trolleys, displays and signs, and living habits of the citizens.

These things are the same in all American cities to an extent that would never be possible in Europe despite the present trend toward uniformity.

And yet, when you come right down to it, local situations in America tend to vary somewhat. Such things as land terrain, a river or the sea, history, and commerce have left their stamp of individuality on the large cities of the East. How much different is Boston, for example, with its aristocratic quarter around the Public Garden and the Common; and the Statehouse with its golden dome—one would look in vain for such a sight in New York. Boston is definitely the most cultured, the most polished, and the most European city on the American continent.

Boston may trail New York as a commercial and shipping center, but there is a tremendous amount of intellectual capital here that flows out to benefit the rest of the country. The wealthy are more solid, older, and better established here in Boston. Commonwealth Avenue, for instance, as an elegant thoroughfare has no competitor anywhere in New York. It has a flavor that usually comes only from people with large amounts of money. But one can learn to live with the self-consciousness of the monied aristocracy when he sees what fine institutions of science, art, and charity all this wealth has produced. Philanthropy for the Americans is commonplace, but here in Boston it has reached its zenith.

Evidence of Bostonian generosity is to be observed almost everywhere—in the galleries built for art collections, the institutions for education, and the buildings for the care of the sick.

The Boston Common and the Public Garden, which is separated from the Common by a boulevard, are both favorite spots in this city. Beautiful old elms cover the rolling terrain and shade the pathways. In the middle of the Common is a memorial, a tall column of white granite, dedicated to the sons of Boston who lost their lives in the Civil War and atop of the pillar is a bronze statue of America. However, the most significant sculpture in these two parks is an equestrian statue of Washington by Thomas Ball.[1] Other monuments of American statesmen have not turned out quite so well, mainly because they are too small for the areas where they are exhibited.

Framed on one side by beautiful private homes and on the other by Boylston Street, a lively business street, these parks could be taken right out of London. They look like St. James's Park. Otherwise the city has no large public squares and the streets are narrower than is usual for American cities. However, a major fire destroyed part of the old city, which subsequently was rebuilt on a broader basis. All traces of the fire have now been cleaned away and the buildings that have risen from the ashes are

[1] The Public Garden, located at the foot of aristocratic Commonwealth Avenue, had been a Boston landmark since it was laid out in the 1860s. There flower beds, grass plots, and shrubs surrounded a pond where during the summer gaily-canopied pleasure boats were much in evidence. At the Arlington Street entrance stood Thomas Ball's giant equestrian statue of George Washington, erected in 1869 and reputed to be the largest of its kind in America. Across Charles Street from the Public Garden was the historic Boston Common, surrounded by a mile-long iron fence, and shaded by over a thousand elms. The Army and Navy Monument, erected to honor the city's sons who fell in the Civil War, was an ugly column of granite seventy feet tall surmounted by a female statue robed in classical drapery. *King's Handbook of Boston Profusely Illustrated* (Cambridge, 1885 edn.), 106–109.

View of the Public Garden and Boston Common

larger and much more glamorous than the older structures.

I first saw the dome of the Statehouse gloriously shining in the morning sun, high on the peak of a hill in the middle of the city.[2] Under close inspection, though, the building lost something of its glamour. It is made of brick, and painted with yellow; only the columns and dome give it splendor. I climbed the steps and walked into the great hall. The interior is completely coated with marble. In glass cases around the walls are the flags of the regiments that Massachusetts contributed to save the Union. After touring the various rooms in the Statehouse, I climbed to the top of the dome. And what a view I had from there: The big city lay at my feet—with its parks, its wide avenues, its straight streets, and its excellent enclosed harbor. All the way down from the border of Maine the coastline has been eroded by the tides and as a result has a wonderful, irregular shape; and so it is in Boston

[2] Massachusetts' famed State House, the "hub of the solar system" according to Bostonians, was built in 1795 from the designs of Charles Bulfinch. Subsequent generations did their best to mar the classical beauty of the original structure; Herr Mohr saw it during its dark ages when its lovely brick walls had been painted yellow. The "Hall of Flags" just inside the main entrance contained the state regimental flags from the Civil War. The great dome, gilded in 1874, rose 110 feet above Beacon Street. "The view from the dome," one guidebook advised, ". . . is very fine, including the city, the harbor and ocean beyond." *Appleton's General Guide*, 88; *King's Handbook of Boston*, 87–90.

also. The beautifully formed shoreline surely attracted the first settlers to Boston. Like New York, it is surrounded on three sides by water. The Charles River to the north hardly merits the name of river since it is more an inlet or bay of the ocean. Similarly on the south side of the Boston peninsula, South Bay extends inland along a tongue of land. On the other shores the suburbs of Cambridge, Charlestown, East Boston and South Boston circle the large city like a big wreath. Boston Harbor is dotted with islands and islets, and only from a very high point, such as in the dome, can one look out beyond them to the sea.

Rising above the motley mixture of houses are many, many churches, most of them bold structures built of stone. Trinity Church is probably the finest example.[3] The view from the dome was truly lovely and for the person better informed it would be even more interesting. Nevertheless, even for me, the foreigner, the panoramic view was practical later when I went into the streets to look at the individual buildings. The golden dome was my landmark and I never let it out of my sight . . . .

[3] Herr Mohr's taste was excellent. Trinity Church, built in 1877 from the designs of Henry H. Richardson, was based on the Romanesque styles of southern France rather than the universally popular Gothic then in vogue, and gave Americans a valuable lesson in the virtues of simplicity. It was, in the opinion of a contemporary, "the finest church edifice in New England, if not in the United States." *King's Handbook of Boston*, 172–173.

Via Charlestown Street I came onto Washington Street, one of the most glorious and lively streets in the city. During the afternoon hours, the crowds here are not different from those on Broadway in New York. The sparkling stores are filled with shoppers and visitors—here in America one can walk into a store without the slightest intention of buying anything. Generally the customers are members of the fair sex, which in this country means the ruling sex. Yet, the type of store, the merchandise, and the manner of display are the same everywhere. Rarely does one see something very distinctive. And the taste in most items seems somewhat dubious. Color combinations, lines, patterns and overall appearance seem to follow an American standard of aesthetics, not ours.

In the matter of women's clothes, it cannot be denied that they do have a certain elegant simplicity. Dark colors are the rule. The cut of the dresses is not very striking and the women use very little jewelry, feathers, or flowers. What patterns and styles I saw in the windows did not look very appealing. For instance, I came upon some strange white brocade material, crocheted over and over with colorful little birds. But for all I know, this might be the latest Paris style, which we will soon be seeing in Bremen . . . .

The city is rich in institutions of art and science as well as in schools and hospitals. Much is still in the developing stage. The Boston Athenaeum, however, is already an institution of remarkable age, at least by American standards. It dates back to the beginning of the century and Franklin's name is linked with its establishment. It has a library of 115,000 volumes and a reading room that is generally restricted to members only.[4] However, others can gain access without too much difficulty. There is also a Historic Genealogical Society that does research on the history of New England and, within its limited sphere, it too has a magnificent library. The collections of both institutions are augmented by the general works in the Boston Public Library. Established through a donation, the Public Library has one of the most significant book collections in the country[5] . . . .

[4] The Boston Athenaeum at 10½ Beacon Street, built between 1847 and 1849, housed an excellent library of 145,000 volumes and was open only to its 1,049 shareholders and their families. Among its treasures was the library of George Washington, purchased in 1848 for $4,000. Although the Athenaeum traced its ancestry to the Anthology Club which had been formed in Boston in 1807 by the father of Ralph Waldo Emerson, its connection with Benjamin Franklin, if any, was remote. *King's Handbook of Boston*, 123-124.

[5] Herr Mohr refers to two of Boston's most venerable institutions. The New England Historic Genealogical Society, incorporated in 1845, maintained an excellent library in a three-story building at 18 Somerset Street; most of its 20,000 volumes and 60,000 pamphlets dealt with local history. The Boston Public Library, then on Boylston Street opposite the Boston Common, was one of the largest in the nation, with 453,935 volumes. *King's Handbook of Boston*, 121-122.

Boston Athenaeum
(central building on right side of Beacon Street)

Likewise excellent is the Society for Natural History and the Society for Technology, each of which was founded and is maintained by both public and private funds.[6] Part of the Technology Institute is

[6] The museum and library of the Boston Society of Natural History was located on Berkeley Street near Boylston, not far from the Massachusetts Institute of Technology, which was on the corner of Boylston and Berkeley Streets. The latter, which had been incorporated in 1861 to operate

an industrial school that teaches young boys and girls the arts of the industrial age. Perhaps nowhere in the world has education in technical matters been offered so equally to boys and girls as here in Massachusetts . . . .

The main center for scientific study in the Boston area is the well-known Harvard University in Cambridge, which can trace its roots back a quarter of a millennium. In the year 1636, six years after the founding of Boston, the college was established in Newton, as the suburb now called Cambridge was then known . . . . In the course of time, it has grown from its modest beginnings to become the most famous university in the New World. The state, the city, former graduates, and friends compete with one another to see who can give the most money to this seat of learning.

About 1,500 students are pursuing here all branches of learning. Instruction is divided into college education, professional education, or graduate studies.[7] Students have their choice to live in either

---

a Society of Arts, a Museum of Arts, and a School of Design, by this time offered courses to seven hundred students in topographical engineering, mechanical engineering, mining, building, and architecture. A School of Mechanical Arts, to which Mohr refers, had recently been added to provide instruction in the manual trades. *King's Handbook of Boston*, 133–134, 148–151.

[7] Harvard University's faculty of 160 was at this time offering instruction to 1,400 students, of whom some 900 were concentrating in the liberal arts and the remainder in professional subjects. Charles W. Eliot, the university's president,

halls or private homes. Also in the selection of their courses they have complete freedom. Required courses did exist earlier, but have been abandoned recently.

For the most part the buildings surround a shady park or quadrangle. These include the halls where the students live, the classroom buildings, and the libraries with their excellent collections. It all looks very untypical of America and yet the buildings are far too modern to be compared to the old grey buildings of Oxford or the English town of Cambridge. Unfortunately my visit was spoiled by a frightful rain storm. The water just poured out of the sky, an icy wind was blowing, and after a few steps from the trolley, I was soaked. Even Memorial Hall, which is the pride of Cambridge, looked washed out. It is a rich Gothic structure that was built in memory of all the sons of Harvard who gave their lives in the Civil War.

Washington

SADDENED that I had only touched the surface of such an interesting city as Boston, I had to leave it. I had the feeling that I could have spent weeks and months getting to know the city—its industry, its commerce, and its intellectual hopes and dreams.

---

had, since he assumed office a dozen years before, been reforming the curriculum to remove rigid requirements, substituting for them an elective system which allowed students to choose their courses, with no prescribed "majors".

Taken from *Frank Leslie's Illustrated Newspaper*

Harvard University campus, with Memorial Hall in foreground

We left Boston in the evening and arrived early the next morning on the Harlem River above New York. A large ferry boat transported that part of the train destined for towns south of New York to the station of the Pennsylvania Railroad, which lies in New Jersey. Our ferry boat unloaded us there. The cars were pulled onto the tracks and hitched to the very next train departing for Philadelphia. Punctuality on American railroads is not very common, so it was not surprising that we missed our train and had to wait for a later one. The advantage of this was that we could make the trip during the day in beautiful sunshine. We rode through the Jersey Heights that ring the city like a wall, then moved on through a rocky cut and out onto a broad plain of uncultivated lowlands.

Next we passed through Newark, a manufacturing city, then through Elizabeth and later Trenton, the capital of New Jersey.

The area is not very appealing until one reaches the vicinity of Philadelphia. Our train passed by Fairmount Park, the pride of Philadelphia, and before we arrived in the station we already had a few good views of the city.[8] At the railroad station we learned that we would be delayed for more than

[8] Fairmount Park, the largest city park in the world, extended along both banks of the Schuylkill River for more than seven miles, and along Wissahickon Creek for another six miles. Its 2,704 acres were maintained in a state of natural beauty, but with occasional zoological gardens and statues. *Appleton's General Guide*, 38–39.

two hours, so we had some time to take a good look around the city.

No sooner had I stepped out of the depot into the street than my eyes became glued to a unique building—the City Hall. It is a rectangular building, the four sides equally proportioned, in the Renaissance style, heavily ornamented but not really in good taste.[9] Grand entrances open onto Market Street and Broad Street, two wide avenues that cross in front. One of the entrances is supposed to be crowned by a tower that will excel in height all other towers in the world and the entire colossal building is to be faced with white marble. However, on the construction site I saw some poured iron ornaments that were painted white to look like marble and destined for high points on the structure. The City Hall has already been under construction for many years and it will take many more before the work is complete. It is clear that Philadelphia likes marble. All the marble I have seen in New York and Boston cannot compare in splendor

[9] Herr Mohr's judgment was good again. The Philadelphia City Hall, planned during the nation's architectural dark ages after the Civil War and under construction for most of the remainder of the century, borrowed its style from the French Renaissance. It had scarcely been completed when public taste for lush architecture shifted so violently that a demand arose that it be torn down. By this time, however, Philadelphians had learned to love their monstrosity and rose in rebellion; instead it was cleaned to reveal a radiant white stone and a bluish slate finish that was startling if not beautiful.

Courtesy of The Free Library of Philadelphia

City Hall, Philadelphia

to what I found in Philadelphia. The buildings themselves, though, do not compare in size with those of New York.

Traveling from Philadelphia to Baltimore, I found the landscape ever more beautiful. In the bright sunshine the forests displayed their rich fall colors—from many shades of red to glowing purple and back to browns and greens. To the left we could see the Delaware River briefly; then it was hidden from view by the city of Wilmington. Leaving Pennsylvania and Delaware, we arrived in the state of Maryland, crossing the Susquehanna River on a long bridge. At this point the river spreads out forming a large bay and its hilly forested banks provided a delightful kaleidoscope of water and colorful trees. After a short stop in Baltimore we moved on toward Washington. The closer we came to the Capital City of the Union, the less attractive was the rural scene. But then suddenly the Capitol became visible before us, rising high into the air and overpowering everything else. The sight was grandiose!

From the first moment, Washington captivates the foreigner. Its wide, hard-surfaced streets are fine and some of them are covered with asphalt. They are lined with trees that shade the sidewalks and there is not that awful rush of people and business. The people here take their time. They walk along as if they were doing it for pleasure and at times you encounter an atmosphere that you would find in a German residential government town.

The city is probably more lively when Congress is in session. I was told that this brings an additional 20,000 people to the city. These thousands are made up of job seekers, politicians, petitioners, curiosity seekers, lobbyists, and the press, all of whom swarm around the Congress. Many of them have time on their hands, so they spend hours on the streets. Thus during the period when the representatives of the people are meeting, the city has a completely different look and the life is far less peaceful than now.

A few weeks before the opening of the session, Washington looks like any major resort city getting ready for its high season. Everybody makes improvements, cleans up, paints, and polishes. Of course there are a multitude of hotels here even though none of them can compare to the major hotels of New York or Chicago. At this time the hotels and apartment buildings are far from filled and the owners do not expect to rent them until December.

Yet, just with its native population, Washington is a large city. The census of 1880, which they say everywhere was far too low, reports the total population for Washington and the District of Columbia as approximately 178,000. This figure includes 60,000 colored people, by which they mean Negroes. Certain streets have only black residents . . . .

From the very beginning Washington was platted on a grand scale and even today the city has not yet grown to the boundaries that were decided upon from the first. The houses seem very low in relation to the width of the streets and this gives the city a scattered appearance. People have given it the nickname of "city of the great distances." In addition to being the city of great distances, Washington is also a city of monuments. Many of the generals and statesmen of this country have been memorialized by great statues and one gets the impression that the Americans are very skillful in making these like true portraits. One of the oddest of the memorials, though, is the Washington Monument, a pillar that juts 600 feet into the air. In its present stage, the square column has already reached a tremendous height and it looks just like the smokestack of a distillery.[10] Although the Congress has allotted the funds for its completion, there is no evidence of any building going on now.

In this capital city the Capitol itself occupies the center of the stage.[11] It stands on a hill about a mile back from the Potomac and ninety feet above it. From this point, avenues radiate in all directions. They cut across the regular checkerboard pattern of the other streets and at the points where they meet at odd angles there are open areas. The Capitol is visible from almost any point, enthroned on its hill and topped by its dazzling white dome . . . . Its columns, steps, frontispiece, and huge dome give the building an idealistic look, well-suited to the

[10] The Washington Monument, standing on the Mall near 14th Street, was planned to stand 600 feet high, but funds were exhausted when it reached 174 feet and work was suspended. Not until 1876 did Congress appropriate the money needed to complete the structure. Construction, as Herr Mohr noted, was soon to be resumed. *Appleton's General Guide*, 57.

[11] The Capitol which crowned Capitol Hill was generally regarded by Americans as "the most magnificent public edifice in the world." It had been under construction since 1815 when its predecessor was destroyed during the War of 1812, following basic designs by Benjamin H. Latrobe. The central dome had only been added between 1856 and 1865. *Appleton's General Guide*, 50.

Courtesy of The Library of Congress

United States Capitol

goals of the governing body. This quality is all the more appealing when contrasted to the realistic interests that dominate American life. The Capitol and other state buildings have been built in either a Graeco-Roman or a Renaissance style, both borrowed from a world that has little in common with the form and substance of the young Republic of the United States.

General Washington would have had difficulty finding the ideals of the Republic either in Athens or in Rome. The American basic principle of government contradicts that of ancient Greece and Rome sharply. While the ancients had a differentiated state system governing society, the United States constitution rests on the universal equality of all citizens. Since the abolition of slavery, and since the Negroes have become citizens, there is no comparison anymore.

Despite all these enigmas, the Capitol projects a fine image. Its dimensions, its position, the material used, all fill the observer with a feeling of reverence. One can hardly escape the thought that the calm and beautiful proportion that exudes from the building itself will somehow inspire the same qualities in the men who sit in it and deliberate about the well-being of their country. Perhaps the day will come when the period of fermentation and impetuosity of young America will have calmed down. When this stage has been reached, the leaders of the country will no longer be swayed by their lower passions. Rather, they will make their decisions here in a spirit of wise and patriotic counsel.

From early morning until dark, when the Congress is not meeting, all of the rooms in the Capitol are open to the public. Large crowds of people come on pilgrimages to wander about in the rooms. The greatest attraction seems to be the rotunda where the sons of the Republic stand captivated by the symbolic recreations of their great historical events. The less the people of this country are affected by history, the more they cling to that which links the present to the past. Many things indicate that the American senses a vacuum in the brevity of his history and by that token tries to preserve what he does have by honoring it with greater reverence and piety . . . .

The White House, as the official residence of the President of the United States is known, is the other attraction in Washington.[12] Even though the Capitol is undeniably beautiful in many respects, it does not fit well into its surroundings. Quite the opposite is true of the White House. It fits in perfectly, but by that token it does not look like the official residence of a President. With its lovely park and garden and the broad view of the Potomac, the house looks just like the rural home of a country gentleman . . . .

Otherwise practically every building that is used by the United States government is classical in style. Yet nowhere else in the city does one find even a modest form of this classical style. It seems that the government buildings do not have the slightest influence on the rest of the architecture of the city. The good and simple citizens of Washing-

[12] The White House was first occupied by President John Adams in 1800. It was extensively rebuilt after the damage done during the War of 1812, and when Herr Mohr saw it, it looked much as it had since 1824 when the north and south porticoes were added.

ton apparently have no understanding of this style, but then they are neither Greeks nor Romans. The sad fact is that the houses in Washington are even more drab—if that is possible—than those in other cities of this country . . . .

Washington is alive only when the Congress is in session. Then it really becomes the capital of the United States. But at any time it is worthy of a visit.

18

Baltimore Back to New York

New York

O<small>N</small> my way back from Washington I took time to pay a visit to Baltimore. I am not really sure why I wanted to go to Baltimore, but somehow I expected to find it a city essentially different from the other American cities. I guess I had imagined that Baltimore would be more of a southern type city. In this I was naturally disappointed. The capital city of Maryland has exactly the same style of buildings, the same layout, and the same appearance as any other American city.

Yet it does have a pretty location. The environs are appealing and the city itself lies on a hilly terrain so that even from the streets there are pleasant and panoramic views over the city. Away from the construction area around the Union Depot, the streets look quite pleasant. They have used a bright red brick and the windows and doors are framed with white granite. Since the steps have been made of the same granite, the city offers a lively contrast of color. In addition, there are red blinds on the windows, which add to the rich display of color. Farther downtown in the older section of the city the reds do not predominate so strongly. In that

Courtesy of the Maryland Historical Society

View of Baltimore

Taken from *A Souvenir of Baltimore*

area, smoke, fumes, and time have taken their toll.

Baltimore is one of the older cities in the country. One hundred and fifty years have passed since its founding. To be sure, in its first years the city developed very slowly. But in the first decades of this century, a large tract of land was platted for the expansion of the city, using the typically American square pattern. So, with few exceptions, all streets run straight and cross each other at right angles . . . .

Baltimore is a significant export center, but it is suffering at present from the competition of New York. The city does a good business in oysters. These are caught in Chesapeake Bay and are brought to the markets to be shipped either inland or to foreign ports. Although trade in all directions does keep Baltimore strong, one still feels the pressure of the Empire City. Due to her great import business, New York is also in a position to draw all export articles into her sphere for shipping, even in cases where great distances do not make that entirely practical. Therefore most people recognize that the future of Baltimore and the state of Maryland is dependent for the most part on the growth of their own industries.

Baltimore has been successful in this respect and it is a joy to learn that among the established firms, many are German. The German element in Baltimore makes up a very large percentage of the population. For the many German merchants there is a Germania Club and its recreation room is adorned with a portrait of the late Consul General Schumacher.[1] He was one of the most respected

[1] Of Baltimore's population of 332,518 in 1880, only 34,051 were German-born, a smaller proportion than in the western cities Herr Mohr had visited. Their Germania Club was housed in a sumptuous building on Lafayette Street where it served as a center for the community's social life, as it had since its founding in 1840. One of its most prominent early members was Albert Schumacher, who had reached

businessmen in Baltimore and his firm continues to be one of the top leaders among the shipping merchants . . . .

The pride of the city is the Druid Hill Park. There art and nature have combined to create a splendid public park in the immediate vicinity of the city.[2] And the city did not have to wait decades before the park would outgrow the character of raw construction and new planting. For one hundred and fifty years these five hundred acres had been in the hands of the Rogers family, who had cultivated and cared for the area with fine taste and true devotion. In 1868 the city bought the property from the family for a half million dollars. At its southern entrance the city has built a large water reservoir, creating a lake with a circumference of more than a mile. Along one forested shore there is a delightful pathway.

Some gracious Germans of Baltimore took me on a tour of the park, then out beyond it to the envi-

the United States from his native Bremen in 1826 and by 1839 achieved wealth and influence as an exporter and business executive. For a time he served as Consul General for both Hamburg and Bremen, and had been president of the Germania Club. Dieter Cunz, *The Maryland Germans* (Princeton, 1948), 229–243.

[2] Druid Hill Park was a pleasure ground of 680 acres on the northern edge of the city, reached by horse car along Madison Avenue. It had been sold to the city in 1868 by Nicholas L. Rogers, and was maintained as a nature sanctuary, with few architectural decorations to add to its natural beauty. A tower at the head of Druid Hill Lake offered a fine view of the city. *Appleton's General Guide*, 47.

rons of Baltimore. I could not get enough of the
charming landscape. It is pleasant and comfortable,
yet covered with vegetation that is in part strange to
us. It is so luxuriant and rich that one marvels how
such delicate plants can endure the grim, cold win-
ters. I must admit that nowhere else in America did
the region so captivate me as the environs of Baltimore, despite the fact that the sunshine was very
thrifty in showing itself.

I will remember with pleasure the pleasant and
interesting company and the hearty welcome which
my German countrymen gave to me in Baltimore.
One thing was most touching: Even though they
have established their homes and found their independence on American soil and even though many
now belong to the highest society, nevertheless
their burning love for the Fatherland has not been
extinguished.

Now, after a week back in this Empire City, I find
the courage to attempt some evaluations of New
York. It is indeed an undertaking, for this is the
principal city not only of the United States but also
of the entire hemisphere. Every walk through the
streets, every glance in a store, every conversation,
every view of the sea, absolutely everything manifests a new perspective on the complexity and the
gigantic dimensions of this city. To us strangers it
all looks so very American, while to the Americans
it looks so European. Paris and London are the

only cities one can compare to New York and yet both of these lie far inland. New York is built on a low, narrow strip of rock, completely surrounded by salt water. In three directions—to the south, west, and east—there can be no further expansion whatever. The Hudson and the East River are so huge that they cannot help but form barriers. And no matter how integrated the cities of Brooklyn, Jersey City, and Hoboken seem to be with the core city of New York, the fact remains that they follow their own development paths. In addition they have their own peculiarities even though they are interdependent with the city of New York.

Together these cities comprise a huge metropolitan complex. New York alone has perhaps one and one half million people, while the other parts together have about one million. This population size presupposes an intricate passenger transportation network to move the large masses of people back and forth. This explains why the streets are always jammed with thousands of vehicles of all types. Some are old fashioned and high-wheeled buses that lumber along on the poor pavement; others are the horsedrawn railway cars. There is also the elevated railroad that runs on tracks supported by steel structures about twenty feet off the ground.

For the same reasons, there is an unbelievably heavy but glorious barge traffic on the waters around New York, all serving inland commerce. The barge traffic is so thick, in fact, that one tends to overlook the heavy traffic of seagoing vessels. Without interruption, monstrous ferries hurry back and forth, carrying men and vehicles across the Hudson and East rivers, or to Staten Island.

The most heavily used traffic artery in the city is Broadway, which is an exception to the regular street pattern. It is most elegant at the point where it intersects Fifth Avenue forming Madison Square. Lower down it is just another street to handle traffic to the warehouses and farther north its character becomes very mixed. Amidst all this feverish movement lies Trinity Church with its cemetery. Below City Hall, Broadway reaches its climactic point in terms of traffic, movement, confusion, and sensations. Then it ends almost idyllically in Bowling Green on the Battery, a square covered with trees and lawns.[3] This is the area of Castle Garden, where the immigrants usually land, and the park surely makes the friendliest impression possible on them. At the fringe of this splendid park is the turnaround for all the elevated railroad lines. Close to Bowling Green the railroads branch out in different directions. They have so nearly covered the streets, one has the impression of looking into a tunnel.

Berlin has its city railroad and London has its

[3] The Battery in those less-crowded days was a pretty little park at the southern tip of Manhattan, with a fine view of the bay, and "adorned with fine trees and verdant lawns." At its southwestern edge was Castle Garden, a large building used at this time as a depot for immigrants arriving in the United States. *Appleton's Complete Guide*, 7.

Park Place, New York City

Taken from Rudolf Cronau's *Von Wunderland zu Wunderland*

underground railways, but neither of these transportation systems has been so inconsiderate of the
people who lived nearby while they were expanding. In New York, the price of land is much too
high to even think of clearing away buildings for a
railroad as was done in Berlin, and the bed rock
underfoot has rendered hopes for an underground
subway unthinkable. So they have simply built the
tramway over the streets at a height that would not
interfere with the normal traffic below. Naturally
all the streets that have been covered have lost their
beauty completely. All the buildings that front on
such streets have their lower stories shadowed in the
dark, and in one way or another they all suffer from
the elevated. For what it can do, though, this kind
of elevated railroad is a fine invention. It is built
with common sense and is so practical that one
grows to like it and uses it often.[4] To be sure the
elevated differs from the buses in that the trains
cannot stop wherever passengers want to get on or
off. At irregular intervals, usually at a point where
an avenue crosses a main thoroughfare, there will be
a platform.

[4] At this time four elevated railroads, all operated by the
Manhattan Elevated Railroad Company, extended length-
wise through the city. Three—the Second, Sixth, and Ninth
Avenue lines—started from the Battery. Trains operated on
a schedule four minutes apart, save during rush hours when
they were only two minutes apart. Fares were five cents during rush hours, and ten cents at other times. Several lines of
horse cars also criss-crossed the city, supplemented by om-
nibuses and hackney coaches. *Appleton's General Guide*, 2.

Loading and unloading are exceptionally quick. This is possible because everybody knows just where to go. When the business of the day is finished, hundreds of people crowd onto each platform. Yet in a jiffy the entire crowd is on board. How often these trains run past a given station I am not certain, but I believe that at certain hours of the day, when the demand is heavy, one train follows on the heels of the next. In spite of the frequency and speed of the trains, they seem to be run with great care and skill.

Not all tracks run the same distance north of the city. The one extending the farthest is on Nineteenth Avenue. It carried us along through the areas of future New York. Below Central Park—that is, to 58th Street—the city is built solidly together. East and west of Central Park are many open spaces for houses still to be built. The park runs from 59th Street to 110th, a distance of about three miles. At the upper end of the park the buildings stop altogether. Here only the outlines of the cross streets are visible. Beyond, the whole landscape looks just like a platted city superimposed on a wild terrain. Not only have the streets been staked out, they have even been provided with street lights. Viewing it from a distance, the area looks like a large-mesh screen made of wires at right angles. Here and there are fully built clusters of dwellings, then again only isolated houses, or a single brick apartment house. For the most part, though, what one sees from the

elevated railroad is just an open field being prepared for the future. In some parts the unbuilt
blocks are used for flower and vegetable gardens.
Sometimes they grow right out in the open, sometimes in greenhouses; and the products no doubt
bring a good price down in the New York markets.
In other blocks, squatters have settled. These are
migrants who, finding difficulty paying rent to a
landlord, throw up temporary board shacks. There
they live until the lot has been sold or excavated for
a building.

It seems that the city of New York has no limits
of growth toward the north. The numbered streets
continue all the way to 155th Street with the avenues running through them from south to north.
There are indications that the streets will someday
continue all the way to the city of Yonkers, which
borders New York on the north.

Two and a half centuries ago, according to the
legend, the island of Manhattan was sold by the
Indians to the Dutch for sixty guilders and New
Amsterdam was founded. We are not so foolish as
to want to know how Manhattan Island will look in
another 250 years. But how will it look in another
fifty if development continues at the same pace as
today? Those who live to see it will probably think
of the New York in our time as being small and lost
in the past, just as New Amsterdam seems to us
today.

19

The Farewell Banquet

New York
October 16, 1883

Eɴᴅᴇ ɢᴜᴛ, ᴀʟʟᴇs ɢᴜᴛ! All's well that ends well, one could say after the farewell celebration yesterday evening. The stately troupe that boarded the *Elbe* in Bremerhafen gathered once more with as many of its original members as could be brought together.

We departed from Germany on the fifteenth of August and after reaching Portland, the party gradually broke apart for individual excursions hither and yon. In the faces and words of everyone present last evening, there was a genuine conviction that we had just concluded a trip that would be a source of satisfaction and enrichment for many years to come. The trip also gave us diversion and pleasure, as well as a broadened knowledge. While these two months included excellent accommodations, they also occasioned minor inconveniences making up a total experience that hardly any of us had ever had before.

Tomorrow the main contingent of our party will depart for Europe on board the *Werra*, another steamer of the North German Lloyd. A few of us have already left, but the rest of us have gathered at

Delmonico's Restaurant which is on Fifth Avenue. This restaurant is considered the finest in New York and probably does not take second place to any in the world.[1]

A large number of the party had gone from Portland to San Francisco to return here via the Central Pacific Railroad. Some of these remained longer in San Francisco, others took a trip to the Yosemite Valley, still others went south to have a look at Colorado and Arizona. Not until they arrived back here were they together again in the Brunswick Hotel, which is the main center for our party . . . .

In New York the German-Americans joined us, swelling our party to more than fifty persons. When we had met at the Ratskeller in Bremen at the start of our journey, the future looked rather uncertain. For most of us, America was still a strange land and we were still strange to each other. Virtually none of us knew one another personally and yet we were to share the joys and sorrows of a two-month journey. Of course we had little or no comprehension about the distance of the trip. How would the people of America receive us? What would they think of us? Countless other questions occurred to every-

[1] The reunited members of the German party were again at the Brunswick Hotel, where they had stayed when they arrived in New York. Delmonico's, directly across the street, was generally acknowledged to be the best restaurant in the United States and, according to Americans, "one of the best restaurants in the world," noted for its elaborate dinners and fine wine cellar. *Appleton's General Guide*, 1.

one and we all had to wait for the future to evolve its answer.

Now we not only knew what the American continent had in store, but we also knew how well we have endured our common test. On the whole we were well satisfied. We could truly say to each other that not the slightest disagreement had disturbed our harmony and that our appearances and actions gave no cause for misunderstanding. The hospitality of the Northern Pacific Railroad in the person of its president, Henry Villard, went far beyond any of our expectations. He never let on how heavily his responsibilities weighed on him and he personally saw to it that all his plans were carried out to the last detail.

Just think for a moment what this meant. At its largest, our party included 361 persons and we traveled a distance of 3,000 to 4,000 miles out and the same back, in regions that were barely opened up to civilization, across a railroad which was just then completed. In one respect we were fortunate. All accidents on the railroad were without serious consequences. Moreover, every one of the accidents was caused by defective equipment or material. The mental composure of the American train personnel in these critical moments was truly admirable. This in itself prevented worse things from happening.

In the course of his eventful life, Henry Villard has surely carried some heavy burdens of worry. Perhaps no moment in his life has given him more cause for relief than seeing his task fulfilled. His guests have gone to the Pacific and returned safely; finally his responsibility for their well-being and safety is over.

Everything that happened in the eventful nine weeks since departing from our homeland filled our minds as we sat down at the horseshoe table in the dining room of Delmonico's. Richly decorated with flowers, china, fine glassware, and lamps, the table was elegant. The restaurant lived up to its worldwide reputation. The food was prepared tastefully and attractively. The wines were splendid.[2] But the habit here of suddenly passing out cigarettes during the meal to whet the appetite for more is a freakish custom which they must have imported from Cuba or Russia. They do not, however, have the custom of delivering speeches during the meals as we in Germany.

The toast of the evening—to our honored guest Henry Villard—was spoken by Privy Councilman Professor Hofmann. Hofmann always speaks with a delightful humor and last night he was better than ever.[3] He began with a quote from George Sand:

[2] So they were; six were served during the meal, which began with Consommé Marie Stuart and Timbales à la Rothschild and ended with Gaufres à la Crème and Soufflé Vanille. A printed menu of the dinner of October 15, given by "his German guests" to honor Henry Villard, is in the Villard Excursion File, Folder 4-7.

[3] Dr. A. W. Hofmann, famed professor of chemistry at the University of Berlin, who spoke so eloquently on this occasion, was himself to be honored at a dinner given by the

"Voyager c'est apprendre, apprendre c'est vivre."[4]
This wise proverb must above all refer to those who
accompanied our honored guest on his triumphal
journey from the shores of the Atlantic to the Pacific Coast. We have indeed lived and learned. In the
first place we have learned to know the triumphant
victor himself. We have also learned to love and
appreciate him. No matter what the speakers say,
they cannot honor Villard in the way he deserves to
be honored. Noting this fact, the speaker refreshed
for our minds a few of the things Villard had shown
us in the past few weeks.

He recalled the high points of our trip from Niagara Falls to Puget Sound and to Yellowstone Park.
He dwelt also for a time on the impressive festival
in Seattle where the main speaker had addressed
Henry Villard and said, "You have released us, Sir,
as it were from solitary confinement." Then, bor-
rowing the words William Evarts used in one of his
speeches, Hofmann apologized by saying, "I do not
recall that I have ever given a short speech, but
neither can I remember ever hearing a short speech
in America." With that, he called on all present to
express heartfelt thanks and good wishes for Henry
Villard's great undertaking, the Northern Pacific

American Chemical Society at the Hotel Brunswick the
next evening. *New York Times*, October 17, 1883, p. 5.

[4] The French novelist George Sand, or Madame Amantine
Lucile Aurore, to use her full name, was quoted as saying
that "To travel is to comprehend, and to comprehend is to
live."

Railroad, that it might continue to grow and flourish. With a powerful outcry we thundered, "*Heinrich Villard, lebe hoch!*" "Long live Henry Villard!"

When the storm of applause finally died down, Villard took the opportunity to say thank you with a few poignant words. He is really no public speaker, but his thoughts slowly worked their way out of his mind in a pleasant, touching way. Until today, he said, he felt like an innkeeper for some thirty or forty Germans and German-Americans. Today, at last, he felt like a guest with that many tourguides looking out for his welfare. He said he liked this new arrangement very well. Then he went on to thank his German guests for accepting the invitation and for participating in the completion of the work that he considered his privilege to bring to its conclusion. He expressed the hope that once back in our homes, we would continue to relay our good feelings toward both the railroad and its president. He admitted that he had to overcome many obstacles in bringing about the completion of the railroad. And even at this very moment he was under heavy siege, but he was confident today as before that he had the strength to ward off the attacks and maintain his great work. With best wishes for a happy return trip, he closed amid an outburst of spontaneous and warm applause.

Others spoke also, including Carl Schurz, who said how much he and his American friends had enjoyed this trip with their compatriots from Germany. He reassured us that we had made a fine and lasting impression on many Americans. Becoming more serious, Schurz expressed the hope that we would carry with us the impression that America is truly a land with a great future, that America is not without a streak of idealism, and that her citizens have an unshakable faith in the greatness of their country.

I myself then spoke a word of thanks on behalf of the press. We parted shortly before midnight.[5]

This evening those of our party sailing with the *Werra* will board their ship, for she is to depart tomorrow morning at five o'clock. Representatives of the press including myself will sail on October 31. We hope that our companions will have a good and fast crossing. Unfortunately the weather does not look very promising, but *navigare necesse est.*

[5] The *New York Times*, which had lavished such publicity on the visiting Villarders when they arrived, failed even to mention their farewell dinner. It did note that the *Werra* was to sail on October 17. *New York Times*, October 17, 1883, p. 5.

EPILOGUE

Nicolaus Mohr as a Foreign Observer of the United States

W HEN Nicolaus Mohr published his *Excursion Through America* he joined a host of foreign observers who used a visit to the New World (sometimes distressingly brief) as a basis for observations and speculations designed to explain to their fellow-countrymen that inexplicable land beyond the seas. When he did so he was in excellent—and numerous—company. Writing travel accounts was a minor industry in Great Britain during the nineteenth century, and attracted a surprising number of authors in both Germany and France. The volumes they produced, numbering into the many hundreds, shed a great deal of light on the American civilization they were describing, but they also reveal a real thirst in the Old World for news about the New.

This was easy to understand. America, virtually since its discovery, had been to Europeans not only a *terra incognita* but a land of promise, beckoning the dispossessed and the discontented with all its unoccupied lands, its abundant opportunities for

economic self-advancement, its less than rigid strati-
fied social structure, and its prospects for adventure
and romance in an untamed wilderness. Yet few
could probe its mysteries; tradition-bound schools
and universities largely ignored the New World until well into the twentieth century, denying the educated classes the in-depth analysis of the American
social order that they wished. Newspapers and magazines published occasional articles about the United States, but the authenticity of such accounts was
rightly suspect. So were the pen-pictures painted by
fiction writers in their novels and stories.

To thousands of Europeans thirsting for news of
the New World, then, the traveler who had visited
there was the only reliable source of authentic information. He could be relied upon, for he was,
after all, an eye-witness observer of the events and
scenes he described. Given this belief, and given
also the overwhelming curiosity of Englishmen and
Frenchmen and Germans concerning the United
States as a possible future home, the demand for
travel books becomes comprehensible. That demand was large, and seemingly endless. Publishers
in London, Paris, Leipzig, or Florence were eager to
print virtually any book-length travel account that
came their way. The prospects of such a market as
this not only stoked the travel industry (for many
made the journey with that well-paying book in
mind), but inspired a good many hundred travelers
to record their impressions, even though many of

those who did so were ill-equipped by training and skill for the task.

The accounts they prepared can be understood only against this background, for their purpose was to answer a number of questions about the United States that Europeans were constantly asking. Most tailored their accounts to these questions, ignoring other aspects of the New World scene just as important. All varied their themes with changing interests; the curiosity of Europeans shifted from point to point with the passing decades, and the astute traveler sought to satisfy the audience for which he was writing. Thus the interests of the members of the Villard party, and of Nicolaus Mohr, were not always those of European pilgrims who had preceded them, but typified the 1880s when they made their excursion.

One constant interest that varied little from the eighteenth century to the twentieth was in the natural wonders of the New World: its flora, its fauna, its land forms, and particularly its native peoples. European curiosity concerning the red Indian began to rise when Columbus told his first tales, and did not begin to abate until the last tribesman was driven onto a reservation. Britain's Royal Society was eager for every crumb of information that could be obtained on unusual plants, unique animal species, different birds, distinctive geological structures, and especially the life and psychology of the red men. So were the learned societies—and the educated intellectual elite—of France and Germany and Italy. This travelers knew, and they did their best to lard their narratives with information and descriptions to satisfy this hunger.

When Professor K. A. Zittel of the University of München [Munich] left the Villard Party to explore Mount Tacoma or led the assault on Mount Mac-Donald in quest of geological information he typified that traditional interest in the unknown new land. So did Professor A. W. Hofmann of the University of Berlin when he branched out by himself to collect "water from the spouting geysers [of Yellowstone National Park] to take back home for analysis." And so also did the artist, Konrad Dielitz, when he left his friends to live for a time among the Crow Indians. By the 1880's America's natural wonders were too well known in Europe to spark the interest that they had a century before, but enough survived to help explain the interests of the party and the nature of Herr Mohr's observations.

No less intriguing to Europeans than the world of nature was the opportunity for adventure and romance offered by the unsettled wastes of the New World. To men and women living in a closed society, where restraints on conduct were commonplace and life on farm or mill increasingly humdrum, the image of America as a land of danger and excitement, where raw strength ruled and men battled for righteousness with fists and six-shooters, was forever fascinating. The American types that captured Europe's imagination were those that personified the hazards of frontier life—the fur trappers, Indian fighters, bad men, and cowboys above all others. This travelers knew, and they were constantly on the look-out for dramatic examples of American lawlessness to spice their pages. When Nicolaus Mohr listened to tall tales of a vigilance committee operating in Helena in 1883 he was engaging in a bit of wishful thinking typical of most of those who wrote about the New World.

If America was an example of disrespect for the law for some Europeans, it was for others the counterpart of the political democracy that they hoped to achieve in their own lands. Until the American Civil War their concern was with the success or failure of the democratic experiment, and travelers shared their prejudices by reporting instances that would bolster pre-conceived beliefs on both sides. After that struggle demonstrated its permanence, observers shifted their interest to an analysis of its institutional structure and reasons for its success. Visitors to the United States, from Alexis de Tocqueville on, wrote endlessly of the federal system, analyzing its strength and weaknesses, and cataloguing the features that explained its endurance. This interest was as alive in the 1880s as it had been a half-century earlier. The primary purpose of some members of the Villard party was to study governmental operations at first hand. Professor Rudolf von Gneist, the best-known representative of the academic world among the group, was an authority on the common law and Anglo-American legal practices. As a leader of the opposition liberal party in the German Reichstag he was searching for models fashioned in the American crucible that could be applied to democratize government practices at home. Both he and most others in the party mirrored the enlightened interest in American institutions common among German liberals of that day, seeking as they were to improve political, industrial, and social procedures in their own land.

Even more intriguing to this group—and to many Europeans—than the democratic example provided by the United States was the prospect of economic gain offered by the exploitation of its untapped resources. During the early nineteenth century, especially, the primary object of travelers had been utilitarian inquiry; they observed, and wrote, with an eye to the needs of the millions of potential emigrants eager to search for a much greater chance for self-advancement outside their homelands. Their reports –stressing the plentiful job opportunities in American farming and the higher standards of living there—had much to do with setting in motion the immigrant tides that added so greatly to the numbers and greatness of the United States. Now, in the closing years of the century, travelers were less concerned with American opportunity for individuals than for its potentials as a seat for investment. German—and English and French and Ital-

Italian—capitalists were well aware that higher profits were obtainable in a developing than in a stabilized economy. Visitors to the United States could tell them where their money would bring the highest return.

The Villard party mirrored this new interest. The bankers and business magnates sprinkled through its ranks had been invited by Henry Villard partly because he wanted to interest them in the economic potentials of the northwestern states; he was well aware that they commanded total assets of $100,000,000 and counted on them to be so impressed with what they saw that a sizable portion of this sum would be diverted into the region served by his railroads. He need not have worried; those German capitalists would have sensed that opportunity under any circumstances, canny investors that they were. Nicolaus Mohr shared their opinion, much to Villard's delight, for his Bremen newspaper was a power in commercial circles in northern Germany. Mohr was also deeply interested in the German-Americans he met in such large numbers during his tour, seeing in their success the success of the emigration policy that had drained central Europe of so much of its manpower during this century.

The Villard party in general, then, and Nicolaus Mohr in particular, typified the interests that motivated most of the European travelers who had visited America in the past. How did they compare with those observers as accurate portrayers of the national scene? That Mohr can be ranked with Alexis de Tocqueville, Harriet Martineau, Matthew Arnold, Alexander MacKay, Charles Dickens, James Bryce, or a dozen others of their ilk cannot be pretended. His visit was too brief, his purpose too utilitarian, his contacts too limited by his inclination to seek out his fellow-Germans, to allow him to probe the depths of the American character or to offer penetrating insights into the nature of the social structure and the elements of democratic institutions. Too, the circumstances under which his book was written—in brief moments snatched from a busy schedule—left little time for the reflections that would have added understanding to his observations. His was but a surface-skimming assignment, confined to the external appearances rather than the molding forces shaping the nation's culture.

Yet to dismiss Nicolaus Mohr as a superficial recorder is to ignore his significant contributions and conceal the fact that he dovetailed surprisingly well into the pattern of European travelers who wrote about the United States. It is also to escape the touches of skepticism that add lightness to his narrative. The very title chosen for his book, *Ein Streifzug durch den Nordwesten Amerikas: Festfahrt zur Northern Pacific-Bahn im Herbste 1883* (literally: *Roaming through the American Northwest: A Festival Journey on the Northern Pacific Railroad in the Fall of 1883*) followed the usual pattern of nineteenth century travel literature by holding out a promise of adventure and exotic revel to the reader. Moreover, Mohr wrote with that typical florid German of the late nineteenth century which allowed a touch of romanticism in his descriptions of the natural scenery. Interspersed throughout, however, were touches of wry humor. He narrated with whimsical exaggeration and with tongue in cheek, especially when he was describing the parades in Minneapolis and St. Paul and Portland celebrating the opening of the railroad.

In this sense, Mohr's account differed from the overly-serious travel reporting about America which was common in the nineteenth century; in other aspects it seems at first glance to follow familiar patterns. It seems, in other words, to be thoroughly ordinary with little to add to the literary form that it represented. Yet it did differ, and in a way that adds to its significance. For Mohr's narrative, *Excursion Through America,* was distinguished by its all-embracing scope, by the fact that it offered readers an unfolding panorama of American life in 1883 from coast to coast.

Viewed in this light, the volume emerges as one of the most comprehensive travel accounts written by a foreign observer during the second half of the nineteenth century. He was, as was often the case with travelers, carried away by his theme: the opening of the Northern Pacific and the colorful series of events accompanying that ceremony. Yet he did not allow this to dominate his narrative; the excursion became simply a medium for a description of a segment of the continent extending from New York to Seattle. This might be hurriedly written, dictated as it was by the pace of the journey, but not too hastily to allow Mohr to express sound judgments and make invaluable comparisons. He, not unlike other travelers, found the latter particularly valuable in giving his readers in Germany a common point of reference. Thus he recorded the observation of the Berliners in the group when they saw the lake resort area outside Minneapolis that they were on their native Wannsee. When Mohr viewed the hillsides near Portland they recalled to him the rolling countryside of the Black Forest. On the Hudson, or steaming up the Columbia River past Vancouver, he was reminded of the Rhine Valley, but with all the landscape on the larger scale of the American West. His report was filled with these comparisons, enlightening his readers and driving home both the similarities and differences of the two lands.

He was, basically, a fact-finding journalist, relying heavily on the guidebooks he carried for a hard core of information of the sort interesting to Germans; the stress in his narrative on the percentage of German-Americans in each city was a case in point. He also had a keen ear for information on investment possibilities, trade developments, and the economic potentialities of the regions he visited; this was a practical concern for a publisher whose *Weser*

Zeitung was noted throughout Germany for its commercial news. Yet Mohr was sensitive to the American spirit of progress; no other facet of the national character was so well portrayed in his book. He heralded the completion of the Northern Pacific as "Ereignis in der Geschichte der Menschheit"—as one of the great events in human history. Nicolaus Mohr—and most of his fellow-guests who witnessed the last-spike ceremony—viewed the event as a triumph of civilization, opening as it did vast new areas to cultivation. Here was the American view of progress, unclouded by any concern with the sacredness of the environment. Mohr mirrored the viewpoint of town-boosters along the right-of-way who enshrined Henry Villard as their hero because he gave them the tool to conquer nature.

He reflected their attitude, too, in his refusal to idealize the American Indian. True, Mohr faithfully recorded Carl Schurz's frequent pleas for a humanitarian treatment of Uncle Sam's wards, but he did so more because a fellow German was voicing these sentiments than because of genuine concern with the plight of the red man. In his eyes there was nothing wrong in confining Indians to reservations (or forcing them to demean themselves by dancing for visitors); this was their just lot if they refused to conform to the superior civilization that was offering them a fine opportunity to better themselves.

In these sentiments there was little reminder of Europeans of a century before who had glorified the noble savage as one of the most enviable of God's creations.

In this sentiment, and in lack of concern with the slaughter of buffalo and the ravaging of nature's riches, Nicolaus Mohr reflected a shift in interest among travelers that was indeed indicative of a changing social order within the United States. Europe was awakening to the fact that the New World's greatest contribution to the future was the technological genius of its people. Travelers responded to this shift by glorifying the city and the factory rather than the wonders of nature. Mohr described the bustling surge of life in New York City with almost Whitmanesque exuberance; he waxed poetic over the energy and hustle of the people there and admired the Brooklyn Bridge as one of the modern wonders of the world. He marveled at such innovations as the elevated railroads in Manhattan and the cable-drawn streetcars in Chicago, just as travelers of a century before had marveled at the beauties of the Hudson River Valley. He, too, admired the Palmer House in Chicago not for the excellence of its service or the superiority of its cuisine but because it was the largest in the world. He cited Chicago as "Beispiel des fabalhaften Aufschwung"—a fine example of the fabulous progress that was skyrocketing the size of American cities. Mohr—and the Americans whose opinions he mirrored—were yet unaware of the problems bred of urban growth. Those nightmare visions of slums, of family dislocation, of pollution, were for the future. Mohr could glow with pride, as could the Americans, with the trend toward the metropolitanism then transforming the landscape.

He revealed this prejudice with the many city portraits that he sketched as he journeyed westward. Each town visited along the tracks of the Northern Pacific Railroad was glowingly described; so were the older cities that he visited on his return journey. Each—St. Louis, Louisville, Cincinnati, Boston, Baltimore, Washington—was a metropolis which was worthy of his notice—and praise. Urban crowding, ever-spreading slums, air contamination, sweatshops, stark poverty, crime and intemperance—all these were urban phenomena in the 1880s, stirring the first reformers into action. But Mohr, and the American elite with whom he associated, closed their eyes to these evils. He could note with satisfaction that he considered Buffalo to be a town with a "big city feeling" and Cleveland as worth seeing because it was "supposedly one of the most charming cities in the United States."

Nicolaus Mohr not only saw the American city through the rose-tinted glasses of his day—and class—but even tried (as most foreign observers did not) to do justice to American cultural achievements. To do so required overcoming a deep traditional prejudice; even though some Europeans of that day were willing to concede the material and economic advances made by the United States, all were reluctant to admit any achievements in the fine arts. Carl Schurz, speaking at the final dinner for Henry Villard at Delmonico's, was almost plaintive when he hoped that the returning dignitaries would carry with them the impression that the Americans were "not without a streak of idealism." This Mohr tried to do. When he visited Boston he noted its many fine libraries, and glorified the role of Harvard University in American education. Commenting on an art exhibit in Louisville, Kentucky he was pleased to discover that the United States had produced many practicing artists, even though the quality of the works did not satisfy Old World standards. Mohr also was aware of the significance of philanthropy in American cultural life, commenting favorably on the vast fortunes left by wealthy Bostonians for worthy causes. Yet, favorable though he might be, he was also honest enough to criticize fashions and architecture that offended his sense of good taste. Here he showed sound judgment, without at the same time displaying the sense of arrogance common among other travelers such as Matthew Arnold who so seriously offended their American hosts.

If Nicolaus Mohr differed from some observers of the American scene by his greater tolerance for the nation's emerging culture, he joined with even more of them in detecting admirable traits in the American character. He noticed the neatness of the small towns through which he passed, the greater affluence of large segments of the people, the uniformity and at the same time the diversity of their customs, the comfort of travel accommodations. He was also impressed, as were most visitors, with the hospitality extended to foreigners and indeed to most strangers. He observed the extent to which society was disciplined, and the power of the herd instinct in shaping social conduct. He was impressed with the patience shown by Americans when inconvenienced by conditions beyond their control; Mohr contrasted the patience and good humor of Villard's guests when forced to wait long hours for overdue trains with what he imagined would be the reaction of his countrymen under similar circumstances. He, in common with many visitors before him, was overwhelmed by the colossal distances of the great West, and felt at times a "terrible monotony" as the Northern Pacific train labored across the continent. Here were sentiments and observations expressed by most travelers who visited in the United States during the nineteenth century, suggesting that Mohr was a competent observer.

So he was. In his *Excursion Through America* he has left for us not only a fascinating account of one of the most exciting events in the history of the Pacific Northwest—the opening of the Northern Pacific Railroad with the pageantry accompanying that ceremony—but a faithful and valuable picture of American life at a time when frontiering was

drawing to a close and the urban-industrial complex emerging as the dominant force in the national
life. Herr Mohr's fascinating narrative deserves an
honorable place among the travel accounts that
have brought the Old World news of the New, and
shed so much light on the emerging civilization of
the United States.

KLAUS LANZINGER
University of Notre Dame

Index

INDEX

List of The Lakeside Classics

The Lakeside Classics